GREAT AMERICAN

MARINE CORPS STORIES

LYONS PRESS CLASSICS

GREAT AMERICAN

MARINE

CORPS

STORIES

EDITED BY

TOM MCCARTHY

LYONS
PRESS

ESSEX, CONNECTICUT

An imprint of The Globe Pequot Publishing Group, Inc.
64 South Main Street
Essex, CT 06426
www.GlobePequot.com

Distributed by NATIONAL BOOK NETWORK

British Library Cataloguing in Publication Information available

Library of Congress Cataloging-in-Publication Data available

ISBN 978-1-4930-8999-4 (paper)
ISBN 978-1-4930-9000-6 (electronic)

CONTENTS

INTRODUCTION

My Rifle

The Creed of a United States Marine

By Major General William H. Rupertus, USMC

Published March 13, 1942, in Marine Corps *Chevron*

*This is my rifle. There are many like it, but this one
is mine.*

*My rifle is my best friend. It is my life. I must master it as
I must master my life.*

*My rifle, without me, is useless. Without my rifle, I am
useless. I must fire my rifle true. I must shoot straighter
than my enemy who is trying to kill me. I must shoot him
before he shoots me. I will . . .*

*My rifle and myself know that what counts in war is not
the rounds we fire, the noise of our burst, nor the smoke
we make. We know that it is the hits that count. We will
hit . . .*

My rifle is human, even as I, because it is my life. Thus, I will learn it as a
brother. I will learn its weaknesses, its strength, its parts, its accessories, its
sights and its barrel. I will ever guard it against the ravages of weather and
damage as I will ever guard my legs, my arms, my eyes, and my heart against
damage. I will keep my rifle clean and ready, even as I am clean and ready.
We will become part of each other. We will . . .
Before God, I swear this creed. My rifle and myself are the defenders of my
country. We are the masters of our enemy. We are the saviors of my life.
So be it, until victory is America's and there is no enemy, but peace!

"Come on, you sons of bitches! Do you want to live forever?"
First Sergeant Dan Daly, leading an assault against German machine guns at Belleau Wood during World War I, captured the essence of the United States Marine Corps precisely.

Marines are not used to run supplies, secure bases, or conduct clandestine operations in the dark of night. Marines are called in when the United States wants the world to know it is coming in hard and it is time to run for cover.

Great American Marine Corps Stories expands on the exhortation of First Sergeant Dan Daly with ten unforgettable stories on the courage and indefatigable spirit of America's finest fighting force.

The United States Marine Corps has fought for freedom for more than 250 years, and never once on American soil.

That was the point.

November 10, 1775, the Continental Congress approved a resolution for the organization of the Corps, creating what would become the Marines, a heroic group of men and women who put their lives on the line in far-flung places around the globe—and yes, from the halls of Montezuma to the shores of Tripoli but in literally hundreds of other locations, from Belleau Wood to Iwo Jima, Inchon, Khe San, Fallujah,

Mogadishu, and beyond. No matter what year, what war or conflict, or what demands placed on these heroic men, a common theme arises.

It was captured best by Admiral Chester Nimitz describing the Marines at the Battle of Iwo Jima.

"Uncommon valor was a common virtue."

Heroics were indeed common. Take this during the Battle of Belleau Wood:

"Floyd Gibbons's left eye had just been shot out of his head, along with part of his skull. With his remaining eye, he watched Major Berry 'rise to his feet and in a perfect hail of lead rush forward and out of my line of vision.'"

Despite his wound, Berry continued to command, led his men in destroying a German machine gun nest.

Or the nonchalance of a Marine under siege at Khe San:

"The Marines of Captain Dabney's I/3/26, located on Hill 881S, provided extremely effective and enthusiastic support throughout the attack. In three hours, Captain Dabney's men pumped out close to 1,100 rounds from only three 81mm mortars, and the tubes became so hot that they actually glowed in the dark."

The spirit—the essence of being a Marine—can be summarized by a comment from Major General Jim "Mad Dog" Mattis to his Marines in Fallujah in 2004 during the heat of a brutal Iraqi assault:

"Keep up the good work, my fine young warriors. You have honored your families, the Corps, and the American people. I am very proud of you."

And the typical Marine response.

"Oooh-rah, sir!!"

Great American Marine Stories offers gripping, real-life stories of sacrifice and courage from wars and conflicts from World War I to Afghanistan in heart-stopping detail. The United States Marine Corps has served in nearly every conflict in United States history and by the early twentieth century would become the most dominant force in warfare.

Here are visceral accounts of iconic battles, unknown conflicts, and forgotten patrols that each have one thing in common: heroism in its purest form.

You will find in this eminently readable collection stories of Marines at Belleau Wood in France during World War I, a victory said by many historians to be the "birth of the modern Marine Corps," and on to breathtaking and heartbreaking action on Iwo Jima.

Here also are Marines making a surprise amphibious landing at the strategic port of Inchon during the Korean War, and the besieged Marines at Khe San in Vietnam, under attack for six months.

There are also stories of unsung heroes in unknown battles: recon Marines on patrol in Vietnam; invading Marines during the First Gulf War; Marine snipers in Haiti, Somalia, and Afghanistan; and a stunning account of life inside the risky missions undertaken by Marines members of the elite Anglicos.

Riveting and inspirational, *Great American Marine Corps Stories* is a must read for historian, Marines, and lovers of adventure.

1

BELLEAU WOOD

ALAN AXELROD

Five in the afternoon, Belleau Wood, France, June 6, 1918. No bugles, *Tribune* correspondent Floyd Gibbons would write. No flashing swords. Just a general advance through fields of wheat toward a former hunting preserve, tangled, overgrown, and now transformed into one big machine gun nest. Gibbons, as well as the 6th Regiment's Colonel Albertus Catlin, remarked on the beauty of the Marines advancing toward the woods in perfect rank and file, as if on parade, a gloriously doomed march into "a veritable hell of hissing bullets," a "death-dealing torrent," against which the Marines bent their heads "as though facing a March gale."

That is how many of the Marines began the attack, in the orthodox "advance in line of sections" they had learned so painstakingly under French tutelage. It was a style of advance born of a very human desire to impose order on chaos, to ward off confusion with method. It did not work for long.

Against Benjamin Berry's 3rd Battalion, 5th Marines, who had to advance across the most extensive stretch of open wheat field—some four hundred yards of it—the German fire was longest and hottest. "The headed wheat bowed and waved in that metal cloud-burst like meadow grass in a summer breeze. The advancing lines wavered, and the voice of a Sergeant was heard above the uproar: 'Come on, you sons of bitches! Do you want to live forever?'"

Marines marched against Belleau Wood in the elaborately choreographed line of sections formation: to make sense of it, to extract some greater meaning from it.

Without such patterns and stories, the Battle of Belleau Wood threatened to emerge into posterity as what Catlin admitted "it has been called"—nothing but "an exaggerated riot," a slaughter, full of sound and fury, signifying—just what?

Even under fire, legends endure far longer than a line of sections. "The ripping fire grew hotter," Catlin wrote. "The machine guns at the edge of the woods were now a bare hundred yards away, and the enemy gunners could scarcely miss their targets. It was more than flesh and blood could stand."

Berry's "men were forced to throw themselves flat on the ground or be annihilated, and there they remained in that terrible hail 'til darkness made it possible for them to withdraw to their original position." Henry Larsen, Berry's adjutant, reported to the brigade after the battle: "three platoons of the 45th Company went over. Only a few returned." And Catlin wrote: "Berry's men did not win that first encounter in the attack on Belleau Wood," which was another way of saying that not a single one of Berry's Marines even reached the edge of the woods, and 60 percent of the battalion became casualties.

Among these was Major Benjamin Berry himself. Floyd Gibbons was there when it happened—and he was more than a witness.

Gibbons, with Berry and many of his men, was making his way down a wooded slope, where midway down was a sunken road, littered with French bodies and "several of our men who had been brought down but five minutes before. We crossed that road hurriedly knowing that it was covered from the left by German machine guns."

Gibbons, Berry, and the Marines came to a V-shaped field, "perfectly flat and . . . covered with a young crop of oats between ten and fifteen inches high." On all sides of the field were dense clusters of trees. Gibbons and the others could hear the machine guns. "We could not see them but we knew that every leaf and piece of greenery there vibrated from their fire and the tops of the young oats waved and swayed with the streams of lead that swept across."

After giving orders to follow him at ten- to fifteen-yard intervals, Berry "started across the field alone at the head of the party. [Gibbons] followed." The woods around the field "began to rattle fiercely," and Gibbons could see "the dust puffs that the bullets kicked up in the dirt around our feet." Berry was well beyond the center of the field when he turned toward Gibbons and the other men: "Get down everybody."

He did not have to repeat the order. "We all fell on our faces. And then it began to come hot and fast," the volleys of lead sweeping the "tops of the oats just over us." As Gibbons "busily engaged [in] flattening [himself] on the ground," he heard a shout. "It came from Major Berry. I lifted my head cautiously and looked forward. The major was making an effort to get to his feet. With his right hand he was savagely grasping his left wrist. 'My hand's gone,' he shouted."

In some ways what really had happened to him was worse. Berry's hand had not been shot off, but a bullet had entered his left arm at the elbow, passing down alongside the bone, "tearing away muscles and nerves to the forearm and lodging itself in the palm of his hand. His pain was excruciating," causing him to stand up as he gripped his arm. Gibbons called to Berry, "Get down. Flatten out, Major," knowing that "he was courting death every minute he stood up." Berry in turn called over to Gibbons, "We've got to get out of here. We've got to get forward. They'll start shelling this open field in a few minutes." Gibbons replied that he was crawling over to him. "Wait until I get there and I'll help you. Then we'll get up and make a dash for it."

Gibbons crawled, pushing "forward by digging in with my toes and elbows extended in front of me. It was my object to make as little movement in the oats as possible."

A bullet had gone through the biceps of the upper arm and come out the other side. Gibbons looked down at his sleeve and could not even see the hole where the bullet had entered.

Then the second one hit. It nicked the top of my left shoulder. And again came the burning sensation, only this time the area affected seemed larger.

Feeling surprisingly little pain, Gibbons continued to crawl toward Berry.

And then the third one struck me. In order to keep as close to the ground as possible, I had swung my chin to the right so that I was pushing forward with my left cheek flat against the ground, and in order to accommodate this position of the head, I had moved my steel helmet over so that it covered part of my face on the right.

Then there came a crash. It sounded to me like someone had dropped a glass bottle into a porcelain bathtub. A barrel of whitewash tipped over and it seemed that everything in the world turned white.

That was the sensation. I did not recognize it because I have often been led to believe and often heard it said that when one receives a blow on the head everything turns black.

Gibbons asked himself, "'Am I dead?' . . . I wanted to know. . . . How was I to find out if I was dead? . . . I decided to try and move my fingers on my left hand. I did so and they moved. I next moved my left foot. Then I knew I was alive."

Floyd Gibbons's left eye had just been shot out of his head, along with part of his skull. With his remaining eye, he watched Major Berry "rise to his feet and in a perfect hail of lead rush forward and out of my line of vision."

Despite his wound, Berry continued to command, led his men in destroying a German machine gun nest, and later received the Distinguished Service Cross from General Pershing. Gibbons remained in the oat field for three hours, until 9:00 p.m., not daring to move until they judged it was sufficiently dark to risk crawling back to the American position.

After a series of agonizing stops at various forward dressing stations, Gibbons was loaded into an ambulance and evacuated to a hospital. Astoundingly, he was on his feet and once again covering the war within ten days of having been wounded.

If the line of sections advance in all its archaic formality failed to work for long, in some places it did not work at all. The poverty of communications and the level of confusion were so profound on the afternoon of June 6 that some units never even formed up to join the "parade." They were not aware of the attack until after it had actually begun.

Lieutenant George Gordon, commanding a platoon in one of Berry's companies, was standing—standing—at the periphery of the wheat field "watching the shells as they dropped along the edge of the woods across the wheatfield." He was talking with a friend, who remarked of the shelling, "I wonder what this is about. . . . They must have something spotted over there." Several minutes passed before Captain Larsen ran up to Gordon and his friend. "Get your platoons ready immediately," he shouted. "You should have started across with the barrage." Gordon later remarked:

This was the first information we had received regarding an attack and did not know one had been planned. No objective was given as to where it was to stop and no maps had been distributed; the only thing we were sure of was the direction and we knew that.

Attacking from Lucy-le-Bocage, well south of Berry, Sibley's 3rd Battalion, 6th Marines was, in Catlin's words, "having better luck." Catlin thrilled at the sight of these men "sweeping across the open ground in four waves, as steadily and correctly as though on parade." As if to justify in some pragmatic terms the ostentatious grandeur of this procession under fire, Catlin explained, "They walked at the regulation pace, because a man is of little use in a hand-to-hand bayonet struggle after a hundred yards dash." The obvious response to this observation would have been to ask the colonel just how much use a dead man was. But who could have dared such impertinence as Catlin looked on? "My hands were clenched and all my muscles taut as I watched that cool, intrepid, masterful defiance of the German spite." He saw "no sign of wavering or breaking."

Interviewed in October 2003 in upstate New York, Eugene Lee—who at age 104 was then the nation's "oldest living Marine"—recalled the grim journey across the wheat field. "They split us out into formation. They had the first wave go so far. They kept on firing in the woods there. The next wave would come and jump over them and they'd go so far, and would fire 'til they got in the edge of the woods."

The object of this leapfrog advance was to allow the first wave to cover the farther advance of the second wave, and the second to cover that of the third, and the third to cover the fourth as it finally reached the woods. Once the fourth had been delivered to the objective, the Marines of the preceding waves—those who survived—would follow it in. Lee was in the third of the four human waves.

Unlike Berry's men, many of Sibley's, who had much less open field to traverse, made it to Belleau Wood. Yet their entry into the objective was somehow anticlimactic. Catlin wrote that the "Marines have a war cry that they can use to advantage when there is need of it. It is a bloodcurdling yell calculated to carry terror to the heart of the waiting Hun. I am told that there were wild yells in the woods that night, when the Marines charged the machine gun nests, but there was no yelling when they went in." Catlin also noted a report that the Marines "advanced on those woods crying, 'Remember the *Lusitania!*' If they did so, I failed to hear it." Quite rightly, he observed that this did not "sound like the sort of thing the Marine says under the conditions." In fact, so far as he could observe, Catlin did not believe "a sound was uttered throughout the length of those four lines. The men were saving their breath for what was to follow."

Having written of this wordless entry into Belleau Wood, an entry bought at the price of many dead and wounded, the colonel of the 6th Marine Regiment feared that he had "given but a poor picture of that splendid advance." True, there "was nothing dashing about it like a cavalry charge," yet it was nevertheless "one of the finest things I have ever seen men do."

Catlin fully appreciated that these Marines "were men who had never before been called upon to attack a strongly held enemy position."

What lay before them was a "dense woods effectively sheltering armed and highly trained opponents of unknown strength." Indeed, within the depths of this dark space "machine guns snarled and rattled and spat forth a leaden death. It was like some mythical monster belching smoke and fire from its lair." Yet these Marines, the vast majority entirely new to combat, marched "straight against it . . . with heads up and the light of battle in their eyes."

Months after the battle, Private W. H. Smith, recovering from wounds in the Brooklyn Naval Hospital, related to Catlin what it had been like marching into Belleau Wood. He said that there "wasn't a bit of hesitation from any man. You had no heart for fear at all. Fight— fight and get the Germans was your only thought. Personal danger didn't concern you in the least and you didn't care."

Smith explained that he and about sixty others had gotten ahead of the rest of the company. "We just couldn't stop despite the orders of our leaders." Reaching the edge of the woods, they "encountered some of the Hun infantry" and then "it became a matter of shooting at mere human targets." At first, it was almost easy. The Marines fixed their rifle sights at three hundred yards and "aiming through the peep kept picking off Germans. And a man went down at nearly every shot." But then the enemy "detected us and we became the objects of their heavy fire."

Colonel Catlin, who had no field telephone, "felt obliged to see what was going on." He took his stand on a "little rise of ground protected by a low line of bushes about 300 yards from the woods." The position was near a road, the point at which the left flank of Thomas Holcomb's battalion made contact with the right flank of Berry's battered battalion.

"The shelter trenches did not cross the road," so Catlin was fully exposed as he watched the advance through his binoculars. "Bullets," he recalled, "rained all around me, the machine gun crews near me forming a target for the Germans."

The "racket of rifle and machine gun fire and bursting shrapnel and high explosives" was "like the continuous roll of some demoniacal drum, with the bass note of the heavy guns that were shelling Lucy." Through his binoculars, Catlin watched "a number of our brave lads fall" as the German machine gunners made sure to aim low, sweeping the ground, thereby "catching most of the men in the legs." Those who were thus disabled "lay right in the line of fire and many of them were killed there on the ground," whereas those "who were able to stand and keep going had the best chance."

Some of these men "went through the whole fight with leg wounds received during the first ten minutes."

Vivid as his perceptions of battle were, Catlin was not destined to be an eyewitness for long. "Just about the time Sibley's men struck the woods a sniper's bullet hit me in the chest. It felt exactly as though someone had struck me heavily with a sledge. It swung me clear around and toppled me over on the ground. When I tried to get up I found that my right side was paralysed." Catlin's French interpreter, Captain Tribot-Laspierre—a "splendid fellow," Catlin called him, "who stuck to me through thick and thin"—had been "begging [Catlin] to get back to a safer place." Now he sprang out of his cover and rushed to Catlin's side. "He is a little man and I am not, but he dragged me head first back to the shelter trench some twenty or twenty-five feet away."

Like Gibbons on Berry's side of the attack, Catlin on Sibley's was more fascinated than horrified by the sensations of being wounded. "I have heard of men getting wounded who said that it felt like a red-hot iron being jammed through them before the world turned black," but nothing of the kind happened to Catlin. "I suffered but little pain and I never for a moment lost consciousness." Nor did he think of death, "though I knew I had been hit in a vital spot. I was merely annoyed at my inability to move and carry on."

The colonel took a peculiarly professional and analytical interest in the circumstances of his wounding, concluding that it had been a "chance shot and not the result of good marksmanship, for the bullet must have come some 600 yards." It passed "clean through" Catlin's right lung, "in at the front and out at the back, drilling a hole straight through me." Catlin related that ballistics experts calculated that a "bullet fired at short range—less than five hundred or six hundred yards—twists [so that] when it strikes an obstacle it wabbles." Catlin therefore reasoned that had he been shot at close range, the bullet would have "torn a piece out of my back as big as my fist." However, had the bullet been fired from a range greater than about six hundred yards, it would have been "already wabbling, and would have made a big hole in the front of my chest and perhaps would not have gone clear through." Because the holes going in and out were both small, Catlin concluded that he had been shot from a range of about six hundred yards.

"[For that] I am thankful."

Catlin calmly sent word of his wounding to the command post, ordering his second in command, Lieutenant Colonel Harry Lee, to assume command of the 6th Regiment. Forty-five minutes elapsed before the regimental surgeon, Dr. Farwell, came under intense fire to Catlin's side. Farwell had brought stretcher bearers with him, but heavy shelling prevented immediate evacuation, and when gas shells began to detonate nearby, the stretcher men put a mask on the colonel. "I never knew before how uncomfortable one of those things could be. It is hard enough for a man to breathe with a lung full of blood without having one of those smothering masks clapped over his face." What gave Catlin comfort was the sound of the fire gradually receding, which told him that "Sibley's men were advancing." However, when the firing grew louder on the left, he "knew that Berry's outfit was being beaten back."

At length, the pace of the shelling eased, and four men raised Catlin's stretcher to their shoulders. "Carrying a 215-pound man on a stretcher over rough country under fire is no joke," Catlin observed, "but they got me to Lucy," then to an ambulance, and on to hospitals at Meaux and Paris. The colonel remained hospitalized until July 22, when he was sent home on leave.

In Catlin's absence, the men on Sibley's left flank, most of them, clawed their way into Belleau Wood, via its southwestern hook. On contact, the combat was a combination of close rifle fire and fierce bayonet work. Both the US Army and the Marine Corps administered bayonet training, and soldiers and Marines made ample use of the bayonet in the Great War—more, certainly, than they had in any previous conflict. Yet US Army soldiers tended to dread the weapon, whereas Marines, at least in the attack, reveled in its use. In a war fought to such a great extent by the weapons of high technology—high-explosive artillery, gas, the machine gun, the airplane, and even the tank—it was as if Marines craved contact at its most warriorlike. The isolated German outposts in the southwestern end of Belleau Wood fell prey to the Marines' bayonets, but the terrain, with its tangle of undergrowth, soon broke up the cohesiveness of the attacking units. Isolated and slowed, Captain Dwight Smith's company of Sibley's Marines, after they had penetrated a few hundred yards into the woods, made easy marks for the German machine guns. The machine gun fire became so intense that the attackers were deflected northward from their due eastward push.

Another of Sibley's companies, led by Lieutenant A. H. Noble, followed Dwight Smith's men into the woods, desperately trying to maintain contact with the lead company but failing to do so amid the rugged terrain and the outpouring of machine gun fire. As if shivered and split by the stream of fire, the left flank of Noble's company sheared off to the north—just as Smith's men had done—but the right flank, advancing along the ravine at the southern tip of Belleau Wood, continued due east. This flank consisted of two platoons, one under Lieutenant Louis Timmerman and another under a lieutenant named Hurley. The attack on the woods, which had begun in parade-order "line of sections," increasingly broke up within Belleau Wood itself. Yet, in doing so, it did not falter or flag. Instead, as companies divided into platoons and platoons into sections and sections into fire teams or even individual Marines, the fragmented fight only intensified.

In Timmerman's case, his platoon soon lost contact with Hurley's, and then the sections of the platoon itself lost contact with one another.

Marines set up machine gun positions within the woods wherever they could. This was necessary, of course, but it also added to the confusion of this most chaotic combat. Timmerman and the men who were still with him passed one Marine machine gun company, so he naturally assumed that the machine gun fire he heard to his rear was coming from them. In fact, what he heard was the sound of German machine gunners pinning down all of Smith's company along with Sibley's other two companies and the two sections of Timmerman's own platoon that had veered to the north. Unaware of this, Timmerman just kept going. In its advance, the platoon stumbled across a German outpost. The Marines and the enemy were equally surprised, but it was the Germans who gave up, and Timmerman sent back the prisoners under a single man while he and the others kept moving.

That's when Timmerman got his second surprise. He was suddenly shocked to discover that he had broken through to the east side of Belleau Wood, finding himself at a point slightly to the north of Bouresches.

Just before the attack, the company commander, Lieutenant Noble, had passed on to his platoon commanders the orders he had received. They were for the platoons on the right flank to move through Belleau Wood and capture Bouresches.

Like all neophyte lieutenants, Timmerman was anxious to follow orders, and he assumed everyone else was too. Finding himself and the two platoon sections with him—about twenty Marines in all—on the east side of Belleau Wood, and entirely unaware that the rest of the Marines in the southern end of the woods were being held down and held back by German machine guns, Timmerman experienced a moment of panic. It was not panic born of an awareness of the actual situation: that he and twenty other Marines were alone in enemy territory, separated from the rest of their unit by a dense woods exploding in hostile fire.

Instead it was panic born of the fear that everyone else had made it through Belleau Wood before him and that he was behind in the assault on Bouresches.

Sending one wounded private—a Marine named Henry—to the rear, Timmerman deployed his two sections into a line of skirmishers, sent a Corporal Larsen and Private Swenson ahead as scouts, then led his men along the ravine they had followed through the woods until they reached a wheat field. On the other side of this field, about two hundred yards away, was Bouresches. As with the wheat fields on the western face of Belleau Wood, this one "was thrashing to and fro with machine gun bullets."

Timmerman watched as Larsen and Swenson reached "a sort of mound of earth parallel to our line of advance." They signaled a halt there, and Timmerman advanced his men to the mound. Suddenly, "[I] noticed that we were coming under fire from all directions," despite being "sheltered from the enemy in front."

Who was firing from the rear?

It was a profoundly disorienting moment. After no more than a minute, however, the disorientation blossomed into disbelief as Private Henry—the wounded Marine Timmerman had sent to the rear—"came running back yelling something."

Timmerman could not make out what Henry was trying to say, so he signaled for him to come over. What he was saying was, "The woods in back of us were full of Germans." At first, the lieutenant simply did not believe him. After all, "[they] had just come through there." But the sight, sound, and sensation of "the bullets kicking up dust and landing all around our side of the barricade" soon made a believer out of him.

Clearly, Timmerman realized, he and his two sections—now reduced from twenty to "about fifteen" men—could not long stay behind a mound that offered no shelter. Timmerman yelled to his Marines, ordering them back into Belleau Wood. "Luckily I hit the edge of the woods just where the Germans were."

There were seventeen German privates and two noncoms manning a pair of machine guns in a patch of low ground that led off from the ravine.

The machine gunners were second-line troops, and they did not expect a swarm of Marines to descend on them from the east. In the lead, Timmerman kicked the faces of the first two Germans he encountered, knocking both unconscious. The others, confronted with the Marines' bayonets, threw down their weapons and laid themselves prostrate before the attackers.

Some tore open their uniform blouses, baring their chests, as if to say in a language that required absolutely no translation, We are unarmed!

At this point, a sergeant from Hurley's platoon broke through Belleau Wood with a couple of Marines. Timmerman put his prisoners into their custody and instructed them to take them to the rear.

Still under the unshakable conviction that most of the other Marines had broken through the woods and were already attacking toward Bouresches, Timmerman could not afford to be encumbered by POWs. He further assumed that capturing the machine gunners had put an end to German resistance in the south end of Belleau Wood.

He therefore resumed his interrupted advance and returned to the mound. This time, machine gun fire opened up from the town, then also from his left flank, coming from a rise just fifty yards off. To this was added fire from Timmerman's left rear as well. "I faced around and saw Swenson lying dead with a bullet hole through the forehead." Timmerman shouted, "Open fire to the right," and pointed "toward the hillock where a terrific fire was coming from." No sooner had he done this than he himself was hit on the left side of the face. "[Timmerman] fell forward thinking, 'I've got mine,'" believing that a bullet had ripped through under his eye. He lost consciousness momentarily but then "felt better."

He said, "[Although] I was covered with blood I realized I had not been dangerously hit." Nevertheless, Timmerman's "men were dropping around there" and so "[Timmerman] told them to follow [him]" and, once again, they "ran back for the shelter of the woods."

Lieutenant Louis Timmerman had begun the advance on Belleau Wood commanding a platoon of fifty Marines as part of a company of some two hundred. This mass of men broke apart inside the woods, leaving Timmerman with fifteen men on the other side. By the time he retreated to the eastern perimeter of Belleau Wood, shot through the face, he commanded just six Marines. They hunkered down in the German machine gun position they had captured minutes ago. Only then did it occur to him that Belleau Wood had neither been taken nor even traversed—at least not by very many of the Marines who had entered it.

Beyond these realizations, the lieutenant knew only that the battle, which had been ahead of him in Belleau Wood when Belleau Wood had been ahead of him, was now ahead of him in the little town of Bouresches. But the battle was also on either side of him and, not least of all, it was raging yet in the ruined tangle of trees, rocks, and ravines that now lay behind him.

TAKING BOURESCHES

Lieutenant Louis Timmerman and a half dozen tired Marines were a crew too small to feed, fire, and defend the two German machine guns they had captured. But by the time they had retreated to this position, a Sergeant Fadden and some other Marines managed to wiggle through Belleau Wood to Timmerman's position. They did so just in time to man the weapons as Timmerman spotted a column of troops approaching no more than forty yards away. Through the smoke, it was difficult to make out their uniforms, but Timmerman was sufficiently persuaded that they were Germans to order his men to let loose with the machine guns. The column quickly broke up.

Because he occupied a covered position at the edge of the woods, was in possession of machine guns, and was staying put, Timmerman suddenly became the nucleus around which ragged Marines gathered in ones and twos and threes. Some ran in from Belleau Wood. Others crawled, wounded. They came from the rear, from the right, and from the left. They were from various platoons and companies, and there were even some men from Berry's battalion who, instead of retreating from the wheat field when that battalion's attack on Belleau Wood failed, had waited for the fire to die down and, one by one, crawled into the woods, eventually emerging in Sibley's sector, well to the south of where Berry's men were supposed to be.

By the time that about forty Marines had gathered around the captured German machine gun position, Sibley's intelligence officer showed up. He told Timmerman to hold on where he was and await reinforcements. It certainly had not been planned like this—of course, very little had been planned—but Timmerman now found himself in possession of the first piece of the first objective that had been assigned to the Marines. Because he had gotten through the woods and was holding ground on the east side of the woods, Timmerman was deemed worthy of reinforcement.

Timmerman's achievement notwithstanding, most of Sibley's battalion was still fighting it out within Belleau Wood, or "Hellwood," as Sibley's Marines had taken to calling it. Albertus Catlin, put out of action by a bullet through the lung, later gathered reports on what happened after he was taken from the field. In his account of the struggle at Belleau Wood, he called Major Berton Sibley "one of the most picturesque characters in the Marine Corps," describing him as short, swarthy, and wiry, "one of those men whose looks are no indication of their age; he might be anywhere from thirty-five to fifty. I fancy that is why he is affectionately known as 'the old man.'" Catlin praised Sibley as "particularly thorough" and impossible to rattle. "His men love him and would follow him anywhere."

Into Belleau Wood, Catlin claimed, "They followed him as warriors of old followed their chieftain."

The reality was not nearly so straightforward. The 79th Company, under Captain Randolph Zane, was one of the first of Sibley's units to penetrate the woods. As it did, it came under what platoon commander Lieutenant Graves B. Erskine called "murderous fire, mainly automatic weapons, some artillery and mortar."

The artillery barrage included gas shells. "My platoon consisted of fifty-eight men in addition to myself when we jumped off. About forty minutes later, five of us were left." It was at this point that Erskine grabbed a wounded Marine as the man made his way to the rear. He asked him to tell Captain Zane, who was some distance in the rear, that the platoon was "pinned down and could advance no further."

After an hour or so, "this poor kid"—he had been badly wounded in the nose—"crawled back to report the captain's words: 'Goddamnit, continue the advance.' This was at early nightfall. We continued the advance."

To the right of Erskine's rapidly dwindling platoon, the men of Captain Donald Duncan's 96th Company were advancing through the ravine at the extreme southern end of Belleau Wood, which led to Triangle Wood, little more than a clump of trees below the tip of Belleau Wood and in line of sight with Bouresches to the northeast.

Firing from Bouresches, German machine guns raked this wooded patch. Duncan deployed three of his platoons to the eastern perimeter of Triangle Wood, then sent his fourth platoon, under Lieutenant Clifton Cates, to shift to the left and make contact with Major Sibley. Cates moved left to Zane's right flank in Belleau Wood proper, then, reasoning that Sibley must already have moved forward of this position, he led his platoon due east to the eastern margin of the woods. Pausing there, he saw before him, nestled at the foot of a gentle seven-hundred-yard slope, the village of Bouresches.

There was Bouresches, but there was no sign of Sibley. It was still possible that Sibley was somewhere ahead, and Cates also knew that Bouresches was one of the day's objectives. Both of these facts argued for a continuation of his advance. Just as he was deciding whether to do this, he saw the rest of Duncan's company on his right beginning to advance east of the woods. That decided him. Cates stepped out of the cover of Belleau Wood and turned to his platoon: "All right, men, the guide is left, remember, hit their line together, boys," and with that, Cates's platoon began its advance on Bouresches.

On Cates's right, a platoon under Lieutenant Lockhart pulled ahead of the entire company. Seeing this, Captain Duncan and his first sergeant, a Marine named Sissler, walked heedlessly through the machine gun and rifle fire pouring out from Bouresches and approached Lockhart's advanced position.

Donald Duncan was a supremely confident, cool, and collected Marine.

In the British fashion, he carried a swagger stick rather than a cane, and regardless of circumstances, he invariably had a straight-stem pipe clenched between his teeth and a smile on his face. He reached

Lockhart's position, halted him, and ordered him to await the rest of the company so that the attack would be with maximum strength.

Sergeant Al Sheridan saw what happened next. A friend who had grown up with Duncan in Kansas, Sheridan wrote a letter to the captain's family. In it, he pictured Duncan "talking to Mr. Lockhart our platoon leader" while "the bullets were singing all around us." He wrote that Lockhart asked the captain "as a joke if he thought we would see much action."

Duncan broadened his smile at this: "Oh! yes we will give and take but be sure you take more than you give." Sheridan elaborated, "I guess he meant lives." Then he went on: "Anyway [Duncan] started away up the hill and it was not a minute till down he went." A heavy machine gun bullet had drilled into Donald Duncan's stomach. First Sergeant Sissler yelled out for a corpsman. Sheridan, together with dental surgeon Weedon Osborne and a navy corpsman, ran through the fire. They carried Duncan "to a small clump of trees, all the time he was gasping, hit through the stomach," Sheridan continued in his letter. "We no more than laid him on the ground when a big 8 in. shell came in and killed all but myself, I was knocked down but my helmet saved me, so I left them and rejoined my platoon."

Duncan's second in command, Lieutenant Robertson, took over the company. Wasting no time, he waved his pistol above his head and shouted, "Come on, let's go."

Hugging the ground, Lieutenant Cates watched. "We really didn't know where we were going but this town was right in front of us."

Rising to his feet, Cates began moving toward Bouresches, the single-file line of his platoon following behind him. Inclined as it was toward Bouresches, the slope offered this procession of Marines to the German gunners in that town as if serving them up on a platter. At every few steps a man dropped. Cates himself went down when a bullet skimmed his British-model washbasin helmet. He fell on his face, nose buried in the earth, whereupon Robertson took the lead.

Despite appearances to the contrary, Cates was not dead. He rose to his knees and felt his head where a large, bloody, and very tender knot had erupted. Finding his dented helmet, he gingerly fitted it back on, then looked around him before coming fully to his feet. The machine gun fire reminded him of hail hitting the ground, and his very first thought—a sane thought, at that—"was to run like hell to the rear." Looking to the rear and then side to side, he saw no one "except the wounded and dead." But then he looked forward. In that direction he saw four men advancing through the ravine. He "beat over to them."

Beat over to them? It was more like stumble-staggering vaguely in their direction. Cates gave the appearance of a man who had been drowning his sorrows in more than a few glasses of beer. The four faces that materialized before his still blurry vision were familiar to Cates, all members of his platoon: a pair of corporals, Finn and Dorrell; Sergeant Belfry; and Private Tom Argaut. Seeing that Cates looked far from alright, Argaut gently lifted the lieutenant's helmet, gasped or grimaced at the clotted lump poking through a thatch of hair, unscrewed the top from his canteen, and poured some of its contents over the wound. It was not water.

"Goddamn it, Tom. Don't pour that wine over my head, give me a drink of it."

And with that, the four men knew their lieutenant was going to be okay.

Seizing a French rifle that had been abandoned on the field much earlier, Cates led his four Marines down the ravine and toward Bouresches.

These men were now the sum total of his entire command.

On the periphery of the village, Cates saw some Germans lurking in the buildings at the southern tip of Bouresches. Turning to his men, he motioned toward them, and the Marines opened fire, scattering the Germans.

When he sees his enemy run, a Marine does not hesitate to fill the resulting vacuum. Cates and the four others quickly exchanged the wheat field for the streets of the village. Looking back, they were surprised to see Lieutenant Robertson leading about two dozen more Marines.

"Come on," Cates called to Robertson. "Let's take the rest of the town. There's no one in there now."

Robertson turned the men over to Cates, telling him that he would run back to fetch reinforcements. Now with about thirty Marines to deploy, Cates divided them into three assault groups. He assigned Gunnery Sergeant Moorey to lead one group from the west to seize the northwest corner of Bouresches. Sergeant Belfry was tasked with leading the second group to take the center. Assuming that the south end of the little village was already reasonably secure, Cates took the others north to occupy the railroad station.

Earlier in the day, some three hundred or four hundred Germans had held Bouresches, using its buildings as cover for the machine guns with which they swept the southern portions of the wheat fields west and south of Belleau Wood. To Cates, the town now appeared mostly empty, the Germans having withdrawn as the Marines fought their way through the woods and began emerging at its east end. But Cates was wrong. As they approached the heart of the village, a machine gun suddenly opened up on them. Several of Cates's Marines fell, and a bullet passed harmlessly through the lieutenant's own already battered helmet. In short order, another tore a hole through his tunic, pinging audibly against his silver lieutenant's bar and cutting a gash into his shoulder.

Ordering his men back, he divided them into a pair of fire teams. He sent one team around the left side of the machine gun position and the other around the right. After a crackling burst of rifle fire, it was all over.

The machine gun was silenced, and the surviving gunner surrendered.

Cates had won—but at a price. The encounter with the machine gun nest had reduced his total occupation force from thirty Marines to twenty-one.

Nevertheless, he did hold the town, becoming the first Marine to attain one of the objectives Degoutte had assigned, and he had accomplished this not with the three companies allocated to the mission—about six hundred men—but with no more than the ragged remnant of a single, shredded platoon.

When Cates declared to himself that the town was his, night had fallen. It was about a quarter to ten.

Lieutenant Clifton Cates deployed his meager resources through the dark streets and environs of the village in four so-called Cossack posts—independent positions, unconnected with one another. One he placed in an apple orchard adjacent to the village, another behind a wall facing the railroad station, and two in the south end of Bouresches. His men were soon joined by the reinforcements Robertson had managed to recruit from a number of shattered platoons still emerging from the woods.

Later in the night, these newcomers were bolstered by survivors of the 79th Company under Captain Randolph Zane, to whom Cates relinquished command.

The reinforcements were sorely needed, for although Colonel Catlin later crowed that Cates's "twenty men started in to clean up that town in approved Marine fashion," there was a full German regiment just north of the town—part of the German 237th Division—and it had started to push back. The fire fight grew hot, and the Marines in Bouresches sent back word that they were running critically short of ammunition. Hearing of the need, Lieutenant William B. Moore, a Princeton athlete, and Sergeant Major John Quick volunteered for the hazardous duty of driving a truck packed with ammunition, under fire and over shell-cratered roads, to Bouresches. From fifty other Marines who volunteered to go with them, Moore selected a small crew. They loaded the truck, piled in, Quick's foot came down on the clutch pedal, his hand shifted the gear, and letting out the clutch slowly, Quick eased the explosives-packed camion into motion.

It was a hellish ride, brilliantly illuminated by the enemy's starburst shells and phosphorous flares, which quite effectively lit up the lumbering, lurching target. "It rolled and careened fearfully over the gullies and craters," Catlin related, "shells shrieked and whistled over their heads and burst on every hand, and as they neared the town they drove straight into the fire of the spouting machine guns." Miraculously, the truck arrived unscathed and, Catlin succinctly observed, "saved the day."

It made for an exciting story—and the heroism of Moore and Quick was later recognized with the appropriate military decorations. Yet their mission was entirely unnecessary. The critical shortage of ammunition at Bouresches was a figment of someone's fevered imagination. The fact was that the defenders of the newly liberated town had so much ammunition on hand that for four full days they left what Moore and Quick had brought exactly where they had hurriedly dumped it: at the edge of town.

Shortly after 11:00 p.m., Captain Zane reported that the Germans had been driven out of Bouresches. A counterattack at 2:30 a.m. on June 7 was "smothered by our machine gun fire."

The town continued to be an object of contention throughout June 7 and even into June 8. But during these two days, US Army engineers helped the Marines dig into secure defensive positions, and fresh reinforcements were put in place. Each German counterattack was repulsed, and by the end of June 8, the garrison of Bouresches had tied in with the line of Sibley's men who were still fighting it out in Belleau Wood, and also with Holcomb's battalion, which extended the line from Bouresches down to Triangle Farm due south of the village.

This American line now enveloped Belleau Wood on its southern end, effectively containing the German forces that were still making existence hellish there.

Colonel Albertus Catlin, who had to content himself with vicarious pride since he had been taken out of the action, remarked that in capturing Bouresches, his Marines "were obliged to get along without direct telephone connection with headquarters" and instead depended entirely on intrepid runners, who dashed "through machine gun and shell fire" to keep "open the lines of communication."

The platoon or battalion runner was invariably a volunteer. He got no glory, but, as Private Elton Mackin made clear in his remarkable memoir *Suddenly We Didn't Want to Die,* the runner did get plenty of opportunities to be killed. Mackin described how, during the Battle of Belleau Wood, his sergeant summoned him.

"Rest your bones, son, maybe I got a job for you. . . . You and me have the same nickname, it seems. Made me think of you." Sergeant "Slim" explained to Private "Slim" that "Battalion wants a new runner. 'Itchy' Fox was killed last night comin' out. They got a vacancy to fill."

"Bad news," Mackin's third-person narrator observed. "Not of Fox. That was just an ordinary matter, another fellow gone. 'Battalion wants another runner.' It came like an easily spoken sentence of death to the lad who heard it." Private Slim suddenly recalled "talk of jobs too dangerous; jobs certain to mean death. Runners didn't last. Everyone knew that." Stirring within him were "fear and protest," and he mentally groped to "find a good excuse. A fellow didn't have to take a runner job. All a fellow had to do was say no. . . . Suicide squad. That's how the fellows spoke of it. A runner didn't have a chance."

For all their heroism, runners were poor substitutes for efficient communication by field telephone on a modern, fluid battlefield. Shot through the lung, Catlin had ample time to collect firsthand information while convalescing after the battle. "It is not the general who wins such a battle," he wrote of Belleau Wood, "but the captain, the sergeant, the private. . . . The men who went through that Turkish bath of fire and steel are the best judges of what it was like." So he collected their stories.

Catlin collected the tale of Private W. H. Smith of Winston-Salem, North Carolina, who was interviewed "after he had been invalided home."

He told how the "German machine guns were everywhere" in Belleau Wood, in "the trees and in small ground holes." To survive, the Marines dug one-man pits to fire from. These, Smith remarked, "gave us just a little protection."

The bullets "came so close at times I could almost feel their touch. My pack was shot up pretty much but they didn't get me." And that fact led Smith to think he was "bullet proof." He "didn't care a damn for all the Germans and their machine guns," he said, but observed that "every blamed tree must have had a machine gunner," the "potting" of whom "became great sport" for the Marines. "Even the officers would seize rifles from wounded Marines and go to it." But one of those machine guns finally got Smith. "Five shots hit right in succession. The elbow was torn into shreds, but the hits didn't hurt. It seemed just like getting five little stings of electricity."

When the captain ordered two men to help him back, Smith responded that he could make it alone, and he "picked up part of the arm that was hanging loose and walked" two miles to the dressing station. "I got nearly to it when everything began to go black and wobbly. I guess it was loss of blood. But I played in luck, for some stretcher bearers were right near when I went down."

Of images such as these was the intimate picture of battle made. They were images of which higher headquarters, hobbled by hasty and inadequate planning (the result of an impulsive attack decision) and crippled by poor communications, was woefully ignorant. General James Harbord, commanding 4th Brigade from his headquarters at La Loge Farm, received only the most fragmentary word from the front, so that he was forced to view the battle as if through a kaleidoscope. And as if the fragmentary nature of the information was not bad enough, those fragments were, more often than not, inaccurate in themselves, almost always glibly optimistic, painting a picture of the Marines's "beautiful deployment in beautiful line," mentioning but "one casualty at the dressing station," giving assurance that "things are going fine."

Confusion, miscommunication, and even the total absence of communication were present from the very beginning of the attack. At the southernmost end of the American line where the Marines tied in with the Army, Colonel Paul Malone, commanding the Army's 23rd Infantry in this sector, ordered the two Marine battalions to his left to attack along with the others at 5:00 p.m. When Malone reported these orders to 3rd Brigade commander E. M. Lewis, the brigadier exploded.

Attack? Malone's regiment and, with it, the two tied-in Marine battalions were supposed to do no more than stand fast, attacking only if Marine action on the left made it necessary for them to do so.

Stunned, Malone tried desperately to communicate with the Marine battalions, to order them back, but without field telephones, he could not reach them in time. The result was a costly advance that achieved nothing.

At 3:15 a.m., June 7, Malone finally got a message through to the majors commanding the two Marine battalions: "It is desired that you merely reoccupy the position which you occupied before the advance this afternoon. . . . No advance is desired." At 3:45, 2nd Division commander Omar Bundy sent one of his staff officers to 3rd Brigade to find out why two battalions had advanced without authorization. General Lewis replied that "he did not know, as it was not intended," and he assured Bundy's staff officer that "he understood perfectly that there was to be no advance," as if that assurance was somehow supposed to make up for 340 men killed and wounded in a ten-hour action that accomplished nothing in the end and that was never supposed to have taken place to begin with.

ARMIES OF THE NIGHT

After nightfall on June 6, amid heroism and sacrifice, the confusion only intensified. General Harbord, operating from a headquarters close enough to the front to be shelled but too far from it to receive a continuous flow of timely and comprehensive reports, struggled to get his arms around the "exaggerated riot" that was the Battle of Belleau Wood. Harbord was an enthusiastic Army commander who had quickly learned to love the Marine brigade assigned to him, but the fog of war was frustrating him, doubtless frightening him, and finally angering him. Earlier, this had led him to send a shrill epistolary lecture to Major Julius Turrill on the importance of liaison.

Now, just before 9:00 p.m., it prompted a message to Lieutenant Colonel Harry Lee, who had assumed command of the 6th Marine Regiment from the wounded Catlin. "I am not satisfied with the way you have conducted your engagement this afternoon," Harbord began. "Your own regimental headquarters and this office have not had a word of report from you as to your orders or your positions."

Harbord complained to Lee that Major Sibley, whose battalion belonged to the 6th Regiment, had been "asking your regimental adjutant for orders." He further complained that Major Berry, whose battalion belonged to the 5th Regiment but "over whom you should have asserted authority," was "reporting to his own Regimental Commander." Figuratively seizing Lee by the shoulders, Harbord scolded, "I want you to take charge and to push this attack with rigor." He then proceeded to give a string of orders, most of which were made irrelevant either by circumstances or developments on the front.

It is probably most fortunate that Lee was in no position to receive Harbord's sputtering message. The very circumstances that prevented his sending reports to headquarters or even communicating effectively with the battalion commanders prevented his getting the general's ill-tempered missive.

The hard fact was that at nightfall, absolutely no one had the true picture of the situation in Belleau Wood. Company- and platoon-level commanders were, on their own, either struggling to survive, holding in place, or grimly pushing through the woods. Those on the extreme right (south), like Clifton Cates, were able to squeeze through. Those farther left were forced by walls of machine gun fire to divert to the north from their eastward push, a turn that left them stranded in the woods and in the thick of the firefight. Those even farther to the left—the men of Berry's battalion—were either killed, disabled by wounds, or turned back in the initial advance. Some, who had been pinned down for hours in the wheat, managed to crawl into the woods and, if they were lucky, linked up with others who were fighting it out.

Harbord received word late in the night that one entire unit of Marines was stuck in a hard fight at the northern edge of the woods, but actually that part of the objective contained no Marines at all. Only the south end was occupied. The truth was that the attack had no cohesion whatsoever.

That fact would have frustrated and alarmed Harbord even more— had he known it. Intended to be an attack of coordinated companies, the Battle of Belleau Wood was now a fight of platoons, squads, and, most of all, of individual Marines. Despite its fragmented nature, however, it was an attack both fierce and determined.

Harbord did not have an accurate picture of the battlefield, but for him there was no uncertainty as to the big picture. He firmly believed that "more than Belleau Wood was at stake, more than standing between the invader and Paris. It was a struggle for psychological mastery." He conceded that the "stage was small"—no more than a patch of French forestland—"but the audience was the world of 1918."

Harbord could also rest assured that everyone saw the same big picture.

Cut off and confused as they now were in the dark realm of Belleau Wood, Turrill and Lee, as well as every Marine noncom and private, understood that the world was watching them—or, rather, reading the headlines they made. Certainly, the Marines fought as if this were the case. At the same time, they had no doubt about their most immediate mission, which was to kill the Germans who were killing them, and to kill them wherever they found them. These were two islands of crystal clarity: the knowledge that they fought upon a world stage but had to deal with death just yards or feet or inches away.

Majors Berton Sibley and Thomas Holcomb struggled to consolidate their positions in the southern end of Belleau Wood. Farther north, on the left, Lieutenant Colonel Logan Feland had yet to lead his attack, although it was almost half past ten. He had earlier requested a preparatory artillery barrage, then asked for another. Harbord replied to Feland that a barrage had been "put down at your request about 8:50. Your later request . . . for barrage cannot be honored because of ignorance of your whereabouts."

Frederic Wise was holding with his entire battalion (except for Lloyd Williams's 51st Company, sent in earlier) in a reserve position, south of Champillon, to the rear and north of Belleau Wood.

During that hellish night, however, that position yielded no safety. German shells rained down on it. Lieutenant E. D. Cooke recalled that one shell landed "right in the headquarters group and three more exploded in the trees overhead." The concussion blew the company runner, a Marine Cooke identified only as Steve, against him, and knocked them both to the ground. "I grabbed him and rolled into a hole, but Steve was dead. Two other fellows were killed and a half dozen more torn and bleeding." In an effort to save the battalion before it was blown to bits waiting to be called in to the attack, Captain Lester Wass "raged about, making men scatter, take cover, dig in." Others "pulled the wounded behind trees. . . . It was a messy ten minutes."

From that point on, "we kept digging and ducking shells. . . . A grim business, crouching in a shallow hole, wondering if it were to prove a self-dug grave." When shortly after midnight the order finally came to move out, to the relief of Berry's beleaguered 3rd Battalion, the Marines advanced into the battle proper "with no regrets."

Wise's Marines may have felt relieved to be out from under the falling shells, but Wise himself was utterly bewildered. His orders from Harbord told him to take three companies "into the line on right of Feland between him and the 3d Battalion." The order went on to explain that "Feland's right is supposed to be about one kilometer south of Hill 126. Berry's left near Hill 133." Then it instructed Wise, when he arrived "approximately in position," to "report by runner to Feland," who would give him further orders.

Flabbergasted, Wise later wrote, "[It] was the damndest order I ever got in my life—or anyone else ever got. It went on the calm assumption that all the objectives of the First and Third Battalion had been secured." Wise was close enough to the action to know that this assumption was quite unwarranted.

Nevertheless, "Starting at two a.m. I was to go along the Lucy-Torcy road, find Colonel Feland, second in command of the Fifth Marines, whose P.C. [post of command] was supposed to be somewhere near Champillon, and get orders from him what to do." Whereas Wise's Marines were happy to leave a place that amounted to a magnet for artillery fire, Wise himself understood that he "was between the devil and the deep sea. If I didn't move, I knew I'd catch hell"—both from the German artillery and General Harbord. "If I did move, I knew I was going right down into Germany."

But given an order to advance, a Marine advances. "It was dark as pitch. Finding Feland would be a miracle."

The Lucy-Torcy road passed to the left of Belleau Wood and paralleled very closely its entire western margin. To get to the road in the absolute darkness, Wise, in company with Lieutenant Bill Mathews and his section of scouts, personally led all three companies in single file northeast toward the road. Each man, bat blind, held onto the man in front of him. Once they reached the road, they had the luxury of shelter to the east. For approximately a half mile north out of Lucy-le-Bocage a slope or ridge separated the road from Belleau Wood. After this, however, the ridge gave way to "sloping grain fields, like a bottle-neck opening into a bottle." Harbord's orders assumed that Wise's advance up the Lucy-Torcy road would be at least somewhat protected by Berry's battalion, which was supposedly holding the north end of the woods.

Of course, Berry's shattered battalion was doing no such thing.

As his column marched sightlessly along the road, Wise called a halt at the "bottleneck." All was quiet.

And that was precisely the problem.

If an entire battalion was positioned just to the right (east), how could there be no noise? Taking his adjutant and two squads, Wise ventured ahead on the road. Within two hundred yards they were met by a burst of rifle fire—not from the right, but from the left. Wise knew from the sound that the rifles were Springfields, not Mausers, and he called out to cease fire.

The shooting stopped. A moment of silence followed. Then someone shouted, "Look out. The Germans are on your right in the Bois de Belleau."

So much for meeting up with Lieutenant Colonel Feland and Berry's battalion.

With his adjutant and squad members, Wise turned to head back to his halted column. At that point, however, the Germans opened up with machine guns and artillery, killing half of Wise's men as they scrambled back to the others. As he approached the officers at the head of his battalion, Wise was professionally laconic, crisply barking out to them, "About face to the rear—on the double."

It is one thing to give such an order to a squad and quite another to relay it to some six hundred Marines—in single file, no less. The order had to be passed down the line, and as it was, the well-trained Marines responded not by instantly executing the order but by returning the regulation reply: "By whose command?" This was a safeguard to prevent unauthorized retreats and other movements. As future Marine commandant Lieutenant Lemuel Shepherd explained, the order traveled down the line and the reply "went all the way back up the line" to be answered with, "By Colonel Wise—we're in the wrong spot."

But that left another very big problem. Lieutenants Gil Jackson and E. D. Cooke, the officers at the rear of column, had been watching German artillery explode behind them just as they received Wise's order. Cooke recalled: "Jackson and I looked at each other inquiringly. We knew there wasn't any such thing as going to the rear because of the shells." In response to the order, they "made the tail of the column stand fast." This brought to them Captain Wass at a dead run. "To the rear!" he bellowed, facing down Jackson and Cooke.

"By order of Lieutenant Colonel Wise. To the rear!" In an instant, the dilemma was resolved. "We couldn't run from the Boche, but if Fritz Wise and Captain Wass said to run it was time to get going," shells or no shells.

Not that the single-file column could get going very quickly. "We could move a few steps and then halt, then a few steps and halt," Cooke later wrote. "This kept up until day was breaking."

Wise's battalion did not run from the Germans. As soon as it had withdrawn down the Lucy-Torcy road to a defensible position alongside the western face of Belleau Wood, Wise again halted the column, turned it back around, and began its deployment. He sent Captain John Blanchfield's 55th Company forward to assume the first position fronting the woods. The company's task was to begin suppressing some of the fire from the woods.

As Blanchfield and Shepherd organized a reconnaissance to locate the source of fire from a projection out of the western face of Belleau Wood, Blanchfield turned toward the sound of the fire. At that moment, another machine gun crackled from the body of the woods. A bullet caught Blanchfield, spinning him around before it knocked him to the ground. He sprawled across the Lucy-Torcy road.

Seeing Blanchfield fall, Private Paul Bonner at first followed his buddies, who scattered at the burst of fire. But "then I thought of Blanchfield and started back. . . . [I] rushed across the road, machine gun bullets whipping the air everywhere, and I made the captain's side. He was still alive."

Like Albertus Catlin, John Blanchfield was a big man, "twice my size," Bonner judged, "but I picked him up and carried him back."

Despite Bonner's efforts, Blanchfield died, and command of the company fell to Lemuel Shepherd. He continued positioning the platoons along the edge of the woods. Suddenly, his orderly, a Private Martin, went down.

When Shepherd bent to help him, he caught a bullet in his hip. "One of my men came along, pulled us back to the edge of the road, then got us to a dressing station."

While 55th Company deployed along Belleau Wood to the right of the road, the other companies took up positions in a small woods on the road's left. Back at brigade headquarters, General Harbord believed this end of the woods had been occupied, if not secured. The Marines to the west of the woods knew this was hardly the case. Now, however, they heard men deploying along the western margin of Belleau Wood and along the Lucy-Torcy road. E. D. Cooke vividly recalled the result this produced. "Daylight came suddenly as we lay alongside of the road." Cooke heard some talking up ahead, "then shouts and the chug-chug of a heavy machine gun. Several other guns joined in and the air was full of bullets." Cooke hollered to the men, "Keep down!" It was a superfluous command. Their noses were already "buried in the dirt." The firing came from "our own guns," from Marines who assumed that anyone at the end of Belleau Wood this far north had to be German.

Panic sent the "blood pounding into my head and emptied my stomach of courage," Cooke admitted. "It was bad enough to be shot at by the Boche but there was no sense in being killed by friendly troops." Worse, Cooke saw that his own men "looked wild and fingered their triggers, ready to return the fire of our other battalion." Cooke knew that "something had to be done and done quick."

"And Captain Wass did it."

Not that he meant to. Wass yelled to Lieutenant Jackson, "Where are you?" The response was "right here. Across the road." To which Wass returned, "Stand up, so I can see you."

Above the "crackling roar of machine gun bullets," Jackson shouted back, "Captain, if you want to see me, you stand up." Suddenly, it was over.

"American humor can lick anything," Cooke observed. "Smothered chuckles ran down the line," and the friendly fire ceased.

It was 6:00 in the morning, June 7. Wise was in position on the western margin of Belleau Wood, roughly along its center. He had managed to tie in with what remained of Berry's battalion, which was deployed to his left, running farther up the woods. With others who soon joined them, they attacked Belleau Wood at this location a little later in the morning. When they did, they discovered that the Germans had withdrawn.

It was by no means a victory, final or intermediate. Belleau Wood was still thickly occupied by the enemy, who had merely pulled back, deeper into its recesses. General Degoutte had ordered that Belleau

Wood be taken. That objective, intended to be achieved in a day and night's fighting, was far from having been attained. But no one knew just how far.

As the morning of June 7 progressed, Harbord began to learn what had been accomplished and what had not. He reported to General Bundy at 8:30 a.m. that his brigade from right (south) to left (north) held a line extending from Triangle Farm to Bouresches "through the wood, then practically a line east and west through the Bois de Belleau from the northern edge of the town Bouresches to about Hill 181" and then "in a line running southeast-northwest to near north edge of woods about two kilometers north of Lucy." Behind the lines either fronting or through portions of Belleau Wood, Harbord reported another line continuous from "southeast of Bussiares to Triangle Farm."

The victory was not final. The mission was not yet completed. At best, it was a start. And considering the impulsiveness of the offensive, commenced on the spur of the moment and virtually without preparation let alone careful reconnaissance, it was a remarkable start. But it was far from a consummation. Moreover, it had a cost—well, Harbord did not yet know: "No numbers as to casualties are available. Losses known to be heavy."

To the Marines fighting in Belleau Wood, June 7 promised to be another day of hard, confusing combat. To General Harbord, June 7 brought a strong dose of harsh reality, as he reported his tentative and rather meager gains to his superior officer, Omar Bundy. But to the correspondents of America's newspapers, this chaotic battle, just barely begun, loomed as a triumphant breakthrough of nearly miraculous proportions.

As early as June 6, the *Chicago Daily Tribune* trumpeted:

U.S. MARINES SMASH HUNS
GAIN GLORY IN BRISK FIGHT ON THE MARNE
CAPTURE MACHINE GUNS, KILL BOCHES, TAKE PRISONERS

On June 7, the *Tribune* continued in this vein:

MARINES WIN HOT BATTLE
SWEEP ENEMY FROM HEIGHTS NEAR THIERRY

Even the customarily more reserved *New York Times* was ecstatic:

OUR MARINES ATTACK, GAIN MILE AT VEUILLY, RESUME DRIVE AT
NIGHT, FOE LOSING HEAVILY

In newspapers across the nation, the headlines run during these two days were similar. The stories they led were not false so much as they were misleading. Or, rather, they were not so much news as they were premature celebrations.

The exuberance of the headlines and the stories was the product of two things. The first was a long frustration among journalists and the public alike with the hitherto modest role of the AEF in Europe, as General Pershing struggled to avoid committing American forces into battle piecemeal and before they had been thoroughly trained. The second contributor to the burst of journalistic rhapsody was, ironically enough, Pershing's strict policy of censorship. Correspondents were forbidden to identify Army divisions or other units by name, nickname, or number. They were forbidden to identify troops as from a particular state or region. They were forbidden to distinguish among the Army's service branches, such as artillery, cavalry, and infantry.

They were forbidden to make reference to the size of a unit, so they could not use such words as "regiment" or "battalion." All of these restrictions made reporting both difficult and unappealing. After all, in any good story it is essential to know the names of the characters, but Pershing's censorship policy enveloped in dull anonymity the entire American enterprise in the Great War.

With one exception. When the US 2nd Division went to Europe, correspondents pointed out to Pershing's press officer that the US Marines were a service separate from the Army. They were not a branch—like the cavalry or the infantry—so it stood to reason that correspondents should be permitted to identify them by name—that is, "Marines" as opposed to "Army." Pershing agreed.

And now America's journalists had a name—and a character, a most remarkable character—to insert into their stories. Given this, the "anonymous" Army receded into obscurity beneath the headlines, more and more of which were devoted to "our Marines."

Many in the US Army were not happy, and with good reason.

Major General Robert Lee Bullard, commanding officer of the 1st Division, complained that the brigade of Marines constituted just one-third of the 2nd Division yet was accorded all the glory for the victory at Belleau Wood.

"To prevent valuable information from reaching the enemy," Bullard explained in his 1925 *Personalities and Reminiscences of the War*, "our censorship regulations prohibited press reports from mentioning organizations. To say 'Marines' did not violate this regulation: It mentioned no organization. So the press reports of the 2nd Division shouted, 'Marines,' 'Marines,' 'Marines,' until the word resounded over the whole earth and made the inhabitants thereof, except a few Americans in the army in France, believe there was nothing in the 2nd Division, and, indeed, nothing in front of the Germans, but Marines."

One evening, while news "reports were resounding at the highest and American readers were acclaiming the Marines as the saviours of

Paris and the war, General Pershing came on a visit to me," Bullard recounted.

"General," I said to him at dinner, "I see that the 2nd Marines (emphasizing the 2nd as though that division was all Marines) have won the war at Belleau Wood."

"Yes," he answered dryly, "and I stopped it yesterday as I passed there."

But had he? He stopped only what was yet to come, not what had already gone forth. That he could not stop, and it was, I say, enough to convince all good enthusiastic Americans that at Belleau Wood there was nothing but Marines and, of course, dead Germans, their victims and theirs alone.

On June 9, the *New York Times* reported that according to "recruiting headquarters in New York . . . application for service [in the Marine Corps] has increased more than 100 percent in the last two days." Young men picked up newspapers, read about the Marine "triumph" at Belleau Wood, and rushed to the recruiting office.

The US Congress was not far behind them. On July 1, 1918—as it turned out, the day after Belleau Wood was finally secured—lawmakers authorized the expansion of the Corps to 3,017 officers and 75,500 men. To be sure, this was still a small and elite force, but it represented a massive increase from the 15,000 men with the Corps who had entered combat, and it brought an absolute end to all talk among legislative as well as executive circles of ever abolishing the Marines.

Even as the newspapers printed their headlines, the 4th Marine Brigade set about collecting and evacuating its wounded and counting its dead. On June 6 alone, thirty-one officers of the brigade became casualties (twenty-five wounded, six killed) as did 1,056 enlisted Marines, of whom 222 were killed in action or later died of their wounds.

2

INFAMOUS DAY

Marines at
Pearl Harbor

ROBERT J. CRESSMAN AND
J. MICHAEL WENGER

OAHU, DECEMBER 7, 1941

Unlike the battleships the enemy had caught moored on Battleship Row, *Pennsylvania*, the fleet flagship, lay on keel blocks, sharing Dry Dock No. 1 at the Navy Yard with *Cassin* and *Downes*—two destroyers side by side ahead of her. Three of *Pennsylvania's* four propeller shafts had been removed, and she was receiving all steam, power, and water from the yard. Although her being in drydock had excused her from taking part in antiaircraft drills, her crew swiftly manned her machine guns after the first bombs exploded among the PBY flying boats parked on the south end of Ford Island. "Air defense stations" then sounded, followed by "general quarters." Men knocked the locks off ready-use ammunition stowage and *Pennsylvania* opened fire about 0802.

The fleet flagship and the two destroyers nestled in the drydock ahead of her led a charmed life until dive bombers from *Soryu* and *Hiryu* targeted the drydock area between 0830 and 0915. One bomb penetrated *Pennsylvania's* boat deck, just to the rear of 5-inch/25 gun no. 7, and detonated in casemate no. 9. Of *Pennsylvania's* Marine detachment, two men (Privates Patrick P. Tobin and George H. Wade Jr.) died outright, thirteen fell wounded, and six were listed as missing. Three of the wounded—Corporal Morris E. Nations, Jesse C. Vincent Jr., and Private First Class Floyd D. Stewart—died later the same day.

Lieutenant Colonel Daniel Russel Fox, USMC, as the Division Marine Officer on the staff of Rear Admiral Isaac C. Kidd, Commander, Battleship Division One, was the most senior Marine officer to die on board *Arizona* on the morning of December 7, 1941. Fox had enlisted in the Marine Corps in 1916. For heroism in France on October 4, 1918, when he was a member of the 17th Company, Fifth Marines, he was awarded the Navy Cross. He also was decorated with the Army's

Distinguished Service Cross and the French Croix de Guerre. Fox was commissioned in 1921 and later served in Nicaragua as well as China.

As the onslaught descended upon the battleships and the air station, Marine detachments hurried to their battle stations on board other ships elsewhere at Pearl. In the Navy Yard lay *Argonne*, the flagship of the Base Force; the heavy cruisers *New Orleans* and *San Francisco*; and the light cruisers *Honolulu*, *St. Louis*, and *Helena*. To the northeast of Ford Island lay the light cruiser *Phoenix*.

Although *Utah* was torpedoed and sunk at her berth early in the attack, her fourteen Marines, on temporary duty at the 14th Naval District Rifle Range, found useful employment combatting the enemy. The Fleet Machine Gun School lay on Oahu's south coast, west of the Pearl Harbor entrance channel, at Fort Weaver. The men stationed there, including several Marines on temporary duty from the carrier *Enterprise* and the battleships *California* and *Pennsylvania*, sprang to action at the first sounds of war. Working with the men from the Rifle Range, all hands set up and mounted guns and broke out and belted ammunition between 0755 and 0810. All those present at the range were issued pistols or rifles from the facility's armory.

Soon after the raid began, Platoon Sergeant Harold G. Edwards set about securing the camp against any incursion the Japanese might attempt from the landward side and also supervised the emplacement of machine guns along the beach. Lieutenant (j.g.) Roy R. Nelson, the officer in charge of the Rifle Range, remembered the many occasions when Captain Frank M. Reinecke, commanding officer of *Utah*'s Marine detachment and the senior instructor at the Fleet Machine Gun School (and, as his Naval Academy classmates remembered, quite a conversationalist), had maintained that the school's weapons would be a great asset if anybody ever attacked Hawaii.

By 0810, Reinecke's gunners stood ready to prove the point and soon engaged the enemy—most likely torpedo planes clearing Pearl Harbor or high-level bombers approaching from the south. Nearby Army units, perhaps alerted by the Marines's fire, opened up soon thereafter. Unfortunately, the eager gunners succeeded in downing one of two SBDs from *Enterprise* that were attempting to reach Hickam Field. An Army crash boat, fortunately, rescued the pilot and his wounded passenger soon thereafter.

On board *Argonne*, meanwhile, alongside 1010 Dock, her Marines manned her starboard 3-inch/23 battery and her machine guns. Commander Fred W. Connor, the ship's commanding officer, later credited Corporal Alfred Schlag with shooting down one Japanese plane as it headed for Battleship Row.

When the attack began, *Helena* lay moored alongside 1010 Dock, the venerable minelayer *Oglala* outboard. A signalman, standing watch on the light cruiser's signal bridge at 0757, identified the planes over Ford Island as Japanese, and the ship went to general quarters.

Before she could fire a shot in her own defense, however, one eight-hundred-kilogram torpedo barreled into her starboard side about a minute after the general alarm had begun summoning her men to their battle stations. The explosion vented up from the forward engine room through the hatch and passageways, catching many of the crew running to their stations, and started fires on the third deck. Platoon Sergeant Robert W. Teague, Privates First Class Paul F. Huebner Jr. and George E. Johnson, and Private Lester A. Morris were all severely burned. Johnson later died.

To the southeast, *New Orleans* lay across the pier from her sister ship *San Francisco*. The former went to general quarters soon after enemy planes had been sighted dive-bombing Ford Island around 0757. At 0805, as several low-flying torpedo planes roared by, bound for Battleship Row, Marine sentries on the fantail opened fire with rifles and .45s. *New Orleans's* men, meanwhile, so swiftly manned the 1.1-inch/75 quads and .50-caliber machine guns, under the direction of Captain William R. Collins, the commanding officer of the ship's Marine detachment, that the ship actually managed to shoot at torpedo planes passing her stern.

San Francisco, however, under major overhaul with neither operative armament nor major caliber ammunition on board, was thus restricted to having her men fire small arms at whatever Japanese planes came within range. Some of her crew, though, hurried over to *New Orleans*, which was near-missed by one bomb, and helped man her 5-inchers.

St. Louis, outboard of *Honolulu*, went to general quarters at 0757 and opened fire with her 1.1 quadruple mounted antiaircraft and .50-caliber machine gun batteries, and after getting her 5-inch mounts in commission by 0830—although without power in train—she hauled in her lines at 0847 and got underway at 0931. With all 5-inchers in full commission by 0947, she proceeded to sea, passing the channel entrance buoys abeam around 1000. *Honolulu*, damaged by a near miss from a bomb, remained moored at her berth throughout the action.

Phoenix, moored by herself in berth C-6 in Pearl Harbor, to the northeast of Ford Island, noted the attacking planes at 0755 and went to general quarters. Her machine gun battery opened fire at 0810 on the attacking planes as they came within range, her antiaircraft battery five minutes later. Ultimately, after two false starts (where she had gotten underway and left her berth only to see sortie signals canceled each time), *Phoenix* cleared the harbor later that day and put to sea.

For at least one Marine, though, the day's adventure was not over when the Japanese planes departed. Search flights took off from Ford Island, pilots taking up utility aircraft with scratch crews, to look for the enemy carriers that had launched the raid. Mustered at the naval air station on Ford Island, *Oklahoma*'s Sergeant Hailey, still clad in his oil-soaked underwear, volunteered to go up in a plane that was leaving on a search mission at around 1130. He remained aloft in the plane, armed with a rifle, for some five hours.

After the attacking planes had retired, the grim business of cleaning up and getting on with the war had to be undertaken. Muster had to be taken to determine who was missing, who was wounded, who lay dead. Men sought out their friends and shipmates. First Lieutenant Cornelius C. Smith Jr., from the Marine Barracks at the Navy Yard, searched in vain among the maimed and dying at the Naval Hospital later that day for his friend Harry Gaver from *Oklahoma*. Death respected no rank. The most senior Marine to die that day was Lieutenant Colonel Daniel R. Fox, the decorated World War I hero and the division Marine officer on the staff of the Commander, Battleship Division One, Rear Admiral Isaac C. Kidd, who, along with Lieutenant Colonel Fox, had been killed in *Arizona*. The tragedy of Pearl Harbor struck some families with more force than others: numbered among *Arizona*'s lost were Private Gordon E. Shive, of the battleship's Marine detachment, and his brother, Radioman Third Class Malcolm H. Shive, a member of the ship's company.

Over the next few days, Marines from the sunken ships received reassignment to other vessels—*Nevada*'s Marines deployed ashore to set up defensive positions in the fields adjacent to the grounded and listing battleship—and the dead, those who could be found, were interred with appropriate ceremony. Eventually, the deeds of Marines in the battleship detachments were recognized by appropriate commendations and advancements in ratings.

Chief among them, Gunnery Sergeant Douglas, Sergeant Hailey, and Corporals Driskell and Darling were each awarded the Navy

Cross. For his "meritorious conduct at the peril of his own life," Major Shapley was commended and awarded the Silver Star. Lieutenant Simensen was awarded a posthumous Bronze Star, while *Tennessee's* commanding officer commended Captain White for the way in which he had directed that battleship's antiaircraft guns that morning.

CAUGHT FLAT-FOOTED

In the officers' mess at Ewa, the officer of the day, Captain Leonard W. Ashwell, noticed two formations of aircraft at 0755. The first looked like eighteen "torpedo planes" flying at one thousand feet toward Pearl Harbor from Barbers Point, but the second, to the northwest, comprised about twenty-one planes, just coming over the hills from the direction of Nanakuli, also at an altitude of about one thousand feet. Ashwell, intrigued by the sight, stepped outside for a better look. The second formation, of single-seat fighters (the two divisions from *Akagi* and *Kaga*), flew just to the north of Ewa and wheeled to the right. Then, flying in a "string" formation, they commenced firing. Recognizing the planes as Japanese, Ashwell burst back into the mess, shouting, "Air Raid . . . Air Raid! Pass the word!" He then sprinted for the guard house to have "Call to Arms" sounded.

At his home on Ewa Beach, three miles southeast of the air station, Captain Richard C. Mangrum, VMSB-232's flight officer, sat reading the Sunday comics. Often residents of that area had heard gunnery exercises, but on a Sunday morning? The chatter of gunfire and the dull thump of explosions, however, drew Mangrum's attention away from the cartoons. As he looked out his front door, planes with red ball markings on the wings and fuselage roared by at very low altitude, bound for Pearl Harbor. Up the valley in the direction of Wheeler Field, smoke was boiling skyward, as it was from Ewa. As he set out for Ewa on an old country road, wives and children of Marines who lived in the Ewa Beach neighborhood began gathering at the Mangrum's house.

Private First Class James W. Mann, the driver assigned to Ewa's 1938 Ford ambulance, had been refueling the vehicle when the attack began. When Lieutenant Thomas L. Allman, Medical Corps, USN, the group medical officer, saw the first planes break into flames, he ordered Mann to take the ambulance to the flight line. Accompanied by Pharmacist's Mate 2nd Class Orin D. Smith, a corpsman from sick bay, they sped off. The Japanese planes seemed to be attracted to the bright red crosses on the ambulance, however, and halted its progress near the mooring mast. Realizing that they were under attack, Mann floored the brake pedal and the Ford screeched to a halt. Rather than leave the vehicle for a safer area, Mann and Smith crawled underneath it so that they could continue their mission as quickly as possible. The strafing, however, continued unabated. Ironically, the first casualty Mann had to collect was the man lying prone beside him. Orin Smith felt a searing pain as one of the Japanese 7.7-millimeter rounds found its mark in the fleshy part of his left calf. Seeing that the corpsman had been hurt, Mann assisted him out from under the vehicle and up into the cab. Despite continued strafing that shot out four tires, Mann pressed doggedly ahead and delivered the wounded Smith to sick bay.

Also watching the smoke beginning to billow skyward was Sergeant Duane W. Shaw, USMCR, the driver of the station fire truck. Normally, during off-duty hours, the truck sat parked a quarter mile from the landing area. Shaw, figuring that it was his job to put out the fires, climbed into the fire engine and set off. Unfortunately, like Private First Class Mann's ambulance, Sergeant Shaw's bright red engine moving across the embattled camp soon attracted strafing Zeroes. Unfazed by the enemy fire that perforated his vehicle in several places, he drove doggedly toward the flight line until another Zero shot out his tires. Only then pausing to make a hasty estimate of the situation, he reasoned that with the fire truck at least temporarily out of service he would have to do something else. Jumping down from the cab, he soon got himself a rifle and some ammunition. Then he set out for the flight line. If he could not put out fires, he could at least do some firing of his own at the men who caused them.

With the parking area cloaked in black smoke, Japanese fighter pilots shifted their efforts to the planes either out for repairs in the rear areas or to the utility planes parked north of the intersection of the main runways. Inside ten minutes' time, machine gun fire likewise transformed many of those planes into flaming wreckage.

Firing only small arms and rifles in the opening stages, the Marines fought back against *Kaga*'s fighters as best they could, with almost reckless heroism. Lieutenant Shiga remembered one particular Leatherneck who, oblivious to the machine gun fire striking the ground around him and kicking up dirt, stood transfixed, emptying his sidearm at Shiga's Zero as it roared past. Years later, Shiga would describe that lone, defiant, and unknown Marine as the bravest American he had ever met.

Overcoming the initial shock of the first strafing attack, Ewa's Marines took stock of their situation. As soon as the last of Itaya's and Shiga's Zeroes had departed, Marines went out and manned stations with rifles and .30-caliber machine guns taken from damaged aircraft and from the squadron ordnance rooms. Technical Sergeant William G. Turnage, an armorer, supervised the setting up of the free machine guns. Technical Sergeant Anglin, meanwhile, took his little boy to the guard house, where a woman motorist agreed to drive Hank home to his mother. As it would turn out, that reunion was not to be accomplished until much later that day, "inasmuch as the distraught mother had already left home to look for her son."

Master Technical Sergeant Emil S. Peters, a veteran of action in Nicaragua, had, during the first attack, reported to the central ordnance tent to lend a hand in manning a gun. By the time he arrived there, however, there were none left to man. Then he saw a Douglas SBD-2, one of two spares assigned to VMSB-232, parked behind the squadron's tents. Enlisting the aid of Private William G. Turner, VMSB-231's squadron clerk, Peters ran over to the ex-*Lexington* machine that still bore her USN markings, 2-B-6, pulled the after canopy forward, and clambered in the after cockpit, stepping hard on the foot pedal to unship the free .30-caliber Browning from its housing in the after fuselage, and then locking it in place. Turner, having obtained a supply of belted ammunition, took his place on the wing as Peters's assistant.

For the better part of an hour, Lieutenant Wilmer E. Gallaher, executive officer of Scouting Squadron 6, had circled fitfully over the Pacific swells south of Oahu, waiting for the situation there to settle down. At about 0945, when he had seen that the skies seemed relatively clear of Japanese planes, Gallaher decided rather than face friendly fire over Pearl he would go to Ewa instead. They had barely stopped on the strip, however, when a Marine ran out to Gallaher's plane and yelled, "For God's sake, get into the air or they'll strafe you, too!" Other *Enterprise* pilots likewise saw ground crews frantically motioning for them to take off immediately. Instructed to "take off and stay in the air until [the] air raid was over," the *Enterprise* pilots took off and headed for Pearl Harbor. Although all seven SBDs left Ewa, only three (Gallaher's; his wingman, Ensign William P. West's; and Ensign Cleo J. Dobson's) would make it as far as Ford Island. A tremendous volume of antiaircraft fire over the harbor rose to meet what was thought to be yet another attack; seeing the reception accorded Gallaher, West, and Dobson, the other four pilots—Lieutenant (j. g.) Hart D. Hilton and

Ensigns Carlton T. Fogg, Edwin J. Kroeger, and Frederick T. Weber—wheeled around and headed back to Ewa, landing around 1015 to find a far better reception that time around. Within a matter of minutes, the Marines began rearming and refueling Hilton's, Kroeger's and Weber's SBDs. The Marines discovered that Fogg's Dauntless had taken a hit that had holed a fuel tank and would require repairs.

Although it is unlikely that even one of the Ewa Marines thought so at the time, even as they serviced the *Enterprise* SBDs that sat on the landing mat, the Japanese raid on Oahu was over. Vice Admiral Nagumo, already feeling that he had pushed his luck far enough, was eager to get as far away from the waters north of Oahu as soon as possible. At least for the time being, the Marines at Ewa had nothing to fear.

"THEY'RE KICKING THE HELL OUT OF PEARL HARBOR"

Over at the Marine Barracks, the officer of the guard, Second Lieutenant Arnold D. Swartz, after having inspected his sentries, had retired to the officer of the day's room to await breakfast. Stepping out onto the lanai (patio) at about 0755 to talk to the field music about morning colors, he noticed several planes diving in the direction of the naval air station. He thought initially that it seemed a bit early for practice bombing, but then he saw a flash and heard the resulting explosion that immediately dispelled any illusions he might have held that what he was seeing was merely an exercise. Seeing a plane with "red balls" on the wings roar by at low level convinced Swartz that Japanese planes were attacking.

Major Harold C. Roberts had earned a Navy Cross as a corpsman assigned to the Marines during World War I, and a second award in

1928 as a Marine officer in Nicaragua. As acting commanding officer of the 3rd Defense Battalion at Pearl Harbor on December 7, he was a veritable dynamo, organizing it to battle the attacking Japanese. He was killed at Okinawa in June 1945 while commanding the 22nd Marines, but not before his performance of duty had merited him the award of his third Navy Cross.

Over in the squad room of Barracks B, First Lieutenant Harry F. Noyes Jr., the range officer for Battery E, 3-inch Antiaircraft Group, 3rd Defense Battalion, heard the sound of a loud explosion coming from the direction of the harbor at about 0750. First assuming that blasting crews were busy—there had been a lot of construction recently—Noyes cocked his ears. The new sounds seemed a bit different, "more higher-pitched, and louder." At that, he sprang from his bed, ran across the room, and peered northward just in time to see a dirty column of water rising from the harbor from another explosion and a Japanese plane pulling out of its dive. The plane, bearing red *hinomaru* (rising sun insignia) under its wings, left no doubt as to its identity.

The explosions likewise awakened Lieutenant Colonel William J. Whaling and Major James "Jerry" Monaghan who, while Colonel Gilder D. Jackson, commanding officer of the Marine Barracks, was at sea in *Indianapolis* (CA-35) en route to Johnston Island for tests of Higgins landing boats, shared his quarters at Pearl Harbor. Shortly before 0800, Whaling rolled over and asked, "Jerry, don't you think the Admiral is a little bit inconsiderate of guests?" Monaghan, then also awake, replied, "I'll go down and see about it." Whaling, meanwhile, lingered in bed until more blasts rattled the quarters' windows. Thinking that he had not seen any 5-inch guns emplaced close to the building and that something was wrong, he got up and walked over to the window that faced the harbor. Looking out, he saw smoke and, turning, remarked, "This thing is so real that I believe that's an oil tank burning right in front there." Both men then dressed and hurried across the parade ground, where they encountered Lieutenant Colonel Elmer E. Hall, commanding officer of the 2nd Engineer Battalion. "Elmer," Whaling said amiably, "this is a mighty fine show you are putting on. I have never seen anything quite like it."

Meanwhile, Swartz ordered the field music to sound "Call to Arms." Then, running into the officer's section of the mess hall, Swartz informed the officer of the day, First Lieutenant Cornelius C. Smith Jr., who had been enjoying a cup of coffee with Marine Gunner Floyd McCorkle when sharp blasts had rocked the building, that the Japanese were attacking. Like Swartz, they ran out onto the lanai. Standing there, speechless, they watched the first enemy planes diving on Ford Island.

Marines began to stumble, eyes wide in disbelief, from the barracks. Some were lurching, on the run, into pants and shirts; a few wore only towels. Swartz then ordered one of the platoon sergeants to roust out the men and get them under cover of the trees outside. Smith, too, then ran outside to the parade ground. As he looked at the rising smoke and the Japanese planes, he doubted those who had derided the "Japs" as "cross-eyed, second-rate pilots who couldn't hit the broad side of a barn door." It was enough to turn his stomach. "They're kicking the hell out of Pearl Harbor," he thought.

Lieutenant (j. g.) William R. Franklin (Dental Corps), USN, the dental officer for the 3rd Defense Battalion's Headquarters and Service Battery, and the only medical officer present, had organized first aid and stretcher parties in the barracks. As the other doctors arrived, Roberts directed them to set up dressing stations at each battalion headquarters and one at sick bay. Elsewhere, Marines vacated one

one-hundred-man temporary barracks, the noncommissioned officer's club and the post exchange, to ready them for casualties. Parties of Marines also reported to the waterfront area to assist in collecting and transporting casualties from the ships in the harbor to the Naval Hospital.

By the time the Marines had gotten their new fire precautions in place, the Japanese second wave attack was in full swing. Although their pilots selected targets exclusively from among the Pacific Fleet warships, the Marines at the barracks in the Navy Yard still were able to take the Japanese planes, most of which seemed to be coming in from the west and southwest, under fire. While Marines were busily setting up the three-inch guns, several civilian yard workmen grabbed up rifles and "brought their fire to bear upon the enemy," allowing Swartz's men to continue their work.

The Japanese eventually put Major Roberts's ingenious fire control methods—the field musics—to the test. After hearing four hearty blasts from the bandsmen, the .50-calibers began hammering out cones of tracer that caught two low-flying dive bombers as they pulled out of their runs over Pearl, prompting Roberts's fear that the ships would fire at them, too, and hit the barracks. One Val slanted earthward near what appeared to be either the west end of the lower tank farm or the south end of the Naval Hospital reservation, while the other, emitting great quantities of smoke, crashed west-southwest of the parade ground.

Although the Marines's success against their tormentors must have seemed sweet indeed, a skeptical Captain Taxis thought it more likely that the crews of the two Vals bagged by the machine gunners had just run out of luck. Most of the firing, in his opinion, had been quite ineffectual, mostly "directed at enemy planes far beyond range of the weapons and merely fired into the air at no target at all." Gunners on board the fleet's warships were faring little better!

Almost simultaneously with the dive-bombing attacks, horizontal bombing attacks began. Major Roberts noted that the eighteen bombers "flew in two Vees of nine planes each in column of Vees and [that] they kept a good formation." At least some of those planes appeared to have bombed the battleship *Pennsylvania* and the destroyers *Cassin* and *Downes* in Dry Dock No. 1. In the confusion, however, Roberts probably saw two divisions of Kates from *Zuikaku* preparing for their attack runs on Hickam Field. A single division of such planes from *Shokaku*, meanwhile, attacked the Navy Yard and the Naval Air Station.

Well removed from the barracks, Marines assigned to the Navy Yards Fire Department rendered invaluable assistance in leading critical firefighting efforts. Heading the department, Sergeant Harold F. Abbott supervised the distribution of the various units and coordinated the flood of volunteers who stepped forward to help.

One of Abbott's men, Private First Class Marion M. Milbrandt, with his one-thousand-gallon pumper, summoned to the Naval Hospital grounds, found that one of *Kaga*'s Kates—struck by machine gun fire from the ships moored in the Repair Basin—had crashed near there. The resulting fire, fed by the crashed plane's gasoline, threatened the facility, but Milbrandt and his crew controlled the blaze.

Other Marine firefighters were hard at work alongside Dry Dock No. 1. *Pennsylvania* had not been the only ship not fully ready for war, because she lay immobile at one end of the drydock. *Downes* lay in the dock, undergoing various items of work, while *Cassin* had been having ordnance alterations at the Yard and thus had none of her 5-inch/38s ready for firing. Both destroyers soon came in for some unwanted attention.

As bombs turned the two destroyers into cauldrons of flames and their crews abandoned ship, two sailors from *Downes*, meanwhile, sprinted over to the Marine Barracks: Gunner's Mate First Class Michael G. Odietus and Gunner's Mate Second Class Curtis P. Schulze. After the order to abandon ship had been given, both had, on their own initiative, gone to the Marine Barracks to assist in the distribution of arms and ammunition. They soon returned, however, each gunner's mate with a Browning Automatic Rifle in hand, to do his part in fighting back.

A 5-inch/25-caliber open pedestal mount antiaircraft gun—manned here by sailors on board the heavy cruiser *Astoria* (CA-34) in early 1942—was the standard battleship and heavy cruiser antiaircraft weapon at Pearl Harbor. The mount itself weighed more than 20,000 pounds, while the gun fired a 53.8-pound projectile to a maximum range (at 45 degrees elevation) of 14,500 yards. It was a weapon such as this that Sergeants Hailey and Wears and Private First Class Curran, after the sinking of their ship, *Oklahoma* (BB-37), helped man on board *Maryland* (BB-46) on December 7, 1941.

Utilizing three of the department's pumpers, meanwhile, the first firefighters from the yard, who included Corporal John Gimson, Privates First Class William M. Brashear, William A. Hopper, Peter Kerdikes, Frank W. Feret, Marvin D. Dallman, and Corporal Milbrandt, among them, soon arrived and began to play water on the burning ships. At about 0915, four torpedo warheads on board *Downes* cooked off and exploded, the concussion tearing the hoses from the hands of the men fighting the blaze and sending fragments everywhere, temporarily forcing all hands to retreat to the nearby road and sprawl there. Knocked flat several times by the explosions, the Marines and other firefighters, including men from *Cassin* and *Downes* and civilian yard workmen, remained on the job.

Explosions continued to wrack the two destroyers, while subsequent partial flooding of the dock caused *Cassin* to pivot on her forefoot and heel over onto her sister ship. Working under the direction of Lieutenant William R. Spear, a fifty-seven-year-old retired naval officer called to the colors, the firemen were understandably concerned that the oil fires burning in proximity to the two destroyers might drift aft in the partially flooded drydock and breach the caisson, unleashing a wall of water that would carry *Pennsylvania* (three of whose four propeller shafts had been pulled for overhaul) down upon the burning destroyers. Preparing for that eventuality, Private First Class Don O. Femmer, in charge of the 750-gallon pumper, stood ready should the conflagration spread to the northeast through the dock.

Fortunately, circumstances never required Femmer and his men to defend the caisson from fire, but the young private had more than his share of troubles when his pumper broke down at what could have been a critical moment. Undaunted, Femmer made temporary repairs and stood his ground at the caisson throughout the raid.

At the opposite end of the drydock, meanwhile, Private First Class Omar E. Hill fared little better with his five-hundred-gallon pumper. As if the firefighting labors were not arduous enough, a ruptured circulating water line threatened to shut down his fire engine. Holding a rag on the broken line while his comrades raced away to obtain spare parts, Hill kept his pumper in the battle.

Meanwhile, firefighters on the west side of the dock succeeded in passing three hoses to men on *Pennsylvania*'s forecastle, where they directed blasts of water ahead of the ship and down the starboard side to prevent the burning oil, which resembled a "seething cauldron," from drifting aft. A second five-hundred-gallon engine crew, led by Private First Class Dallman, battled the fires at the southwest end of the drydock, despite the suffocating oily black smoke billowing forth from *Cassin* and *Downes*. Eventually, by 1035, the Marines and other volunteers—who included the indomitable Tai Sing Loo—had succeeded in quelling the fires on board *Cassin*; those on board *Downes* were put out early that afternoon.

More work, however, lay in store for Corporal Milbrandt and his crew. Between 0755 and 0900, three Vals had attacked the destroyer *Shaw*, which shared *YFD-2* with the little yard tug *Sotoyomo*. All three scored hits. Fires ultimately reached *Shaw*'s forward magazines and triggered an explosion that sent tendrils of smoke into the sky and severed the ship's bow. Several other volunteer units were already battling the blaze with hose carts and two 350-gallon pumpers sent in from Honolulu. Milbrandt, aided as well by the Pan American Airways fire boat normally stationed at Pearl City, ultimately succeeded in extinguishing the stricken destroyer's fires.

In the meantime, after having pounded the military installations on Oahu for nearly two hours, between 0940 and 1000 the Japanese planes made their way westward to return to the carrier decks from whence they had arisen. With the respite offered by the enemy's departure (no one knew for sure whether or not they would be back), the Marines at last found time to take stock of their situation. Fortunately, the Marine Barracks lay some distance away from what had interested the Japanese the most: the ships in the harbor proper. Although some "shell fragments literally rained at times," the material loss sustained by the barracks was slight. Moreover, it had been American gunfire from the ships in the harbor, rather than bombs from Japanese planes overhead, that had inflicted the damage; at one point that morning a 3-inch antiaircraft shell crashed through the roof of a storehouse—the only damage sustained by the barracks during the entire attack.

Considering the carnage at the airfields on Oahu, and especially among the units of the Pacific Fleet, only four men of the 3rd Defense

Battalion had been wounded: Sergeant Samuel H. Cobb Jr. of the 3rd Defense Battalion's 3-inch Antiaircraft Group suffered head injuries serious enough to warrant his being transferred to the Naval Hospital for treatment, while Private First Class Jules B. Maioran and Private William J. Whitcomb of the Machine Gun Group and Sergeant Leo Hendricks II of the Headquarters and Service Battery suffered less serious injuries. In addition, two men sent with the trucks to find ammunition for the 3-inch batteries suffered injuries when they fell off the vehicles.

In their subsequent reports, the defense battalion and barracks officers declined to single out individuals, noting no outstanding individual behavior during the raid—only the steady discharge of duty expected of Marines. To be sure, great confusion existed, especially at first, but the command quickly settled down to work and "showed no more than the normal excitement and no trace of panic or even uneasiness." If anything, the Marines tended to place themselves at risk unnecessarily, as they went about their business coolly and, in many cases, "in utter disregard of their own safety." Major Roberts recommended that the entire 3rd Defense Battalion be commended for "their initiative, coolness under fire, and [the] alacrity with which they emplaced their guns."

Commendations, however, were not the order of the day on December 7. Although the Japanese had left, the Marines expected them to return and finish the job they had begun (many Japanese pilots, including Fuchida, wanted to do just that). If another attack was to come, there was much to do to prepare for it. As the skies cleared of enemy planes, the Marines at the barracks secured their establishment and took steps to complete the work already begun on the defenses. At 1030, the 3rd Defense Battalion's corporal of the guard moved to the barracks and set the battalion's radio to the Army Information Service frequency, thus enabling them to pass "flash" messages to all groups. The Marines also distributed gas masks to all hands.

The morning and afternoon passed quickly, the men losing track of time. The initial confusion experienced during the opening moments of the raid had by that point given way to at least some semblance of order, as officers and noncoms arrived from leave and began to sort out their commands. At 1105, the 3rd Defense Battalion's Battery G deployed to makeshift defense positions as an infantry reserve in some ditches dug for building foundations. All of the messmen, many of whom had taken an active hand in the defense of the barracks against the Japanese attack, returned to the three general mess halls and opened up an around-the-clock service to all comers, including "about 6,000 meals . . . to the civilian workmen of the navy yard," a service discontinued only "after the food supply at the regular established eating places could be replenished."

By 1100, at least some of the 3-inch batteries were emplaced and ready to answer any future Japanese raids. At the north end of the parade ground, the 3rd Defense Battalion's Battery D stood ready for action at 1135, while another battery, consisting of three guns and an antiaircraft director (the one originally earmarked for Midway), lay at the south end. At 1220, Major Roberts organized his battalion's strength into six task groups. Task group no. 1 was to double the Navy Yard guard force, no. 2 was to provide antiaircraft defense, and no. 3 was to provide machine gun defense. No. 4 was to provide infantry reserve and firefighting crews, no. 5 was to coordinate transportation, and no. 6 was to provide ammunition and equipment, as well as messing and billeting support.

By 1300, meanwhile, all of the fires in Dry Dock No. 1 had been extinguished, permitting the Marine and civilian firefighters to secure their hard-worked equipment. Although the two battered destroyers, *Cassin* and *Downes*, appeared to be total losses, those who had battled the blaze could take great satisfaction in knowing that they had not only spared *Pennsylvania* from serious fire damage but had also played a major role in saving the drydock. As Tai Sing Loo recounted later, "The Marines of the Fire Department of the Navy Yard are the Heroes of the Day of Dec. 7, 1941 that save the *Cassin* and *Downes* and USS *Pennsylvania* in Dry Dock No. 1."

Later that afternoon, Battery D's four officers and sixty-eight enlisted men, with four .30-caliber machine guns sent along with them for good measure, moved from the barracks over to Hickam Field to provide the Army installation some measure of antiaircraft protection. Hickam also benefitted from the provision of the 2nd Engineer Battalion's service and equipment. After the attack, the battalion's dump truck and two bulldozers lumbered over to the stricken air base to assist in clearing what remained of the bombers that had been parked wingtip to wingtip, and filling bomb craters.

Around 1530, a Marine patrol approached Tai Sing Loo, a familiar figure about the Navy Yard, and asked him to do them a favor. They had had no lunch; some had had no breakfast because of the events of the day. Going to the garage, Loo rode his bright red "putput" over to the 3rd Defense Battalion mess hall and related to his old friend Technical Sergeant Joseph A. Newland the tale of the hungry Marines. Newland and his messmen prepared ham and chicken sandwiches and Loo made the rounds of all the posts he could reach.

In the afternoon and early evening hours of December 7, the men received reports that their drinking water was poisoned and that various points on Oahu were being bombed and/or invaded. In the absence of any real news, such alarming reports—especially when added to the already nervous state of the defenders—only fueled the fear and paranoia prevalent among all ranks and rates. In addition, most of the men were exhausted after their exertions of the morning and afternoon. Dog tired, many would remain on duty for thirty-six hours without relief. Drawn, unshaven faces and puffy eyes were common. Tense, expectant, and anxious Marines and sailors at Pearl spent a fitful night on December 7.

It is little wonder that mistakes would be made that would have tragic consequences, especially in the stygian darkness of that first blacked-out Hawaiian night following the raid. Still some hours away from Oahu, the carrier *Enterprise* and her air group had been flying searches and patrols throughout the day, in a so-far fruitless effort to locate the Japanese carrier force. South of Oahu, one of her pilots spotted what he thought was a Japanese ship and *Enterprise* launched a thirty-one-plane strike at 1642. Nagumo's fleet, however, was homeward bound. While *Enterprise* recovered the torpedo planes and dive bombers after their fruitless search, she directed the fighters to land at NAS Pearl Harbor.

Machine guns on board the battleship *Pennsylvania* opened fire on the flight as it came for a landing, though, and soon the entire harbor exploded into a fury of gunfire as cones of tracers converged on the incoming "Wildcats." Three of the F4Fs slanted earthward almost immediately; a fourth crashed a short time later. Two managed to land at Ford Island. The 3rd Defense Battalion's journalist later recorded that "six planes with running lights under 400 feet altitude tried Ford Island landing and were machine gunned." It was a tragic footnote to what had been a terrible day indeed.

The Marines at Pearl Harbor had been surprised by the attack that descended upon them, but they rose to the occasion and fought back in the "best traditions of the naval service." While the enemy had attacked with tenacity and daring, no less so was the response from the

Marines on board the battleships and cruisers, at Ewa Mooring Mast Field, and at the Marine Barracks. One can only think that Admiral Isoroku Yamamoto's worst fears of America's "terrible resolve" and that he had awakened a sleeping giant would have been confirmed if he could have peered into the faces, so deeply etched with grim determination, of the Marines who had survived the events of that December day in 1941.

3

TAKING MOUNT SURIBACHI

COLONEL JOSEPH H. ALEXANDER

D-DAY

Weather conditions around Iwo Jima on D-day morning, February 19, 1945, were almost ideal. At 0645 Admiral Turner signaled, "Land the landing force!"

Shore bombardment ships did not hesitate to engage the enemy island at near-point-blank range. Battleships and cruisers steamed as close as two thousand yards to level their guns against island targets. Many of the "Old Battleships" had performed this dangerous mission in all theaters of the war. Marines came to recognize and appreciate their contributions. It seemed fitting that the old *Nevada*, raised from the muck and ruin of Pearl Harbor, should lead the bombardment force close ashore. Marines also admired the battleship *Arkansas*, built in 1912, and recently returned from the Atlantic where she had battered German positions at Pointe du Hoc at Normandy during the epic Allied landing on June 6, 1944.

Lieutenant colonels Donald M. Weller and William W. "Bucky" Buchanan, both artillery officers, had devised a modified form of the "rolling barrage" for use by the bombarding gunships against beachfront targets just before H-hour. This concentration of naval gunfire would advance progressively as the troops landed, always remaining four hundred yards to their front. Air spotters would help regulate the pace. Such an innovation appealed to the three division commanders, each having served in France during World War I. In those days, a good rolling barrage was often the only way to break a stalemate.

The shelling was terrific. Admiral Hill would later boast that "there were no proper targets for shore bombardment remaining on Dog-Day morning." This proved to be an overstatement, yet no one could deny the unprecedented intensity of firepower Hill delivered against the areas surrounding the landing beaches. As General

Kuribayashi would ruefully admit in an assessment report to Imperial General Headquarters, "we need to reconsider the power of bombardment from ships; the violence of the enemy's bombardments is far beyond description."

The amphibious task force appeared from over the horizon, the rails of the troopships crowded with combat-equipped Marines watching the spectacular fireworks. The Guadalcanal veterans among them realized a grim satisfaction watching American battleships leisurely pounding the island from just offshore. The war had come full cycle from the dark days of October 1942, when the 1st Marine Division and the Cactus Air Force endured similar shelling from Japanese battleships.

The Marines and sailors were anxious to get their first glimpse of the objective. Correspondent John P. Marquand, the Pulitzer Prize–winning writer, recorded his own first impressions of Iwo: "Its silhouette was like a sea monster, with the little dead volcano for the head, and the beach area for the neck, and all the rest of it, with its scrubby brown cliffs for the body." Lieutenant David N. Susskind, USNR, wrote down his initial thoughts from the bridge of the troopship Mellette: "Iwo Jima was a rude, ugly sight. . . . Only a geologist could look at it and not be repelled." As described in a subsequent letter home by US Navy lieutenant Michael F. Keleher, a surgeon in the 25th Marines:

The naval bombardment had already begun, and I could see the orange-yellow flashes as the battleships, cruisers, and destroyers blasted away at the island broadside. Yes, there was Iwo—surprisingly close, just like the pictures and models we had been studying for six weeks. The volcano was to our left, then the long, flat black beaches where we were going to land, and the rough rocky plateau to our right.

The commanders of the 4th and 5th Marine Divisions, Major Generals Clifton B. Cates and Keller E. Rockey, respectively, studied the island through binoculars from their respective ships. Each division would land two reinforced regiments abreast. From left to right, the beaches were designated Green, Red, Yellow, and Blue. The 5th Division would land the 28th Marines on the left flank, over Green Beach, the 27th Marines over Red. The 4th Division would land the 23rd Marines over Yellow Beach and the 25th Marines over Blue Beach on the right flank. General Schmidt reviewed the latest intelligence reports with growing uneasiness and requested a reassignment of reserve forces with General Smith. The 3rd Marine Division's 21st Marines would replace the 26th Marines as corps reserve, thus releasing the latter regiment to the 5th Division. Schmidt's landing plan envisioned the 28th Marines cutting the island in half, then returning to capture Suribachi, while the 25th Marines would scale the Rock Quarry and then serve as the hinge for the entire corps to swing around to the north. The 23rd Marines and 27th Marines would capture the first airfield and pivot north within their assigned zones.

General Cates was already concerned about the right flank. Blue Beach Two lay directly under the observation and fire of suspected Japanese positions in the Rock Quarry, whose steep cliffs overshadowed the right flank like Suribachi dominated the left. The 4th Marine Division figured that the 25th Marines would have the hardest objective to take on D-day. Said Cates, "If I knew the name of the man on the extreme right of the right-hand squad, I'd recommend him for a medal before we go in."

The choreography of the landing continued to develop. Iwo Jima would represent the pinnacle of forcible amphibious assault against a heavily fortified shore, a complex art mastered painstakingly by the Fifth Fleet over many campaigns. Seventh Air Force Martin B-24 Liberator bombers flew in from the Marianas to strike the smoking island. Rocket ships moved in to saturate nearshore targets.

Then it was time for the fighter and attack squadrons from Mitscher's Task Force 58 to contribute. The navy pilots showed their skills at bombing and strafing, but the troops naturally cheered the most at the appearance of F4U Corsairs flown by Marine Fighter Squadrons 124 and 213, led by Lieutenant Colonel William A. Millington from the fleet carrier Essex. Colonel Vernon E. Megee, in his shipboard capacity as air officer for General Smith's Expeditionary Troops staff, had urged Millington to put on a special show for the troops in the assault waves.

"Drag your bellies on the beach," he told Millington.

The Marine fighters made an impressive approach parallel to the island, then virtually did Megee's bidding, streaking low over the beaches, strafing furiously. The geography of the Pacific War since Bougainville had kept many of the ground Marines separated from their own air support, which had been operating in areas other than where they had been fighting, most notably the Central Pacific. "It was the first time a lot of them had ever seen a Marine fighter plane," said Megee. The troops were not disappointed.

The planes had barely disappeared when naval gunfire resumed, carpeting the beach areas with a building crescendo of high-explosive shells. The ship-to-shore movement was well under way, an easy thirty-minute run for the tracked landing vehicles (LVTs). This time there were enough LVTs to do the job: 68 LVT(A)4 armored amtracs mounting snub-nosed 75mm cannon leading the way, followed by 380 troop-laden LVT 4s and LVT 2s.

The waves crossed the line of departure on time and chugged confidently toward the smoking beaches, all the while under the climactic bombardment from the ships. Here there was no coral reef, no killer neap tides to be concerned with. The navy and Marine frogmen had reported the approaches free of mines or tetrahedrons. There was no premature cessation of fire. The "rolling barrage" plan took effect. Hardly a vehicle was lost to the desultory enemy fire.

The massive assault waves hit the beach within two minutes of H-hour. A Japanese observer watching the drama unfold from a cave on the slopes of Suribachi reported, "At nine o'clock in the morning several hundred landing craft with amphibious tanks in the lead rushed ashore like an enormous tidal wave." Lieutenant Colonel Robert H. Williams, executive officer of the 28th Marines, recalled that "the landing was a magnificent sight to see—two divisions landing abreast; you could see the whole show from the deck of a ship." Up to this point, so far, so good.

The first obstacle came not from the Japanese but from the beach and the parallel terraces. Iwo Jima was an emerging volcano; its steep beaches dropped off sharply, producing a narrow but violent surf zone. The soft black sand immobilized all wheeled vehicles and caused some of the tracked amphibians to belly down. The boat waves that closely followed the LVTs had more trouble. Ramps would drop, a truck or jeep would attempt to drive out, only to get stuck. In short order a succession of plunging waves hit the stalled craft before they could completely unload, filling their sterns with water and sand, broaching them broadside. The beach quickly resembled a salvage yard.

The infantry, heavily laden, found its own "foot mobility" severely restricted. In the words of Corporal Edward Hartman, a rifleman with the 4th Marine Division, "The sand was so soft it was like trying to run in loose coffee grounds." From the 28th Marines came this early, laconic report: "Resistance moderate, terrain awful."

The rolling barrage and carefully executed landing produced the desired effect, suppressing direct enemy fire, providing enough shock and distraction to enable the first assault waves to clear the beach and begin advancing inward. Within minutes six thousand Marines were ashore. Many became thwarted by increasing fire over the terraces or down from the highlands, but hundreds leapt forward to maintain assault momentum.

The 28th Marines on the left flank had rehearsed on similar volcanic terrain on the island of Hawaii. Now, despite increasing casualties among their company commanders and the usual disorganization of landing, elements of the regiment used their initiative to strike across the narrow neck of the peninsula. The going became progressively costly as more and more Japanese strongpoints along the base of Suribachi seemed to spring to life.

Within ninety minutes of the landing, however, elements of the 1st Battalion, 28th Marines, had reached the western shore, seven hundred yards across from Green Beach. Iwo Jima had been severed—"like cutting off a snake's head," in the words of one Marine. It would represent the deepest penetration of what was becoming a very long and costly day.

The other three regiments experienced difficulty leaving the black sand terraces and wheeling across toward the first airfield. The terrain was an open bowl, a shooting gallery in full view from Suribachi on the left and the rising tableland to the right. Any thoughts of a "cakewalk" quickly vanished as well-directed machine gun fire whistled across the open ground and mortar rounds began dropping along the terraces. Despite these difficulties, the 27th Marines made good initial gains, reaching the southern and western edges of the first airfield before noon.

The 23rd Marines landed over Yellow Beach and sustained the brunt of the first round of Japanese combined arms fire. These troops crossed the second terrace only to be confronted by two huge concrete pillboxes, still lethal despite all the pounding. Overcoming these positions proved costly in casualties and time.

More fortified positions appeared in the broken ground beyond. Colonel Walter W. Wensinger's call for tank support could not be immediately honored because of congestion problems on the beach. The regiment clawed its way several hundred yards toward the eastern edge of the airstrip.

No assault units found it easy going to move inland, but the 25th Marines almost immediately ran into a buzz saw trying to move across Blue Beach. General Cates had been right in his appraisal. "That right flank was a bitch if there ever was one," he would later say. Lieutenant Colonel Hollis W. Mustain's 1st Battalion, 25th Marines, managed to scratch forward three hundred yards under heavy fire in the first half-hour, but Lieutenant Colonel Chambers's 3rd Battalion, 25th Marines, took the heaviest beating of the day on the extreme right, trying to scale the cliffs leading to the Rock Quarry.

Chambers landed fifteen minutes after H-hour. "Crossing that second terrace," he recalled, "the fire from automatic weapons was coming from all over. You could've held up a cigarette and lit it on the stuff going by. I knew immediately we were in for one hell of a time."

This was simply the beginning.

While the assault forces tried to overcome the infantry weapons of the local defenders, they were naturally blind to an almost imperceptible stirring taking place among the rocks and crevices of the interior highlands. With grim anticipation, General Kuribayashi's gunners began unmasking the big guns—the heavy artillery, giant mortars, rockets, and antitank weapons held under tightest discipline for this precise moment. Kuribayashi had patiently waited until the beaches were clogged with troops and material. Gun crews knew the range and deflection to each landing beach by heart; all weapons had been preregistered on these targets long ago. At Kuribayashi's signal, these hundreds of weapons began to open fire. It was shortly after 10:00 a.m.

The ensuing bombardment was as deadly and terrifying as any the Marines had ever experienced. There was hardly any cover. Japanese artillery and mortar rounds blanketed every corner of the three-thousand-yard-wide beach. Large-caliber coast defense guns and dual-purpose antiaircraft guns firing horizontally added a deadly scissors of direct fire from the high ground on both flanks. Marines stumbling over the terraces to escape the rain of projectiles encountered the same disciplined machine gun fire and minefields that had slowed the initial advance. Casualties mounted appallingly.

Two Marine combat veterans observing this expressed a grudging admiration for the Japanese gunners. "It was one of the worst blood-lettings of the war," said Major Karch of the 14th Marines. "They rolled those artillery barrages up and down the beach—I just didn't see how anybody could live through such heavy fire barrages."

Said Lieutenant Colonel Joseph L. Stewart, "The Japanese were superb artillerymen. . . . Somebody was getting hit every time they fired." At sea, Lieutenant Colonel Weller tried desperately to deliver naval gunfire against the Japanese gun positions shooting down at 3rd Battalion, 25th Marines, from the Rock Quarry. It would take longer to coordinate this fire: The first Japanese barrages had wiped out the 3rd Battalion, 25th Marines's entire shore fire control party.

As the Japanese firing reached a general crescendo, the four assault regiments issued dire reports to the flagship. Within a ten-minute period, these messages crackled over the command net:

1036: (From 25th Marines) "Catching all hell from the quarry. Heavy mortar and machine gun fire!"

1039: (From 23rd Marines) "Taking heavy casualties and can't move for the moment. Mortars killing us."

1042: (From 27th Marines) "All units pinned down by artillery and mortars. Casualties heavy. Need tank support fast to move anywhere."

1046: (From 28th Marines) "Taking heavy fire and forward movement stopped. Machine gun and artillery fire heaviest ever seen."

The landing force suffered and bled but did not panic. The profusion of combat veterans throughout the rank and file of each regiment helped the rookies focus on the objective. Communications remained effective. Keen-eyed aerial observers spotted some of the now-exposed gun positions and directed naval gunfire effectively. Carrier planes screeched in low to drop napalm canisters. The heavy Japanese fire would continue to take an awful toll throughout the first day and night, but it would never again be so murderous as that first unholy hour.

Marine Sherman tanks played hell getting into action on D-day. Later in the battle these combat vehicles would be the most valuable weapons on the battlefield for the Marines; this day was a nightmare. The assault divisions embarked many of their tanks on board medium landing ships (LSMs), sturdy little craft that could deliver five Shermans at a time. But it was tough disembarking them on Iwo's steep beaches. The stern anchors could not hold in the loose sand; bow cables run forward to "deadmen" LVTs parted under the strain. On one occasion the lead tank stalled at the top of the ramp, blocking the other vehicles and leaving the LSM at the mercy of the rising surf. Other tanks bogged down or threw tracks in the loose sand.

Many of those that made it over the terraces were destroyed by huge horned mines or disabled by deadly accurate 47mm antitank fire from Suribachi. Other tankers kept coming. Their relative mobility, armored protection, and 75mm gunfire were most welcome to the infantry scattered among Iwo's lunar-looking, shell-pocked landscape.

Both division commanders committed their reserves early. General Rockey called in the 26th Marines shortly after noon. General Cates ordered two battalions of the 24th Marines to land at 14:00; the 3rd Battalion, 24th Marines, followed several hours later. Many of the reserve battalions suffered heavier casualties crossing the beach than the assault units, a result of Kuribayashi's punishing bombardment from all points on the island.

Mindful of the likely Japanese counterattack in the night to come—and despite the fire and confusion along the beaches—both divisions also ordered their artillery regiments ashore. This process, frustrating and costly, took much of the afternoon. The wind and surf began to pick up as the day wore on, causing more than one low-riding DUKW truck to swamp with its precious 105mm howitzer cargo. Getting the guns ashore was one thing; getting them up off the sand was quite another. The 75mm pack howitzers fared better than the heavier 105s. Enough Marines could readily hustle them up over the terraces, albeit at great risk. The 105s seemed to have a mind of their own in the black sand. The effort to get each single weapon off the beach was a saga in its own right.

Somehow, despite the fire and unforgiving terrain, both Colonel Louis G. DeHaven, commanding the 14th Marines, and Colonel James D. Waller, commanding the 13th Marines, managed to get batteries in place, registered, and rendering close fire support well before dark, a singular accomplishment.

Japanese fire and the plunging surf continued to make a shambles out of the beachhead. Late in the afternoon, Lieutenant Michael F. Keleher, USNR, the battalion surgeon, was ordered ashore to take over the 3rd Battalion, 25th Marines, aid station from its gravely wounded surgeon. Keleher, a veteran of three previous assault landings, was appalled by the carnage on Blue Beach as he approached: "Such a sight on that beach! Wrecked boats, bogged-down jeeps, tractors and tanks; burning vehicles; casualties scattered all over."

On the left center of the action, leading his machine gun platoon in the 1st Battalion, 27th Marines's attack against the southern portion of the airfield, the legendary "Manila John" Basilone fell mortally wounded by a Japanese mortar shell, a loss keenly felt by all Marines on the island. Farther east, Lieutenant Colonel Robert Galer, the other Guadalcanal Medal of Honor Marine (and one of the Pacific War's earliest fighter aces), survived the afternoon's fusillade along the beaches and began reassembling his scattered radar unit in a deep shell hole near the base of Suribachi.

Late in the afternoon, Lieutenant Colonel Donn J. Robertson led his 3rd Battalion, 27th Marines, ashore over Blue Beach, disturbed at the intensity of fire still being directed on the reserve forces this late on D-day. "They were really ready for us," he recalled. He watched with pride and wonderment as his Marines landed under fire, took casualties, and stumbled forward to clear the beach. "What impels a young guy landing on a beach in the face of fire?" he asked himself. Then it was Robertson's turn. His boat hit the beach too hard; the ramp wouldn't drop. Robertson and his command group had to roll over the gunwales into the churning surf and crawl ashore, an inauspicious start.

The bitter battle to capture the Rock Quarry cliffs on the right flank raged all day. The beachhead remained completely vulnerable to enemy direct fire weapons from these heights; the Marines had to storm them before many more troops or supplies could be landed. In the end, it was the strength of character of Captain James Headley and Lieutenant Colonel "Jumping Joe" Chambers who led the survivors of the 3rd Battalion, 25th Marines, onto the top of the cliffs. The battalion paid an exorbitant price for this achievement, losing twenty-two officers and five hundred troops by nightfall.

The two assistant division commanders, brigadier generals Franklin A. Hart and Leo D. Hermle, of the 4th and 5th Marine Divisions, respectively, spent much of D-day on board the control vessels, marking both ends of the Line of Departure, four thousand yards offshore. This reflected yet another lesson in amphibious techniques learned from Tarawa: having senior officers that close to the ship-to-shore movement provided landing force decision making from the most forward vantage point.

By dusk General Leo D. Hermle opted to come ashore. At Tarawa he had spent the night of D-day essentially out of contact at the fire-swept pierhead. This time he intended to be on the ground. Hermle had the larger operational picture in mind, knowing the corps commander's desire to force the reserves and artillery units onshore despite the carnage in order to build credible combat power. Hermle knew that whatever the night might bring, the Americans now had more troops on the island than Kuribayashi could ever muster. His presence helped his division to forget about the day's disasters and focus on preparations for the expected counterattacks.

Japanese artillery and mortar fire continued to rake the beachhead. The enormous spigot mortar shells (called "flying ashcans" by the troops) and rocket-boosted aerial bombs were particularly scary—loud, whistling projectiles, tumbling end over end. Many sailed completely over the island; those that hit along the beaches or the south runways invariably caused dozens of casualties with each impact. Few Marines could dig a proper foxhole in the granular sand ("like trying to dig a hole in a barrel of wheat"). Among urgent calls to the control ship for plasma, stretchers, and mortar shells came repeated cries for sandbags.

Veteran Marine combat correspondent Lieutenant Cyril P. Zurlinden, soon to become a casualty himself, described that first night ashore:

> At Tarawa, Saipan, and Tinian, I saw Marines killed and wounded in a shocking manner, but I saw nothing like the ghastliness that hung over the Iwo beachhead. Nothing any of us had ever known could compare with the utter anguish, frustration, and constant inner battle to maintain some semblance of sanity.

Personnel accounting was a nightmare under those conditions, but the assault divisions eventually reported the combined loss of 2,420 men to General Schmidt (501 killed, 1,755 wounded, 47 dead of wounds, 18 missing, and 99 combat fatigue). These were sobering statistics, but Schmidt now had 30,000 Marines ashore. The casualty rate of 8 percent left the landing force in relatively better condition than at the first days at Tarawa or Saipan. The miracle was that the casualties had not been twice as high. General Kuribayashi had possibly waited a little too long to open up with his big guns.

The first night on Iwo was ghostly. Sulfuric mists spiraled out of the earth. The Marines, used to the tropics, shivered in the cold, waiting for Kuribayashi's warriors to come screaming down from the hills. They would learn that this Japanese commander was different. There would be no wasteful, vainglorious banzai attacks, this night or any other. Instead small teams of infiltrators, which Kuribayashi termed "Prowling Wolves," probed the lines, gathering intelligence. A barge full of Japanese special landing forces tried a small counter landing on the western beaches and died to the man under the alert guns of the 28th Marines and its supporting LVT crews.

Otherwise, the night was one of continuing waves of indirect fire from the highlands. One high velocity round landed directly in the hole occupied by the 1st Battalion, 23rd Marines's commander, Lieutenant Colonel Ralph Haas, killing him instantly. The Marines took casualties throughout the night. But with the first streaks of dawn, the veteran landing force stirred. Five infantry regiments looked north; a sixth turned to the business at hand in the south: Mount Suribachi.

SURIBACHI

The Japanese called the dormant volcano Suribachi-yama; the Marines dubbed it "Hotrocks." From the start the Marines knew their drive north would never succeed without first seizing that hulking rock dominating the southern plain. "Suribachi seemed to take on a life of its own, to be watching these men, looming over them," recalled one observer, adding, "the mountain represented to these Marines a thing more evil than the Japanese."

Colonel Kanehiko Atsuchi commanded the two thousand soldiers and sailors of the Suribachi garrison. The Japanese had honeycombed the mountain with gun positions, machine gun nests, observation sites, and tunnels, but Atsuchi had lost many of his large-caliber guns in the direct naval bombardment of the preceding three days. General Kuribayashi considered Atsuchi's command to be semiautonomous, realizing the invaders would soon cut communications across the island's narrow southern tip. Kuribayashi nevertheless hoped Suribachi could hold out for ten days, maybe two weeks.

Some of Suribachi's stoutest defenses existed down low, around the rubble-strewn base. Here nearly seventy camouflaged concrete block-houses protected the approaches to the mountain; another fifty bulged from the slopes within the first hundred feet of elevation. Then came the caves, the first of hundreds the Marines would face on Iwo Jima.

The 28th Marines had suffered nearly four hundred casualties in cutting across the neck of the island on D-day. On D+1, in a cold rain, they prepared to assault the mountain. Lieutenant Colonel Chandler Johnson, commanding the 2nd Battalion, 28th Marines, set the tone for the morning as he deployed his tired troops forward: "It's going to be a hell of a day in a hell of a place to fight the damned war!" Some of the 105mm batteries of the 13th Marines opened up in support, firing directly overhead. Gun crews fired from positions hastily dug in the black sand directly next to the 28th Marines command post. Regimental executive officer Lieutenant Colonel Robert H. Williams watched the cannoneers fire at Suribachi "eight hundred yards away over open sights."

As the Marines would learn during their drive north, even 105mm howitzers would hardly shiver the concrete pillboxes of the enemy. As the prep fire lifted, the infantry leapt forward, only to run imme-diately into very heavy machine gun and mortar fire. Colonel Harry

B. "Harry the Horse" Liversedge bellowed for his tanks. But the 5th Tank Battalion was already having a frustrating morning. The tankers sought a defilade spot in which to rearm and refuel for the day's assault. Such a location did not exist on Iwo Jima those first days. Every time the tanks congregated to service their vehicles they were hit hard by Japanese mortar and artillery fire from virtually the entire island. Getting sufficient vehicles serviced to join the assault took most of the morning. Hereafter the tankers would maintain and reequip their vehicles at night.

This day's slow start led to more setbacks for the tankers; Japanese antitank gunners hiding in the jumbled boulders knocked out the first approaching Shermans. Assault momentum slowed further. The 28th Marines overran forty strongpoints and gained roughly two hundred yards all day. They lost a Marine for every yard gained. The tankers unknowingly redeemed themselves when one of their final 75mm rounds caught Colonel Atsuchi as he peered out of a cave entrance, killing him instantly.

Elsewhere, the morning light on D+1 revealed the discouraging sights of the chaos created along the beaches by the combination of Iwo Jima's wicked surf and Kuribayashi's unrelenting barrages. In the words of one dismayed observer:

> The wreckage was indescribable. For two miles the debris was so thick that there were only a few places where landing craft could still get in. The wrecked hulls of scores of landing boats testified to one price we had to pay to put our troops ashore. Tanks and half-tracks lay crippled where they had bogged down in the coarse sand. Amphibian tractors, victims of mines and well-aimed shells, lay flopped on their backs. Cranes, brought

ashore to unload cargo, tilted at insane angles, and bulldozers were smashed in their own roadways.

Bad weather set in, further compounding the problems of general unloading. Strong winds whipped sea swells into a nasty chop; the surf turned uglier. These were the conditions faced by Lieutenant Colonel Carl A. Youngdale in trying to land the 105mm-howitzer batteries of his 4th Battalion, 14th Marines. All twelve of these guns were preloaded in DUKWs, one to a vehicle. Added to the amphibious trucks' problems of marginal seaworthiness with that payload was contaminated fuel. As Youngdale watched in horror, eight DUKWs suffered engine failures, swamped, and sank, with great loss of life. Two more DUKWs broached in the surf zone, spilling their invaluable guns into deep water. At length Youngdale managed to get his remaining two guns ashore and into firing position.

General Schmidt also committed one battery of 155mm howitzers of the corps artillery to the narrow beachhead on D+1. Somehow these weapons managed to reach the beach intact, but it then took hours to get tractors to drag the heavy guns up over the terraces. These, too, commenced firing before dark, their deep bark a welcome sound to the infantry.

Concern with the heavy casualties in the first twenty-four hours led Schmidt to commit the 21st Marines from corps reserve. The seas proved to be too rough. The troops had harrowing experiences trying to debark down cargo nets into the small boats bobbing violently alongside the transports; several fell into the water. The boating process took hours. Once afloat, the troops circled endlessly in their small Higgins boats, waiting for the call to land. Wiser heads prevailed. After six hours of awful seasickness, the 21st Marines returned to its ships for the night.

Even the larger landing craft, the LCTs and LSMs, had great difficulty beaching. Sea anchors needed to maintain the craft perpendicular to the breakers rarely held fast in the steep, soft bottom. "Dropping those stern anchors was like dropping a spoon in a bowl of mush," said Admiral Hill.

Hill contributed significantly to the development of amphibious expertise in the Pacific War. For Iwo Jima, he and his staff developed armored bulldozers to land in the assault waves. They also experimented with hinged Marston matting, used for expeditionary airfields, as a temporary roadway to get wheeled vehicles over soft sand. On the beach at Iwo, the bulldozers proved to be worth their weight in gold. The Marston matting was only partially successful—LVTs kept chewing it up in passage—but all hands could see its potential.

Admiral Hill also worked with the Naval Construction Battalion (NCB) personnel—Seabees, as they were called—in an attempt to bring supply-laden causeways and pontoon barges ashore. Again the surf prevailed, broaching the craft, spilling the cargo. In desperation, Hill's beach masters turned to round-the-clock use of DUKWs and LVTs to keep combat cargo flowing.

Once the DUKWs got free of the crippling load of 105mm howitzers, they did fine. LVTs were probably better, because they could cross the soft beach without assistance and conduct resupply or medevac missions directly along the front lines. Both vehicles suffered from inexperienced LST crews in the transport area who too often would not lower their bow ramps to accommodate LVTs or DUKWs approaching after dark. In too many cases, vehicles loaded with wounded Marines thus rejected became lost in the darkness, ran out of gas, and sank. The amphibian tractor battalions lost 148 LVTs at Iwo Jima. Unlike Tarawa, Japanese gunfire and mines accounted for less than 20 percent of this total. Thirty-four LVTs fell victim to Iwo's crushing surf; eighty-eight sank in deep water, mostly at night.

Once ashore and clear of the loose sand along the beaches, the tanks, half-tracks, and armored bulldozers of the landing force ran into the strongest minefield defenses yet encountered in the Pacific War. Under General Kuribayashi's direction, Japanese engineers had planted irregular rows of antitank mines and the now-familiar horned antiboat mines along all possible exits from both beaches. The Japanese supplemented these weapons by rigging enormous make-shift explosives from five-hundred-pound aerial bombs, depth charges, and torpedo heads, each triggered by an accompanying pressure mine. Worse, Iwo's loose soil retained enough metallic characteristics to render the standard mine detectors unreliable. The Marines were reduced to using their own engineers on their hands and knees out in front of the tanks, probing for mines with bayonets and wooden sticks.

While the 28th Marines fought to encircle Suribachi and the beach masters and shore party attempted to clear the wreckage from the beaches, the remaining assault units of the VAC resumed their collective assault against Airfield No. 1. In the 5th Marine Division's zone, the relatively fresh troops of the 1st Battalion, 26th Marines, and the 3rd Battalion, 27th Marines, quickly became bloodied in forcing their way across the western runways, taking heavy casualties from time-fused air bursts fired by Japanese dual-purpose antiaircraft guns zeroed along the exposed ground. In the adjacent 4th Division zone, the 23rd Marines completed the capture of the airstrip, advancing eight hundred yards but sustaining high losses.

Some of the bitterest fighting in the initial phase of the landing continued to occur along the high ground above the Rock Quarry on the right flank. Here the 25th Marines, reinforced by the 1st Battalion,

24th Marines, engaged in literally the fight of its life. The Marines found the landscape, and the Japanese embedded in it, unreal.

The second day of the battle had proven unsatisfactory on virtually every front. To cap off the frustration, when the 1st Battalion, 24th Marines, finally managed a breakthrough along the cliffs late in the day, their only reward was two back-to-back cases of "friendly fire." An American air strike inflicted eleven casualties; misguided salvos from an unidentified gunfire support ship took down ninety more. Nothing seemed to be going right.

The morning of the third day, D+2, seemed to promise more of the same frustrations. Marines shivered in the cold wind and rain; Admiral Hill twice had to close the beach due to high surf and dangerous undertows. But during one of the grace periods, the 3rd Division's 21st Marines managed to come ashore, all of it extremely glad to be free of the heaving small boats. General Schmidt assigned it to the 4th Marine Division at first.

The 28th Marines resumed its assault on the base of Suribachi—more slow, bloody fighting, seemingly boulder by boulder. On the west coast, the 1st Battalion, 28th Marines, made the most of field artillery and naval gunfire support to reach the shoulder of the mountain. Elsewhere, murderous Japanese fire restricted any progress to a matter of yards. Enemy mortar fire from all over the volcano rained down on the 2nd Battalion, 28th Marines, trying to advance along the eastern shore. Recalled rifleman Richard Wheeler of the experience, "It was terrible, the worst I can remember us taking."

That night the amphibious task force experienced the only significant air attack of the battle. Fifty kamikaze pilots from the 22nd Mitate special attack unit left Katori Airbase near Yokosuka and flung themselves against the ships on the outer perimeter of Iwo Jima. In desperate action that would serve as a prelude to Okinawa's fiery engagements, the kamikazes sank the escort carrier *Bismarck Sea* with heavy loss of life and damaged several other ships, including the veteran *Saratoga*, finally knocked out of the war. All fifty Japanese planes were expended.

It rained even harder on the fourth morning, D+3. Marines scampering forward under fire would hit the deck, roll, and attempt to return fire—only to discover that the loose volcanic grit had combined with the rain to jam their weapons. The 21st Marines, as the vanguard of the 3rd Marine Division, hoped for good fortune in its initial commitment after relieving the 23rd Marines. The regiment instead ran headlong into an intricate series of Japanese emplacements that marked the southeastern end of the main Japanese defenses. The newcomers fought hard all day to scratch and claw an advance of two hundred net yards. Casualties were disproportionate.

On the right flank, Lieutenant Colonel Chambers continued to rally the 3rd Battalion, 25th Marines, through the rough pinnacles above the Rock Quarry. As he strode about directing the advance of his decimated companies that afternoon, a Japanese gunner shot him through the chest. Chambers went down hard, thinking it was all over: "I started fading in and out. I don't remember too much about it except the frothy blood gushing out of my mouth. . . . Then somebody started kicking the hell out of my feet. It was [Captain James] Headley, saying, 'Get up; you were hurt worse on Tulagi!'"

Captain Headley knew Chambers's sucking chest wound portended a grave injury. He sought to reduce his commander's shock until they could get him out of the line of fire. This took doing. Lieutenant Michael F. Keleher, USNR, now the battalion surgeon, crawled forward with one of his corpsmen. Willing hands lifted Chambers on a stretcher. Keleher and several others, bent double against the fire, carried him down the cliffs to the aid station, and eventually on board a DUKW, making the evening's last run out to the hospital ships.

All three battalion commanders in the 25th Marines had now become casualties. Chambers would survive to receive the Medal of Honor; Captain Headley would command the shot-up 3rd Battalion, 25th Marines, for the duration of the battle. By contrast, the 28th Marines on D+3 made commendable progress against Suribachi, reaching the shoulder at all points. Late in the day, combat patrols from the 1st Battalion, 28th Marines, and the 2nd Battalion, 28th Marines, linked up at Tobiishi Point at the southern tip of the island. Recon patrols returned to tell Lieutenant Colonel Johnson that they found few signs of live Japanese along the mountain's upper slopes on the north side.

At sundown Admiral Spruance authorized Task Force 58 to strike Honshu and Okinawa, then retire to Ulithi to prepare for the Ryukyuan campaign. All eight Marine Corps fighter squadrons thus left the Iwo Jima area for good. Navy pilots flying off the ten remaining escort carriers would pick up the slack. Without slighting the skill and valor of these pilots, the quality of close air support to the troops fighting ashore dropped off after this date. The escort carriers, for one thing, had too many competing missions, namely combat air patrols, antisubmarine sweeps, searches for downed aviators, and harassing strikes against neighboring Chichi Jima. Marines on Iwo Jima complained of slow response time to air support requests, light payloads (rarely greater than one-hundred-pound bombs), and high delivery altitudes (rarely below 1,500 feet). The navy pilots did deliver a number of napalm bombs. Many of these failed to detonate, although this was not the fault of the aviators; the early napalm "bombs" were simply old wing tanks filled with the mixture, activated by unreliable detonators. The Marines also grew concerned about these notoriously inaccurate area weapons being dropped from high altitudes.

By Friday, February 23 (D+4), the 28th Marines stood poised to complete the capture of Mount Suribachi. The honor went to the 3rd Platoon (reinforced), Company E, 2nd Battalion, 28th Marines, under the command of 1st Lieutenant Harold G. Schrier, the company executive officer. Lieutenant Colonel Johnson ordered Schrier to scale the summit, secure the crater, and raise a fifty-four-by-twenty-eight-inch American flag for all to see. Schrier led his forty-man patrol forward at 0800.

The regiment had done its job, blasting the dozens of pillboxes with flame and demolitions, rooting out snipers, and knocking out the masked batteries. The combined arms pounding by planes, field pieces, and naval guns the past week had likewise taken its toll on the defenders. Those who remained popped out of holes and caves to resist Schrier's advance, only to be cut down. The Marines worked warily up the steep northern slope, sometimes resorting to crawling on hands and knees.

Part of the enduring drama of the Suribachi flag raising was the fact that it was observed by so many people. Marines all over the island could track the progress of the tiny column of troops during its ascent ("Those guys oughta be getting flight pay," said one wag). Likewise, hundreds of binoculars from the ships offshore watched Schrier's Marines climbing ever upward. Finally, they reached the top and momentarily disappeared from view. Those closest to the volcano could hear distant gunfire. Then, at 10:20 there was movement on the summit; suddenly the Stars and Stripes fluttered bravely.

Lusty cheers rang out from all over the southern end of the island. The ships sounded their sirens and whistles. Wounded men propped themselves up on their litters to glimpse the sight. Strong men wept unashamedly. Navy Secretary Forrestal, thrilled by the sight, turned to Holland Smith and said, "The raising of that flag means a Marine Corps for another five hundred years."

Three hours later an even larger flag went up to more cheers. Few would know that Associated Press photographer Joe Rosenthal had just captured the embodiment of the American warfighting spirit on film. Leatherneck magazine photographer Staff Sergeant Lou Lowery had taken a picture of the first flag raising and almost immediately got in a firefight with a couple of enraged Japanese. His photograph would become a valued collector's item. But Rosenthal's would enthrall the free world.

Captain Thomas M. Fields, commanding officer of Company D, 2nd Battalion, 26th Marines, heard his men yell, "Look up there!" and turned in time to see the first flag go. His first thought dealt with the battle still at hand: "Thank God the Japs won't be shooting us down from behind anymore."

The 28th Marines took Suribachi in three days at the cost of more than five hundred troops (added to its D-day losses of four hundred men). Colonel Liversedge began to reorient his regiment for operations in the opposite direction, northward. Unknown to all, the battle still had another month to run its bloody course.

4

ASSAULTING INCHON

Korea 1950

**LYNN MONTROSS AND CAPTAIN
NICHOLAS A. CANZONA, USMC**

On September 15, 1950, a US Marines force made a surprise amphibious landing at the strategic port of Inchon, on the west coast of Korea, about one hundred miles south of the 38th parallel and twenty-five miles from Seoul.

Aboard the *Henrico* and *Cavalier* in the Inchon narrows were the 1st and 2nd Battalions, 5th Marines, yanked out of the Pusan Perimeter ten days earlier. Having had no time for a rehearsal and only a few days for planning on the basis of admittedly sketchy intelligence, these two units would scale the sea wall of Red Beach and plunge into the dense waterfront area of the sprawling seaport.

The mission of the 5th Marines was to seize the O-A Line, a three-thousand-yard arc encompassing Cemetery Hill on the left (north), Observatory Hill in the center, and thence extending the last one thousand yards through a maze of buildings and streets to terminate at the inner tidal basin. Each battalion would land in a column of companies, Lieutenant Colonel George R. Newton's 1st, on the left, seizing Cemetery Hill and the northern half of Observatory Hill, while Lieutenant Colonel Harold S. Roise's 2nd secured the remainder of the latter, the hill of the British Consulate, and the inner tidal basin.

With H-hour only minutes away, the sky above the objective was murky and the wind whipped rain as well as stinging spray into the faces of the Marines in the assault waves. Only the Marine and navy flyers upstairs could see the panorama of the waterborne attack—the cruisers and destroyers standing silent in the background, LSMR rocket flashes stabbing the false twilight ashore, the landing craft trailing pale wakes behind them like the tails of comets. The pilots observed the LCVPs to the left of Wolmi-do fan out at the line of departure and touch the sea wall of Red Beach minutes later. To the right of the little island, however, they saw the leading waves of the 1st Marines disappear in a blanket of gloom. For while the smoke- and moisture-laden air had obscured parts of the 5th Marines's zone of action ashore, it had completely blotted out Blue Beach and half the length of the 1st Regiment's boat lanes.

Eight LCVPs had crossed the line of departure at H-minus 8 and sped toward Red Beach with the first wave of the 5th Marines. Starting from the left, boats numbered one through four carried parts of two assault platoons of Company A, 1st Battalion, whose mission was to seize Cemetery Hill and anchor the regimental left. In boats five through eight were troops of Company E, 2nd Battalion, whose task included clearing the right flank of the beach and taking the hill of the British Consulate.

From Wolmi-do 3/5s machine guns, mortars, and supporting M-26s cut loose with a hail of bullets and high explosives to cover the landing. Technical Sergeant Knox led an engineer team forward to clear the causeway, in order that the detachment of Able Company Tanks could advance to the mainland after the initial assault waves hit the beach.

As the landing craft passed the midway point of the 2,200-yard boat lane, the heaving LSMRs ceased firing, so that Lieutenant Colonel Walter E. Lischeid and Major Arnold A. Lund could lead in VMFs-214 and -323 for final strikes on both Red and Blue Beaches. Navy Skyraiders joined in at the request of Captain John R. Stevens, commander of Company A; and the FAC of 1/5, First Lieutenant James W. Smith, controlled their strafing passes as the first wave came within thirty yards of the sea wall.

Although the tide was racing in fast, the wall still projected about four feet above the ramps of the landing craft. The Marines readied their scaling ladders. On the right the boats of Company E touched the revetment at 1731. Up went the ladders as the assault troops hurled grenades over the wall. Following the explosions, the Marines from the four boats scrambled to the top of the barrier one by one. The ladders slipped and swayed as the LCVPs bobbed next to the wall. But they served their purpose, and in short order every man of Second Lieutenant Edwin A. Deptula's 1st Platoon was on the beach.

There were no casualties from the few stray bullets cracking through the air. Filtering through smoke and wreckage, the platoon moved inland to cover the landing of the second and third waves, carrying the remainder of Easy Company.

On the north of Red Beach, three of the four LCVPs with the leading elements of Company A bumped the sea wall at 1733. Boat number one, carrying Technical Sergeant Orval F. McMullen and half of his 1st Platoon, was delayed offshore by an engine failure. The remainder of the 1st, under the platoon guide, Sergeant Charles D. Allen, scaled the wall from boat number two in the face of heavy fire from the north flank and from submachine guns in a bunker directly ahead. Several Marines were cut down immediately, the others being unable to advance more than a few yards inland.

Boat number three, with Second Lieutenant Francis W. Muetzel and a squad of his 2nd Platoon, touched a breach in the sea wall under the muzzle of an enemy machine gun protruding from a pillbox. The weapon did not fire as the Marines scrambled through the gap and onto the beach. A second squad and a 3.5-inch rocket section joined from boat number four. Gunfire crackled far off on the left, barely audible amid the roar of fighter planes strafing fifty yards ahead. Muetzel and his men jumped into a long trench that paralleled the sea wall a few feet away. It was empty. Two Marines threw grenades into the silent pillbox, and the six bloody North Koreans who emerged in the wake of the hollow explosions were left under guard of a Marine rifleman.

Just beyond the beach loomed Cemetery Hill, its seaward side an almost vertical bluff. To avoid getting trapped if the enemy opened up from the high ground, Muetzel attacked toward his objective, the Asahi Brewery, without waiting for the remainder of his men in the tardy second wave. The skirmish line raced across the narrow beach, ignoring padlocked buildings and flaming wreckage. Passing to the south of Cemetery Hill, the 2nd Platoon entered the built-up area of the city and marched unopposed up a street to the brewery.

On the left of Company A's zone, the beached half of the 1st Platoon made no progress against the flanking fire and the Communist bunker to the front. The 3rd Platoon, under First Lieutenant Baldomero Lopez, landed in the second wave, and McMullen finally got ashore with the other half of the 1st. Both units crowded into the restricted foothold and casualties mounted rapidly. Enemy guns had felled Lopez as he climbed ashore and moved against the bunker with a grenade. Unable to throw the armed missile because of his wound, the young officer was killed when he smothered the explosion with his body to protect his men. Two Marines attacked the emplacement with flame throwers. They were shot down and their valuable assault weapons put out of action.

The Marines moved rapidly up the incline, flushing out about a dozen Red soldiers who surrendered meekly. Gaining the summit, they drove forward and saw the entire crest suddenly come alive with infantry crewmen of the 226th NKPA Regiment's mortar company. Spiritless and dazed from the pounding by air and naval gunfire, the North Koreans to a man threw down their weapons, filed quietly from trenches and bunkers, and marched to the base of the hill where a small detachment kept them under guard. Hardly a shot had been fired by the 2nd Platoon, still without a single casualty, and the capture of Cemetery Hill had required about ten minutes.

During the attack on the high ground, Eubanks had taken the situation in hand on the left of the beach. He first bested the bunker's occupants in a grenade duel, then ordered the emplacement fired by a flame thrower. Just as Muetzel prepared to dispatch assistance from the top of Cemetery Hill, the 1st and 3rd Platoons broke out of the pocket, drove inland to the edge of the city, and made physical contact with the 2nd.

After landing in 2/5's first wave, the 1st Platoon of Company E pushed inland one hundred yards to the railroad tracks against no resistance whatsoever. Captain Samuel Jaskilka was ashore with the rest of the Company by H-plus 10, and reorganization took place quickly near the Nippon Flour Company buildings, just south of the beach. Deptula's platoon then moved unopposed down the railroad tracks and seized the British Consulate, Regimental Objective C, at 1845. Simultaneously, another platoon cleared the built-up area across the tracks on the lower slopes of Observatory Hill. These rapid accomplishments secured the 5th Marines's right flank, giving an added measure of protection to twenty-two more waves of landing craft and LSTs scheduled for Red Beach.

Still in enemy hands, however, was Observatory Hill, reaching well over two hundred feet above the center of the regimental zone to buttress the arc of the O-A Line. Company C of the 1st Battalion, landing in the fourth and fifth waves shortly before 1800, was to take Objective A, northern half of the critical terrain feature. To Dog Company of 2/5 was charged the southern half, designated Objective B.

That the attack did not go off as planned stemmed from a series of mishaps that began as far out as the line of departure. Despite the fact that Lieutenant Commander Schneeloch was using standard control procedures from the *Bass*, including radio contact with the beach, there was a mixing of waves starting with number four. This development reflected the lack of a rehearsal in the hurried preparations for the operation, and the end result was that parts of Companies

C and D, both in the second assault echelon, landed over the wrong beaches. After landing, Charlie Company had the added disadvantage of being without its company commander for a crucial twelve minutes. Captain Poul F. Pedersen was delayed when the fifth-wave commander, who shared his boat, decided to tow a stalled LCVP left behind by the preceding formation. When he finally reached his company, the job of reorganization was much more difficult than it would have been had he arrived at the beach on schedule. With troops pouring over the sea wall from succeeding waves, what had begun as intermingling at the point of overlap in the center of the landing area had grown to temporary congestion and confusion.

RED BEACH

Out in the channel, the first of eight LSTs heralded the climax of the ship-to-shore movement at 1830 by crossing the line of departure and heading for the sea wall. Prior to the approach, ships' officers had spotted the close fighting on the north flank of Red Beach as they peered through binoculars from their respective bridges.

Later, noting the growing knot of Marines in the center of the waterfront area, they concluded that the assault troops could not advance inland. This impression was strengthened by an abrupt procession of gun flashes on Observatory Hill where, owing to the delay in the attack by Companies C and D, a handful of enemy soldiers had recovered from shock sufficiently to set up machine guns. A few North Korean mortar crews in the city also came to life and manned their weapons.

LST 859, leading the pack, came under mortar and machine gun fire as it waddled toward its berth about 1835. Gun crews on the ship reacted by opening up with 40mm and 20mm cannon, spraying

Cemetery and Observatory Hills and the right flank of the beach. Next in the column of ships, LSTs 975 and 857 likewise commenced firing after taking hits from mortars and machine guns. Enemy automatic weapons touched off a fire near ammunition trucks on LST 914, trailing fourth, but sailors and Marines quickly brought the blaze under control. Guns on the latter ship remained silent as a result of dispatch orders received by the captain after leaving the line of departure.

Lieutenant Muetzel and his platoon were chased by LST fire from the crest of Cemetery Hill to the slope facing Inchon—where they came under fire from a Red machine gun in a building on Observatory Hill. Fortunately, a 40mm shell from one of the LSTs crashed into the building and obliterated the enemy position. There were no casualties in Muetzel's outfit, but Lieutenant Colonel Roise's 2nd Battalion did not fare as luckily from the misdirected shooting by the American ships. Weapons and H&S Companies of 2/5 had landed about 1830 and were just proceeding inland when LST fire seared their ranks, killing one Marine and wounding twenty-three others. "If it hadn't been for the thick walls of the Nippon Flour Company," remarked Roise later, "the casualties might have been worse."

On the beach, meanwhile, Second Lieutenant Byron L. Magness had reorganized his 2nd Platoon of Company C and, on his own initiative, attacked Observatory Hill. Second Lieutenant Max A. Merritt's 60mm mortar section followed closely behind, but the rest of the company remained fragmented in the landing area. Sparked by Technical Sergeant Max Stein, who was wounded while personally accounting for a North Korean machine gun, the provisional force advanced rapidly in the gathering darkness and at 1845 seized the saddle between Objectives A and B on Observatory Hill. This was just about the time when the LSTs stopped firing.

Because their single flare misfired and they were not able to raise Lieutenant Pedersen by radio, Magness and Merritt were unable to inform the beach of their success. In the meantime, Company B, 1/5's reserve, had landed in the 2nd Battalion zone, the waves having swerved to that area to avoid small arms fire peppering their assigned approach on the left. Captain Francis I. Fenton Jr. led the unit through a mixed group on the waterfront to an assembly area near the base of Cemetery Hill. When he discussed the beach situation by radio with the battalion commander, Lieutenant Colonel Newton ordered him to take over Charlie Company's mission and assault the northern half of Observatory Hill.

Darkness had fallen when Company B drove up the slopes of Objective A in a two-pronged attack. Six Marines were wounded in brief skirmishes with North Korean die-hards along the way. Gaining the summit at 2000, Fenton deployed three platoons on line, making contact with the Magness-Merritt force dug in on the saddle to the right. With Objective A seized and Able Company deployed on top and to the flanks of Cemetery Hill, Newton radioed the 5th Marines at 2240 that 1/5's segment of the O-A Line was secured.

In the right of the 5th Marines's zone, the 2nd Battalion had also been making gains, despite the handicaps of mixed boat waves, LST fire, poor visibility, and, finally, enemy action. It will be recalled that Company E suffered no casualties in landing and clearing the water-front as far south as Objective C, the British Consulate. Next to hit the beach was First Lieutenant H. J. Smith's Company D, part of which went ashore in 1/5's zone. Assembling later near the base of Observatory Hill, the unit prepared to carry out its mission of seizing Objective B, the southern half of the big ridge.

Although 2nd Battalion overlays show that Easy Company bore no responsibility for the crest of Observatory Hill, Smith's men somehow got the impression that part of Jaskilka's force was already on the summit. Its tactics based on this misunderstanding, Company D formed a simple route column, with Second Lieutenant Ray Heck's 1st Platoon leading the way, and marched up a street to the top of the hill. The vanguard troops cleared the first peak in the company zone without opposition and continued along the road to the second, expecting to meet men of Company E. They were greeted, however, by machine gun fire from an enemy squad entrenched to the right of the street.

The Marines tumbled into positions on the left. Grenades and small arms fire flew back and forth across the road during a brisk exchange that lasted about fifteen minutes. One of Heck's men was killed and three others wounded. The company corpsman was hit but refused evacuation until he had first administered to the other casualties and seen them off to safety. Company D's executive officer, First Lieutenant Michael J. Dunbar, went forward with Lieutenant Colonel Roise, the battalion commander, and was wounded by a ricochet.

The enemy troops were driven off just as darkness closed in, leaving the Marines to grope for night defensive positions on unfamiliar ground. Eventually Lieutenant Smith formed a line with all three rifle platoons deployed on the forward slopes of Objective B. Out of battalion reserve came Second Lieutenant Harry J. Nolan's platoon of Company F to bridge the gap between Company D and the Magness-Merritt positions in 1/5's zone on the left.

With Cemetery and Observatory Hills secured, the only portion of the O-A Line not yet under control was the extreme right, anchored on the inner tidal basin. Because the night was pitch black, Roise felt apprehensive about sending troops any farther into the city. In answer to a query, Lieutenant Colonel Murray, whose regimental headquarters had landed at 1830 and set up near the terminus of the Wolmi-do causeway, emphasized to Roise that where the O-A Line could not actually be defended from a suitable tactical standpoint, it must at least be outposted. The battalion commander forthwith dispatched a two-squad patrol from Fox Company to the tidal basin, and the small force returned from the one-thousand-yard prowl into the city at 2300, having seen no sign of the enemy. Roise reacted by committing Company F, less its platoon on Observatory Hill, to a defensive perimeter on the right flank. Shortly after midnight, Captain Uel D. Peters deployed the company next to the tidal basin as ordered; and the 5th Marines's O-A Line, though not manned in entirety, came as close to tactical reality as the tangled black depths of the seaport would allow.

BLUE BEACH

In recalling the situation ashore as of 1800 (H-plus 30), Colonel Lewis B. Puller, the regimental commander, later observed, "I personally landed on Blue Beach with the 3d wave. My reason for doing so was, exactly, that there was a strong possibility of confusion and disorganization under the circumstances: namely, the unavoidable necessity of landing the regiment without a rehearsal, without even a CPX. . . . The reorganization of the assault battalions was accomplished with remarkable speed and effectiveness. I recall being, at the time, extremely gratified that my prior concern in this connection was not warranted. Despite the initial delays at the ditch and sea wall, Companies G and I cleared the beach rapidly. Of the few casualties taken during the first 30 minutes ashore, most were caused by an enemy machine gun in a tower about 500 yards inland. LVT fire silenced the weapon, and the Marine infantry plunged forward through a labyrinth of blazing buildings and smoke-filled streets. On the left, George Company groped almost straight ahead toward the lowland corridor as Item veered sharply southward to attack Objective CHARLIE, the seaward tip of Hill 233."

While the assault units fought inland, the gathering darkness created one more formidable handicap for the last wave serials leaving the line of departure far out in the channel. The four Navy guide boats, mentioned earlier as having escorted the first wave, were exactly twenty-eight short of the number prescribed by amphibious doctrine for a landing of the Inchon assault's magnitude. For this reason the guide boats took station on either side of the boat lanes after the initial run, because it was manifestly impossible for them to help out in any other way. The limited visibility, however, just about negated their worth as stationary markers, owing to the fact that some landing craft formations were losing their direction even before they entered the boat lanes.

In describing the situation as it developed at the line of departure Lieutenant Clark later commented, "The BLUE Beach Control Officer was unable to contact LVT wave commanders or wave guide officers by radio at any time during the initial assault. The control officer was aware that waves or groups of LVTs and boats were landing at the wrong places but was helpless to prevent it without communications. As a last resort, Casualty and Salvage landing craft were dispatched to assist the initial wave guides (members of UDT 1) in rounding up vehicles and leading or directing them to BLUE Beach."

Because current and smoke fought relentlessly against tractors seaward of the line of departure, not all of the vehicles could find the control ship. If they did, it was next to impossible to come in close enough to get instructions shouted from the bridge. Thus many wave commanders, amtrac officers, and infantry leaders gave orders to head shoreward on their own initiative. They went in with waves and fragments of waves, displaying the kind of leadership that made the operation an overwhelming success in spite of the obstacles. This was the case with the three waves of 2/1 that failed to arrive at Blue One. They found their way ashore, some of the LVTs landing on Blue Two, others diverted to Blue Three; but the important thing was that they got there.

The most serious error of the day, again offset by initiative and decision, involved Lieutenant Colonel Jack Hawkins's 1st Battalion, landing in regimental reserve. About H-hour, Puller radioed Hawkins and ordered him to cross the line of departure with LCVP waves 21 through 25, carrying the whole of 1/1. Had the approach to the beach gone smoothly, the battalion would have begun landing at approximately H-plus 45 (1815).

Because of conditions in the channel and boat lanes, as already described, a searchlight on the control ship now beamed the supposed course to the beach. Actually, the whole area had become so clouded that the light was mistakenly pointed toward the outer tidal basin, some forty-five degrees off course to the northeast.

Moving in the designated direction, the first two of the reserve waves reached the sea wall of the basin; and the Marines, believing they were at the revetment of Blue Two, began debarking. Hawkins, following in the third wave (wave 23), caught the error as his boat passed within sight of two outlying islands between the basin and the salt evaporator jutting out from the left of Blue One. About the same time, Lieutenant Colonel Robert W. Rickert, executive officer of the 1st Marines, noticed some of the errant landing craft from his free boat between the line of departure and Blue One. He intercepted a group of the LCVPs and reoriented them.

In the meantime, Hawkins cruised the length of the basin wall and shouted instructions to the troops of the first two waves. Most of Company B had already debarked and a few of the empty boats had left for the channel. Able Company, having just begun to land, promptly reembarked in its LCVPs. In short order, the battalion reformed at sea and headed toward Blue Two. Owing to the lack of boats, one platoon of Baker Company remained on the tidal basin all night. Hiking to rejoin the company on the mainland next morning, this platoon rounded up an impressive bag of prisoners.

Upon reaching Blue Two in darkness, Hawkins found Company C, which had avoided the detour owing to the sixth sense of a boat coxswain, organizing and setting up local security. The battalion commander led most of 1/1 forward to a night assembly area along the railroad tracks, half a mile inland. Major David W. Bridges, battalion S-3, was left behind to organize latecomers as they arrived from the tidal basin.

The tactical situation ashore had meanwhile begun to crystallize for the 1st Marines. In the 2nd Battalion zone, Dog Company occupied Objective A, the road intersection, at 2000. Two hours later, Fox Company reported that it occupied enough of Objective D, Hill 117, so that it could cover the Inchon-Seoul highway with fire.

The attack from the beach had cost Sutter's unit one KIA and 19 WIA as compared to enemy losses of fifteen prisoners and an estimated fifty dead.

On the right of the regimental zone, Ridge's 3rd Battalion was also making good progress against light resistance. Item Company reported at 1900 that it was on Objective C, the western nose of Hill 233. Half an hour later, George Company began deploying in blocking positions across the corridor and road at the center of the O-1 Line. This movement was completed about 2030.

The 1st Platoon of How Company passed seaward of Item at 2030 and pressed a night attack against a company of North Koreans on Objective B, the small cape topped by Hill 94. After a token resistance, the Reds abandoned their well-prepared entrenchments, leaving thirty dead and wounded to be counted by the Marines.

How Company (less 1st and 2nd Platoons) covered the low ground between George and Item, finally occupying a blocking position about four hundred yards behind the O-1 Line.

With the seizure of Hill 94, the critical portions of the O-1 Line were secured. There was, however, a good deal of activity within the perimeter for several more hours. Major Bridges of 1/1 collected about one hundred latecomers at Blue Three and led them forward in search of the battalion assembly area. Composed of men from H&S, Able, and Baker Companies, the little force not only missed its destination but made one of the deepest penetrations of the day, finally halting on a hill to the left of George Company's front lines.

Shortly after Bridges set up a defensive position for the night, his position was invaded by an Easy Company contingent in search of the 2nd Battalion. Reoriented to some degree, the visitors reached Dog Company's intersection much later. The 2nd Battalion CP had meanwhile intercepted a group from Major Whitman S. Bartley's Weapons Company at the trail junction selected in the darkness for the initial battalion CP. At one or the other of these points, the misdirected portions of Sutter's battalion were directed to their parent units. All personnel were present or accounted for before dawn.

Two other troop movements completed the tactical mosaic of the 1st Marines. The 2nd Platoon of How Company was to pass through Item's lines on Objective C at 2330 and outpost the summit of Hill 233, some two thousand yards farther along the ridge and beyond the regimental front. After setting out on schedule, the small unit covered about half of its rugged journey upon reaching Hill 180, an intermediate height. With most of the night gone and his troops wearied by the climb, the platoon leader radioed for permission to halt and his request was granted.

Another venture into the unknown was made by an even smaller unit. Second Lieutenant Bruce F. Cunliffe's 60mm section of Fox Company had somehow mingled with 3rd Battalion troops during the drive inland. When he led his men through the darkness in search of 2/1, the section ranged forward of friendly lines and into unexplored territory near Hill 117.

The surprise was mutual when these Marines stumbled into a small NKPA patrol. But a brief fire fight in the darkness was enough for the Red soldiers, who took to their heels and left three dead. Cunliffe's force, which had no casualties, spent the rest of the night in uneventful isolation.

SECURING THE BEACHHEAD

Of all the calculated risks taken at Inchon, perhaps the most daring was the decision to ground eight LSTs abreast on Red Beach immediately after the assault troops landed. The navy workhorses were vulnerable enough at best, and on this narrow strip of waterfront they were lined up so close to one another that shots fired by a blindfolded enemy could scarcely have missed.

Not all the NKPA shells and bullets did miss, for that matter. But fortune as usual blessed the bold, and such enemy rounds as found their targets did not touch off tons of napalm, gasoline, and ammunition.

Only with reluctance had the planners accepted the risk of landing thin-skinned supply vessels before the immediate battle area was secured. But Inchon was not a typical amphibious operation. The tremendous tidal range created an unprecedented situation; and if vital supplies were not landed on the evening high tide, the assault troops must pass a precarious first night without adequate quantities of ammunition, water, and gasoline.

Dusk had fallen, with visibility further reduced by smoke and rain squalls, when the vessels wallowed into Red Beach. The reconnaissance element of Shore Party Group Able had gone ahead with the assault troops to erect landing guides during the last moments of daylight. While the men were working under fire, one of the beach markers was riddled by enemy machine guns as it was being erected.

The H&S Company of Lieutenant Colonel Henry P. Crowe's 1st Shore Party Battalion came in with the first of the LSTs, and other elements of Groups Able and Baker followed in short order. Each of the eight vessels brought a cargo consisting of fifty tons of ammunition, thirty tons of rations, fifteen tons of water, and five tons of fuel. These special loads were in addition to the normal cargo of engineer and shore party equipment and combat vehicles. Every LST was limited to five hundred short tons, however, in order to ensure that it could be beached without trouble.

The last of the LCMs had not yet unloaded and retracted on Red Beach when the first of the LSTs appeared slightly ahead of schedule. Naval officers managed to hold the LSTs back until the beach had cleared, and the eight vessels made a successful landing in spite of treacherous currents combined with low visibility. Two of them grounded momentarily on the mud flats but butted their way through to the beach. And though the sea wall temporarily prevented several vessels from lowering bow ramps effectively, the LSTs at each end of the line were able to discharge cargo over their ramps.

Bulldozers were first on the beach. They moved along the sea wall under enemy fire, pushing down sections of masonry that interfered with unloading operations.

LST 973 had no more than grated ashore when a Red Korean mortar shell exploded among the drums of motor fuel. Gasoline flooded the main deck and leaked down to the crew quarters through holes made by shell fragments. Orders were given to cut off electric motors and enforce all possible precautions, and the vessel miraculously escaped a conflagration even though it took further hits from enemy machine gun fire.

LST 857 ran into a ROK PC boat while heading in toward the beach, but no harm was done to either vessel. Hits from NKPA mortar and machine gun fire punctured eight drums of gasoline without any of them bursting into flame. This was one of the LSTs that fired back at enemy gun flashes. During the exchange a sailor was killed and another knocked unconscious when an enemy projectile damaged one of the LST's gun mounts.

LST 859, which had a sailor wounded by enemy mortar fragments, hit Red Beach with all guns blazing away. When the vessel beached, it was immediately boarded by Marines who helped themselves to ammunition while shouting to sailors in the well deck to stop firing. The same message was slammed home more authoritatively when First Lieutenant William J. Peter Jr. appeared on deck, as directed by Lieutenant Colonel Newton, and demanded that the LST's guns cease at once.

This put an end to the bombardment of shore positions. "No LSTs fired after my ship beached," commented Lieutenant Trumond E. Houston, USN, commander of LST 799 at the extreme left of the line. "Earlier LSTs beaching had opened fire on targets unknown to me, but my command had received very firm orders not to open fire due to the danger of firing into our own forces."

As dusk shaded into darkness, the Marines on and around Cemetery Hill extended their lines into the city. Even at the climax of the military drama there was an unexpected note of comedy—assault troops were to discover shortly that among the ammunition brought by the LSTs, some useless .22 caliber cartridges testified to the haste of departure from Camp Pendleton. There was enough M-1 ammunition, however, so that the enemy had no cause to complain of being neglected by the Marines.

5

SUPPLYING THE EMBATTLED MARINES AT KHE SANH

CAPTAIN MOYERS S.
SHORE II, USMC

"ATTENTION TO COLORS."

The order having been given, Captain William H. Dabney, a product of the Virginia Military Institute, snapped to attention, faced the jerry-rigged flagpole, and saluted, as did every other man in Company I, 3rd Battalion, 26th Marines. The ceremony might well have been at any one of a hundred military installations around the world except for a few glaring irregularities. The parade ground was a battle-scarred hilltop to the west of Khe Sanh and the men in the formation stood half submerged in trenches or foxholes. Instead of crisply starched utilities, razor sharp creases, and gleaming brass, these Marines sported scraggly beards, ragged trousers, and rotted helmet liner straps.

The only man in the company who could play a bugle, Second Lieutenant Owen S. Matthews, lifted the pock-marked instrument to his lips and spat out a choppy version of "To the Colors" while two enlisted men raced to the RC-292 radio antenna that served as the flagpole and gingerly attached the Stars and Stripes. As the mast with its shredded banner came upright, the Marines could hear the ominous "thunk," "thunk," "thunk" to the southwest of their position, which meant that North Vietnamese 120mm mortar rounds had left their tubes. They also knew that in twenty-one seconds those "thunks" would be replaced by much louder, closer sounds, but no one budged until Old Glory waved high over the hill.

When Lieutenant Matthews sharply cut off the last note of his piece, Company I disappeared; men dropped into trenches, dove headlong into foxholes, or scrambled into bunkers. The area that moments before had been bristling with humanity was suddenly a ghost town. Seconds later explosions walked across the hilltop spewing black smoke, dirt, and debris into the air. Rocks, splinters, and spent shell fragments rained on the flattened Marines, but, as usual, no one was hurt. As quickly as the attack came, it was over.

While the smoke lazily drifted away, a much smaller banner rose from the Marines's positions. A pole adorned with a pair of red silk panties—Maggie's Drawers—was waved back and forth above one trenchline to inform the enemy that he had missed again. A few men stood up and jeered or cursed at the distant gunners; others simply saluted with an appropriate obscene gesture. The daily flag-raising ceremony on Hill 881 South was over.

This episode was just one obscure incident that, coupled with hundreds of others, made up the battle for Khe Sanh. The ceremony carried with it no particular political overtones but was intended solely as an open show of defiance toward the Communists as well as a morale booster for the troops. The jaunty courage, quiet determination, and macabre humor of the men on Hill 881S exemplified the spirit of the US and South Vietnamese defenders who not only defied the enemy but, in a classic seventy-seven-day struggle, destroyed him.

The Khe Sanh Combat Base (KSCB) sat atop a plateau in the shadow of Dong Tri Mountain and overlooked a tributary of the Quang Tri River. The base had a small dirt airstrip, which had been surfaced by a US Navy Mobile Construction Battalion (Seabees) in the summer of 1966; the field could accommodate helicopters and fixed-wing transport aircraft. Artillery support was provided by Battery F. The Khe Sanh area of operations was also within range of the 175mm guns of the US Army's 2nd Battalion, 94th Artillery, at Camp Carroll and the Rockpile. In addition, there was a Marine Combined Action Company (CAC) and a Regional Forces company located in the village of Khe Sanh, approximately 3,500 meters south of the base.

The enemy had much to gain by taking Khe Sanh. If the garrison fell, the defeat might well turn out to be the coup de grace to

American participation in the war. At first, the Marines anticipated a major pitched battle, similar to the one in 1967, but the enemy continued to bide his time and the battle at Khe Sanh settled into one of supporting arms.

At Khe Sanh, the periodic showers of enemy artillery shells were, quite naturally, a major source of concern to Commanding Officer Colonel David E. Lownds, who placed a high priority on the construction of stout fortifications. Understandably, not every newcomer to Khe Sanh immediately moved into a thick bunker or a six-foot trench with overhead cover. The colonel had spent most of his tour with a one-battalion regiment and had prepared positions for that battalion; then, almost overnight, his command swelled to five battalions. The new units simply had to build their own bunkers as quickly as they could.

The average bunker usually started as an eight-by-eight-foot dugout with one six-by-six-inch timber inserted in each corner and the center for support. The overhead consisted of planks, a strip of runway matting, sandbags, loose dirt, and more sandbags. Some enterprising Marines piled on more loose dirt, then took discarded 105mm casings and drove them into the top of the bunker like nails. These casings often caused predetonation of the heavier-caliber rounds. The combat engineers attached to the 26th Marines could build one of these bunkers in three or four days; the average infantrymen took longer.

The Marines were also faced with another question concerning their defenses: "How large an artillery round could you defend against and still remain within the realm of practicality?" Because the 26th Marines was supplied solely by air, building material was a prime consideration. Matting and sandbags were easy enough to come by, but lumber was at a premium. Fortifications that could withstand a hit from an 82mm mortar were a must because the North Vietnamese had an ample supply of these weapons, but the base was also being pounded, to a lesser degree, by heavier-caliber guns. With the material available to the 26th Marines, it was virtually impossible to construct a shelter that was thick enough or deep enough to stop the heavy stuff.

Colonel Lownds decided to build a new regimental CP bunker. The engineers supplied the specifications for an overhead that would withstand a 122mm rocket; to be on the safe side, the colonel doubled the thickness of the roof. The day before the CP was to be occupied, a 152mm round landed squarely on top of the bunker and penetrated both layers.

The massing of enemy artillery made the hill outposts that much more important. Had they been able to knock the Marines from those summits, the North Vietnamese would have been able to fire right down the throats of the base defenders and make their position untenable. As it was, the companies on Hills 881S, 861, 861A, and 558 not only denied the enemy an unobstructed firing platform from which to pound the installation, they also served as the eyes for the rest of the regiment in the valley, which was relatively blind to enemy movement.

While the 60mm and 82mm mortars were scattered around in proximity of the combat base, the NVA rocket sites and artillery pieces were located well to the west, southwest, and northwest, outside of friendly counterbattery range. One particularly awesome and effective weapon was the Soviet-built 122mm rocket. When fired, the projectile was fairly accurate in deflection but, because it was powered by a propellant, the biggest margin of error was in range. The North Vietnamese preferred to position their launching sites so their gunners could track along the long axis of a given target; longs and shorts would land "in the ballpark."

The KSCB hugged the airstrip and was roughly in the shape of a rectangle with the long axis running east and west. This made the optimum firing positions for the 122mm rocket either to the east or west of the base in line with the runway. To the west, Hills 881S or 861 would have been ideal locations because in clear weather those vantage points provided an excellent view of Khe Sanh and were almost directly on line with the airstrip.

Unfortunately for the NVA, the Marines had squatters' rights on those pieces of real estate and were rather hostile to claim jumpers. As an alternative, the North Vietnamese decided on 881N, but this choice had one drawback because the line of sight between that northern peak and the combat base was masked by the top of Hill 861.

Because of their greater range, the enemy's 130mm and 152mm artillery batteries were located even further to the west. These guns were cleverly concealed in two main firing positions. One was on Co Roc Mountain, which was southwest of where Route 9 crossed the Laotian border; the other area was 305, so called because it was on a bearing of 305 degrees (west-northwest) from Hill 881S at a range of about ten thousand meters. While the heavy caliber artillery rounds that periodically ripped into the base were usually referred to as originating from Co Roc, 305 was the source of about 60 to 70 percent of this fire, probably because it was adjacent to a main supply artery. Both sites were vulnerable only to air attack and were extremely difficult to pinpoint because of the enemy's masterful job of camouflage, their cautious employment, and the extreme distance from friendly observation posts. The NVA gunners fired only a few rounds every hour so that continuous muzzle flashes did not betray their positions and, after each round, quickly scurried out to cover the guns with protective nets and screens. Some pieces, mounted on tracks, were wheeled out of caves in Co Roc Mountain, fired, and returned immediately. Though never used in as great a quantity as the rockets and mortars, these shells wreaked havoc at Khe Sanh because there was very little that they could not penetrate; even duds went about four feet into the ground.

At the base the Marines had devised a crude but effective early warning system for such attacks. Motor transport personnel had mounted a horn from a two-and-a-half-ton truck in the top of a tree and the lead wires were attached to two beer can lids. When a message was received from 881S, a Marine, who monitored the radio, pressed the two lids together and the blaring horn gave advanced warning of the incoming artillery rounds. The radio operator relayed the message over the regimental net and then dived into a hole. Men in the open usually had from five to eighteen seconds to find cover or just hit the deck before "all hell broke loose." When poor visibility obscured the view between 881S and the base, the radio operator usually picked himself up, dusted off, and jokingly passed a three-word message to Company I that indicated that the rounds had arrived on schedule: "Roger India . . . Splash."

The firing position that plagued the Marines the most was located to the southwest of the hill in a U-shaped draw known as "the Horseshoe." There were at least two NVA 120mm mortars in this area that, in spite of an avalanche of American bombs and artillery shells, were either never knocked out or were frequently replaced. These tubes were registered on the hill and harassed Company I constantly. Anyone caught above ground when one of the 120s crashed into the perimeter was almost certain to become a casualty because the explosion produced an extremely large fragmentation pattern.

The only thing that the Marines had going for them was that they could frequently spot a tell-tale flash of an artillery piece or hear the "thunk" when a mortar round left the tube, but the heavy shells took their toll. On Hill 881S alone, forty Marines were killed throughout the siege and over 150 were wounded at least once.

Considering the sheer weight of the bombardment, enemy shells caused a relatively small number of fatalities at the base. Besides the solid fortifications, there were two factors that kept casualties to a minimum. The first was the flak jacket—a specially designed nylon vest reinforced with overlapping fiberglass plates. The jacket would not stop a high-velocity bullet, but it did protect a man's torso and most vital organs against shell fragments. The bulky vest was not particularly popular in hot weather when the Marines were on patrol, but in a static, defensive position the jacket was ideal. The second factor was the high quality of leadership at platoon and company level. Junior officers and staff noncommissioned officers (NCOs) constantly moved up and down the lines to supervise the younger, inexperienced Marines, many of whom had only recently arrived in Vietnam.

The veteran staff NCOs, long known as the "backbone of the Corps," knew from experience that troops had to be kept busy. A man who was left to ponder his problems often developed a fatalistic attitude that could increase his reaction time and decrease his lifetime. The crusty NCOs did not put much stock in the old cliche, "If a round has your name on it, there's nothing you can do." Consequently, the Marines worked; they dug trenches, filled sandbags, ran for cover, and returned to fill more sandbags. Morale remained high and casualties, under the circumstances, were surprisingly low.

Although the NVA encircled the KSCB and applied constant pressure, the defenders were never restricted entirely to the confines of the perimeter. The term "siege," in the strictest sense of the word, was somewhat of a misnomer because the Allies conducted a number of daily patrols, often as far as five hundred meters from their own lines.

One vital area was the drop zone. When the weather turned bad in February, the KSCB was supplied primarily by parachute drops. Colonel Lownds set up his original zone inside the FOB-3 compound but later moved it several hundred meters west of Red Sector because he was afraid that the falling pallets might injure someone.

The fight on Hill 861A was extremely bitter. At 0305 the North Vietnamese opened up on American positions with a tremendous 82mm mortar barrage. This was followed by continuous volleys of RPG rounds that knocked out several Marine crew-served weapons and shielded the advance of the NVA sappers and assault troops. The North Vietnamese blew lanes through the barbed wire along the northern perimeter and slammed into the Company E lines. Second Lieutenant Donald E. Shanley's 1st Platoon bore the brunt of the attack and reeled back to supplementary positions. Quickly the word filtered back to the company CP that the enemy was inside the wire, and Captain Earle G. Breeding ordered that all units employ tear gas in defense, but the North Vietnamese were obviously "hopped up" on some type of narcotic and the searing fumes had very little effect. Following the initial assault there was a brief lull in the fighting. The NVA soldiers apparently felt that, having secured the northernmost trenchline, they owned the entire objective and stopped to sift through the Marine positions for souvenirs. Magazines and paperbacks were the most popular. Meanwhile, the temporary reversal only served to enrage the Marines. Following a shower of grenades, Lieutenant Shanley and his men charged back into their original positions and swarmed all over the surprised enemy troops.

The counterattack quickly deteriorated into a melee that resembled a bloody, waterfront barroom brawl—a style of fighting not completely alien to most Marines. Because the darkness and ground fog drastically reduced visibility, hand-to-hand combat was a necessity. Using their knives, bayonets, rifle butts, and fists, the men of the 1st Platoon ripped into the hapless North Vietnamese with a vengeance. Captain Breeding, a veteran of the Korean conflict who had worked his way up through the ranks, admitted that, at first, he was concerned over how his younger, inexperienced Marines would react in their first fight. As it turned out, they were magnificent.

The captain saw one of his men come face to face with a North Vietnamese in the inky darkness; the young American all but decapitated his adversary with a crushing, roundhouse right to the face, then leaped on the flattened soldier and finished the job with a knife.

Another man was jumped from behind by a North Vietnamese who grabbed him around the neck and was just about to slit his throat when one of the Marine's buddies jabbed the muzzle of his M-16 between the two combatants. With his selector on full automatic, he fired off a full magazine; the burst tore huge chunks from the back of the embattled Marine's flak jacket, but it also cut the North Vietnamese in half. Because the fighting was at such close quarters, both sides used hand grenades at extremely short range. The Marines had the advantage because of their armored vests, and they would throw a grenade, then turn away from the blast, hunch up, and absorb the fragments in their flak jackets and the backs of their legs. On several occasions, Captain Breeding's men used this technique and "blew away" enemy soldiers at less than ten meters.

No one engaged in the donnybrook was exactly sure just how long it lasted—all were too busy fighting to check their watches. More than likely, the enemy was inside the wire less than a half hour. During the fighting, Captain Breeding fed fire team–sized elements from the 2nd and 3rd Platoons into the fray from both flanks of the penetration. The newcomers appeared to be afraid that they might miss all the action and tore into the enemy as if they were making up for lost time. Even though the E/2/26 company commander was no newcomer to blood and gore, he was awed by the ferocity of the attack. Captain Breeding later said, "It was like watching a World War II movie. Charlie didn't know how to cope with it . . . we walked all over them." Those dazed NVA soldiers who survived the vicious onslaught retreated into another meatgrinder; as they ran from the hill, they were blasted by recoilless rifle fire from 2/26, which was located on Hill 558.

At approximately 0610, the North Vietnamese officers rallied the battered remnants and tried again, but the second effort was also stopped cold. By this time, Captain Breeding, who was busier than the proverbial one-armed paper hanger, was assisting in the coordination of fire support from five separate sources.

The Marines of Captain Dabney's I/3/26, located on Hill 881S, provided extremely effective and enthusiastic support throughout the attack. In three hours, Captain Dabney's men pumped out close to 1,100 rounds from only three 81mm mortars, and the tubes became so hot that they actually glowed in the dark. Again, the bulk of the heavy artillery fire, along with radar-controlled bombing missions, was placed on the northern avenues leading to the hill positions. The enemy units, held in reserve, were thus shredded by the bombardment as they moved up to continue the attack.

After the second assault fizzled out, the North Vietnamese withdrew, but enemy gunners shelled the base and outposts throughout the day. At 1430, replacements from 2/26 were helilifted to Hill 861A. Captain Breeding had lost seven men, most of whom were killed in the opening barrage, and another thirty-five were medevaced, so the new arrivals brought E/2/26 back up to normal strength.

On the other hand, the NVA suffered 109 known dead; many still remained in the 1st Platoon area where they had been shot, slashed, or bludgeoned to death. As near as Captain Breeding could tell, he did not lose a single man during the fierce hand-to-hand struggle; all American deaths were apparently the result of the enemy's mortar barrage and supporting fire. The Marines never knew how many other members of the North Vietnamese had fallen as a result of the heavy artillery and air strikes but the number was undoubtedly high. All in all, it had been a bad day for the Communists.

The North Vietnamese took their revenge in the early morning hours of February 7; their victims were the defenders of the Special Forces camp at Lang Vei. At 0042, an American advisor reported that the installation was under heavy attack by enemy tanks. This was the first time that the NVA had employed its armor in the south and, within thirteen minutes, nine PT-76 Soviet-built tanks churned through the defensive wire, rumbled over the antipersonnel minefields, and bulled their way into the heart of the compound.

A North Vietnamese battalion, equipped with satchel charges, tear gas, and flamethrowers, followed with an aggressive infantry assault that was coordinated with heavy attacks by fire on the 26th Marines. Colonel Lownds placed the base on Red Alert and called in immediate artillery and air in support. Although the Marines responded quickly, the defensive fires had little effect because, by that time, the enemy had overrun the camp. The defenders who survived buttoned themselves up in bunkers and, at 0243, called for artillery fire to dust off their own positions.

Part of Colonel Lownds's mission as coordinator of all friendly forces in the Khe Sanh area was to provide artillery support for Lang Vei and, if possible, to reinforce the camp in case of attack. Under the circumstances, a relief in strength was out of the question. Any column moving down the road, especially at night, would undoubtedly have been ambushed. If the Marines went directly over the mountains, they would have to hack through the dense growth and waste precious hours. A large-scale heliborne effort was ruled out because the North Vietnamese apparently anticipated such a move and withdrew their tanks to the only landing zones near the camp that were suitable for such an operation. Even with tactical aircraft providing suppressive fire, a helo assault into the teeth of enemy armor was ill advised. The most important factor, however, was that NVA units in the area greatly outnumbered any force Colonel Lownds could commit.

Because a relief in force was undesirable, plans for a hit and run rescue attempt were quickly drawn up. Major General Norman J. Anderson, commanding the 1st MAW, and Colonel Jonathan F. Ladd of the US Army Special Forces worked out the details. Two major points agreed upon were that the helicopters employed in the operation would be those that were not essential to the 26th Marines at the moment and that Marine fixed-wing support would be provided.

As soon as it was light, the survivors of the Lang Vei garrison managed to break out of their bunkers and work their way to the site of an older camp some four to five hundred meters to the east. Later that same day, a raiding party boarded Quang Tri–based MAG helicopters and took off for Lang Vei. A flight of Huey gunships, led by Lieutenant Colonel William J. White, Commanding Officer of Marine Observation Squadron 6, as well as jet aircraft escorted the transport choppers. While the jets and Hueys covered their approach, the helicopters swooped into a small strip at the old camp and took on survivors, including fifteen Americans. In spite of the heavy suppressive fire provided by the escorts, three transport helos suffered battle damage during the evacuation. One overloaded chopper, flown by Captain Robert J. Richards of Marine Medium Helicopter Squadron 262, had to make the return trip to Khe Sanh at treetop level because the excess weight prevented the pilot from gaining altitude.

There was a large number of Indigenous personnel—both military and civilian—who could not get out on the helicopters and had to move overland to Khe Sanh. A portion of these were members of the Laotian Volunteer Battalion 33, which on January 23 had been overrun at Ban Houei San, Laos (near the Laotian/South Vietnam border), by three NVA battalions. The remnants fled across the border and took refuge at Lang Vei, and when the Special Forces camp fell, the Laotians continued their trek to the east with a host of other refugees. At 0800 on February 8, about three thousand approached the southern perimeter at Khe Sanh and requested admittance. Colonel Lownds, fearing that NVA infiltrators were in their midst, denied them entrance until each was searched and processed. This took place near the FOB-3 compound, after which some of the refugees were evacuated. The Laotians were eventually returned to their own country.

Also on the morning of February 8, the North Vietnamese launched the first daylight attack against the 26th Marines. At 0420, a reinforced battalion hit the 1st Platoon, A/1/9, which occupied Hill 64 some five hundred meters west of the 1/9 perimeter. Following their usual pattern, the North Vietnamese tried to disrupt the Marines's artillery support with simultaneous bombardment of the base. To prevent friendly reinforcements from reaching the small hill the enemy also shelled the platoon's parent unit and, during the fight, some 350 mortar and artillery rounds fell on the 1/9 positions. North Vietnamese assault troops launched a two-pronged attack against the northwestern and southwestern corners of the A/1/9 outpost and either blew the barbed wire with Bangalore torpedoes or threw canvas on top of the obstacles and rolled over them. The enemy soldiers poured into the trenchline and attacked the bunkers with RPGs and satchel charges. They also emplaced machine guns at the edge of the penetrations and pinned down those Marines in the eastern half of the perimeter who were trying to cross over the hill and reinforce their comrades.

The men in the northeastern sector, led by the platoon commander, Second Lieutenant Terence R. Roach Jr., counterattacked down the trenchline and became engaged in savage hand-to-hand fighting.

While rallying his troops and directing fire from atop an exposed bunker, Lieutenant Roach was mortally wounded. From sheer weight of numbers, the North Vietnamese gradually pushed the Marines back until the enemy owned the western half of the outpost. At that point, neither side was able to press the advantage. Preregistered mortar barrages from 1/9 and artillery fire from the KSCB had isolated the NVA assault units from any reinforcements, but at the same time the depleted 1st Platoon was not strong enough to dislodge the enemy.

One Marine had an extremely close call during the fight but lived to tell about it. On the northern side of the perimeter, Private First Class Michael A. Barry of the 1st Squad was engaged in a furious hand grenade duel with the NVA soldiers when a ChiCom grenade hit him on top of the helmet and landed at the young Marine's feet. PFC Barry quickly picked it up and drew back to throw, but the grenade went off in his hand. Had it been an American M-26 grenade, the private would undoubtedly have been blown to bits, but ChiCom grenades frequently produced an uneven frag pattern. In this case, the bulk of the blast went down and away from the Marine's body; Barry had the back of his right arm, his back, and his right leg peppered with metal fragments, but he did not lose any fingers and continued to function for the rest of the battle.

In another section of the trenchline, Lance Corporal Robert L. Wiley had an equally hair-raising experience. Wiley, a shell-shock victim, lay flat on his back in one of the bunkers that had been overrun by the enemy. His eardrums had burst, he was temporarily paralyzed, and his glazed eyes were fixed in a corpse-like stare, but the Marine was alive and fully aware of what was going on around him.

Thinking that Wiley was dead, the North Vietnamese were only interested in rummaging through his personal effects for souvenirs. One NVA soldier found the Marine's wallet and took out several pictures, including a snapshot of his family gathered around a Christmas tree. After pocketing their booty, the North Vietnamese moved on; Lance Corporal Wiley was later rescued by the relief column.

At 0730, Lieutenant Colonel Mitchell committed a second platoon, headed by the Company A commander, Captain Henry J. M. Radcliffe, to the action. By 0900, the relief force had made its way to the eastern slope of the small hill and established contact with the trapped platoon. During the advance, Companies B and D, along with one section of tanks, delivered murderous direct fire to the flanks and front of Captain Radcliffe's column, breaking up any attempt by the enemy to interdict the linkup. After several flights of strike aircraft had pasted the reverse slope of the hill, the company commander led his combined forces in a frontal assault over the crest and, within fifteen minutes, drove the North Vietnamese from the outpost.

Automatic weapons chopped down many North Vietnamese as they fled from the hill. The battered remnants of the enemy force retreated to the west and, once in the open, were also taken under fire by the rest of the Marine battalion. In addition, the artillery batteries at KSCB contributed to the slaughter, and when the smoke cleared, 150 North Vietnamese were dead. Although the platoon lines were restored, Colonel Lownds decided to abandon the position and, at 1200, the two units withdrew with their casualties. Marine losses that morning on the outpost were twenty-one killed and twenty-six wounded; at the base, five were killed and six wounded.

During the next two weeks, the NVA mounted no major ground attack but continued to apply pressure on the KSCB. There were daily clashes along the Marine lines, but these were limited to small fire fights, sniping incidents, and probes against the wire. A decrease in activity along the various infiltration routes indicated that the enemy had completed his initial buildup and was busily consolidating positions from which to launch an all-out effort. The Allies continued to improve their defenses, and by mid-February most units occupied positions with three or four layers of barbed wire, dense minefields, special detection devices, deep trenches, and mortar-proof bunkers. The battle reverted to a contest of supporting arms, and the North Vietnamese stepped up their shelling of the base, especially with direct fire weapons. Attempts to silence the enemy guns were often frustrated because the Marines were fighting two battles during February—one with the NVA, the other with the weather.

The weather at Khe Sanh throughout February could be characterized in one word: miserable. The northeast monsoons had long since spilled over into the Khe Sanh Valley, and every morning the base was shrouded with ground fog and low scud layers that dissipated around 1000 or 1100. When the sun finally managed to burn through, the cloud ceiling retreated slightly but still hovered low enough to prevent the unrestricted use of airborne artillery spotters and strike aircraft. It was during these periods, when the overcast was between one hundred and five hundred feet, that enemy artillery, rocket, and mortar fire was the heaviest. North Vietnamese forward observers, perched along the lower slopes of the surrounding hills, called in and adjusted barrages with little fear of retaliation against their own gun positions. Later in the afternoon, when the fog rolled in again and obscured the enemy's view, the incoming tapered off.

The Marines adjusted their schedule accordingly. They usually worked under the cover of the haze in the morning, went underground during the midday shelling, and returned to their duties later in the afternoon. While the extremely low cloud cover occasionally befriended the men at the base, it constantly plagued the pilots whose mission was to resupply the 26th Marines.

The job of transporting enough "bullets, beans, and bandages" to sustain the 6,680 Khe Sanh defenders fell to the C-130s of Marine Aerial Refueler Transport Squadron 152 and the US Air Force 834th Air Division; the C-123s of the 315th Air Commando Wing; the UH-34, CH-46, and UH-1E helicopters of Marine Aircraft Group 36 (MAG-36); and the CH-53 choppers of MAG-16.

Even under ideal circumstances, the airlift would have been a massive undertaking. The difficulties, however, were compounded by the poor visibility, which was below minimum for airfield operations 40 percent of the time, and the heavy volume of antiaircraft and artillery fire directed at the incoming transports. The North Vietnamese had moved several antiaircraft units into the hills east of the airstrip forcing the C-130 Hercules, the C-123 Providers, and the helicopters to run the gauntlet during their final approach. Under cover of the heavy fog, some audacious North Vietnamese gun crews positioned their antiaircraft weapons just off the eastern threshold of the runway and fired in the blind whenever they heard the drone of incoming planes. Several aircraft were hit while on GCA final and completely in the soup. Immediately after touchdown, the aircraft were subjected to intense mortar and rocket fire; in fact, the incoming was so closely synchronized with their arrival that the fixed-wing transports were nicknamed "mortar magnets" by the Marines.

The key to survival for the pilots was a steep approach through the eastern corridor, a short roll-out, and a speedy turnaround after landing. A small ramp paralleled the western end of the strip that the transport crews used as an unloading point. After roll-out, the pilot turned off the runway onto the easternmost taxiway, then wheeled onto the ramp while the loadmasters shoved the pallets of supplies out the back. All outgoing passengers were loaded on the double because the seventy-six planes rarely stopped rolling. The pilot completed the loop by turning back onto the runway via the western taxiway and took off in the opposite direction from which he landed. It was not uncommon for the entire circuit to be completed within three minutes; even then, the planes were tracked by exploding mortar rounds.

On February 10, a tragedy occurred that resulted in a drastic alteration of the unloading process. A Marine C-130, heavily laden with bladders of fuel for the 26th Marines, was making its approach to the field under intense fire. Just before the giant bird touched down, the cockpit and fuel bags were riddled by enemy bullets. With flames licking at one side, the stricken craft careened off the runway 3,100 feet from the approach end, spun around, and was rocked by several muffled explosions. The C-130 then began to burn furiously. Crash crews rushed to the plane and started spraying it with foam.

The pilot, Chief Warrant Officer Henry Wildfang, and his copilot suffered minor burns as they scrambled out the overhead hatch in the cockpit. Firefighters in specially designed heat suits dashed into the flaming debris and pulled several injured crewmen and passengers to safety—rescue attempts came too late for six others. One of those killed in the crash, Lieutenant Colonel Carl E. Peterson, the 1st MAW Engineer Officer, was a reserve officer who only a few months before had volunteered for active duty. As a result of this accident and damage sustained by other transports while on the ground, C-130 landings at Khe Sanh were suspended.

With the field closed to C-130s, a US Air Force innovation—the Low Altitude Parachute Extraction System, or LAPES—was put into effect. This self-contained system, which had been used extensively during the renovation of the airstrip in the fall of 1967, enabled the aircraft to unload their cargo without landing. When making a LAPES run, the Hercules pilot made his approach from the east, during which he opened the tail ramp and deployed a reefed cargo parachute.

Prior to touchdown, he added just enough power to hold the aircraft about five feet above the ground. As the plane skimmed over the runway and approached the intended extraction point, the pilot electrically opened the streaming chute, which was attached to the roller-mounted cargo pallets. The sudden jolt of the blossoming chute snatched the cargo from the rear hatch and the pallets came to a skidding halt on the runway. The pilot then jammed the throttles to the firewall, eased back on the yoke, and executed a high-angle, westerly pull-out to avoid ground fire while the Marines moved onto the runway with forklifts and quickly gathered in the supplies.

The system was quite ingenious and allowed the aircraft to pass through the V-ring in a matter of seconds. Even though the airmen could not control the skidding pallets after release, some pilots perfected their individual technique and were able to place the cargo on a twenty-five-meter square with consistency. On one occasion, however, an extraction chute malfunctioned and the cargo rocketed off the western end of the runway; the eight-ton pallet of lumber smashed into a mess hall located near the end of the strip and crushed three Marines to death.

Another technique—the Ground Proximity Extraction System or GPES—was also used but to a lesser degree than the LAPES (fifteen GPES deliveries during the siege as compared to fifty-two LAPES). Both utilized the low approach, but with GPES the cargo was extracted by a hook extended from a boom at the rear of the aircraft. As the C-130 swooped low over the runway, the pilot tried to snag an arresting cable similar to the one used on aircraft carriers, only his hook was attached to the cargo bundles and not the plane. Upon engagement, the pallets were jerked from the rear hatch and came to a dead stop on the runway. With the GPES, the chance of a pallet skidding out of control or overturning was greatly reduced. The only problem that occurred was not with the system itself but with faulty installation.

The Marines who initially emplaced the GPES were frequently chased away from their work by incoming mortar rounds, and as a result of the periodic interruptions, the cable was not anchored properly. The first C-130 that snagged the wire ripped the arresting gear out by the roots. After the initial bugs were remedied, the system worked so successfully that, on one pass, a load containing thirty dozen eggs was extracted without a single eggshell being cracked.

Most of the time, however, the low overcast precluded the use of either extraction system and the preponderance of supplies was delivered by paradrops. This technique called for close air/ground coordination, and the C-130 pilots relied on the Marine Air Traffic Control Unit (MATCU) at Khe Sanh to guide them into the drop zones. The Marine ground controller lined the aircraft up on the long axis of the runway for a normal instrument approach, and when the Hercules passed a certain point over the eastern threshold of the field, the controller called, "Ready, Ready, Mark." At "Mark," the pilot pushed a stopwatch, activated his Doppler navigational system, turned to a predetermined heading, and maintained an altitude of between five hundred and six hundred feet.

The Doppler device indicated any deviation from the desired track to the drop zone, which was west of Red Sector, and the release point was calculated by using the stopwatch—twenty to twenty-six seconds from "Mark," depending on the winds. At the computed release point, the pilot pulled the C-130 into an eight-degree nose-up attitude and sixteen parachute bundles, containing fifteen tons of supplies, slid from the rear of the aircraft and floated through the overcast into the three-hundred-meter-square drop zone. Under Visual Flight Rules (VFR), the average computed error for the drops was only ninety-five meters. Even when these missions were executed completely under Instrument Flight Rules (IFR), the average distance that the bundles landed from the intended impact point was 133 meters—well inside the drop zone. On a few occasions, however, the parachute bundles missed the zone and drifted far enough away from the base to preclude a safe recovery. In these rare instances, friendly artillery and air strikes were brought to bear on the wayward containers to keep them from falling into the hands of the enemy. During the siege, Air Force C-130 crews conducted a total of 496 paradrops at Khe Sanh.

Although the paradrops were sufficient for bulk commodities such as rations and ammunition, there were certain items that had to be delivered or picked up personally. Medical supplies, special ammunition, and other delicate cargo would not withstand the jolt of a parachute landing. In addition, there were replacements to be shuttled into the base and casualties to be evacuated. With the cancellation of all C-130 landings, this job was left up to the sturdy C-123 Providers of the 315th Air Commando Wing as well as MAG-36 and MAG-16 helicopters.

The choppers could maneuver around areas of heavy ground fire, land, unload, take on medevacs, and depart very quickly, but their payloads were limited. On the other hand, the C-123s had a larger cargo capacity but were restricted to a more rigid approach and provided better targets both in the pattern and on the ground. The Providers, however, required much less runway from which to operate than the C-130s and could land and take off using only 1,400 of the 3,900-foot strip. This saving feature enabled the pilots to make a steep approach, short roll-out, and rapid turnaround. The crews still had to undergo those frantic moments on the ground when the geysers of dirty black smoke bracketed their aircraft. Nevertheless, the dauntless

C-123 crews continued their perilous missions throughout the siege with great success.

No discussion of the airlift would be complete without mention of the MAG-36 and MAG-16 helicopter pilots who flew in and out of Khe Sanh daily delivering supplies, delicate cargo, reinforcements, and evacuating casualties. The chopper crews were faced with the same problems that plagued the fixed-wing transports—low ceilings and enemy ground fire—but to a greater degree because of their slow speed and vulnerability. MAG-36 operated primarily from Quang Tri and Dong Ha and was reinforced from the group's main base at Phu Bai. These valiant pilots and crewmen in their Huey gunships, CH-46 transports, and UH-34s flew long hours, day and night, in all kinds of weather to sustain the Marines in and around Khe Sanh. The CH-53s of Da Nang–based MAG-16, with their heavier payload, also made a sizeable contribution to this effort.

The resupply of the hill outposts was a particularly hazardous aspect of the overall mission. Approximately 20 percent of Colonel Lownds's personnel occupied these redoubts and, for all practical purposes, were cut off from the rest of the garrison. The road north of the base was not secure and the perimeters atop the hills were too small and irregular for parachute drops; the only way that the isolated posts could be sustained was by helicopter. When the dense monsoon clouds rolled into the valley, the mountaintops were the first to become submerged and, as the overcast lifted, the last to reappear. During February, several of the outposts were completely obscured for more than a week and resupply was impossible.

During these periods, the North Vietnamese took advantage of the reduced visibility and emplaced heavy automatic weapons along the neighboring peaks and waited for the ceiling to lift, which invariably heralded the arrival of helicopters. As a result, the UH-1Es, UH-34s, and CH-46s were subjected to a hail of enemy bullets during each mission.

When the helicopters proceeded to the hills singly or in small groups, each mission was a hair-raising experience for both the chopper crews and the men on the ground. A good example of what often transpired during those frantic moments occurred early in the siege on Hill 881S when Captain Dabney called for a chopper to evacuate a badly wounded Marine.

One corporal was assigned as a stretcher bearer because he had a badly impacted wisdom tooth and, once aboard, he could ride out on the helicopter and have the tooth extracted at the main base. Because of the 120mm mortars located in the Horseshoe and the antiaircraft guns that ringed the hill, the men on 881S had to employ a variety of diversions to keep the enemy gunners from getting the range of the incoming choppers. In this instance, they threw a smoke grenade a good distance away from the actual landing zone in hopes that the gunners would register on the smoke and the helicopter would be in and out before the North Vietnamese could readjust. This meant that the helo had about nineteen seconds to get off the ground.

The ruse did not come off as planned. The stretcher bearers had barely loaded the wounded man aboard the helicopter, a CH-46, when 120mm mortar rounds bracketed the aircraft and spurred the pilot to action. The helo lurched into the air, and the sudden jolt rolled the corporal with the bad tooth over the edge of the tail ramp; he held on desperately for a few seconds but finally let go and fell about twenty feet to the ground. Cursing to himself, the young man limped back to his trench and waited for another chance.

Later that day, a UH-34 swooped in to pick up another casualty, and the prospective dental patient quickly scrambled aboard. This trip also covered about twenty feet—ten feet up and ten feet down—because the tail rotor of the UH-34 was literally sawed off by a burst from an enemy machine gun just after the bird became airborne. After the swirling craft came to rest, the passengers and the three-man crew quickly clamored out the hatch and dived into a nearby trench. A heavy mortar barrage ensued during which several more men were hit.

By the time another CH-46 arrived on the scene, the passenger list had grown to fourteen, including ten casualties, the crew of the downed helo, and the original dental case. Because of the heavy concentration of enemy fire in the original zone, the Marines had blasted out another landing site on the opposite side of the hill. The chopper touched down, and thirteen of the fourteen Marines boarded before the crew chief stated emphatically that the aircraft was full. As luck would have it, the young Marine with the swollen jaw was the fourteenth man. Thoroughly indignant, the three-time loser returned to his position and mumbled that he would rather suffer from a toothache than try and get off the hill by helicopter.

It was the consensus of both the ground commanders and pilots alike that the problem of getting helicopters to and from the hills was becoming critical. The technique then employed was resulting in casualties among both the air crews and the infantry units, as well as a rapid rise in the attrition of MAG-36 helicopters. The Huey gunships, though putting forth a valiant effort, did not possess the heavy volume of fire required to keep the approach lanes open. As a result, the 1st MAW adopted another system that provided more muscle.

The solution was basically a page out of the Fleet Marine Force Manual for Helicopter Support Operations. All helicopter flights to the hill outposts were to be escorted by strike aircraft that would provide suppressive fire. The A-4 Skyhawks of Chu Lai–based MAG-12 were selected as the fixed-wing escorts, and the little jet was perfect for the job. Affectionately referred to as "Scooters" by their pilots, the A-4 was a highly maneuverable attack aircraft; its accuracy, dependability, and varied ordnance load had made it the workhorse of Marine close air support for many years.

The operation went into effect on February 24. Because of the large number of aircraft utilized in each mission—twelve A-4s, one TA-4, twelve CH-46s, and four UH-1E gunships—the overall effort was nicknamed the Super Gaggle by its planners. The difficulty in execution was primarily one of coordination and control because of the various agencies involved. Additional factors that had to be considered were departure weather, destination weather, and coordination of friendly artillery and air strikes around Khe Sanh. Lieutenant Colonel Carey, the 1st MAW Operations Officer and one of the planners, later described the mechanics of the Super Gaggle:

Success of the effort was predicated on timing, coordination, and often times luck. Luck, as used, refers to the ability to guess whether the weather would hold long enough to complete an effort once it got underway. The effort began with the TA-4 on station determining if sufficient ceiling existed for the "Scooters" of MAG-12 to provide sufficient suppressive fires to assure success. . . . Once the TA-4 called all conditions go, an "H" hour was set and the Super Gaggle began. Twelve A-4s would launch from Chu Lai while simultaneously one hundred miles to the north twelve to sixteen helos would launch from the Quang Tri helo base and proceed to the Dong Ha LSA (Logistics Support Area) for supply pickup. The object was for all aircraft to arrive in the objective area on a precise schedule. So the operation generally consisted as follows: (1) Softening up known enemy positions by four A-4s, generally armed with napalm and bombs; (2) two A-4s armed with CS (tear gas) tanks saturate enemy antiaircraft and automatic weapons positions; (3) thirty to forty seconds prior to final run in by the helos two A-4s lay a smoke screen along selected avenues of approach. . . . (4) while helos make final run into the target, four A-4s with bombs, rockets, and 20mm guns provide close-in fire suppression. . . . Once the helos commenced their descent the factors of weather, their four-thousand-pound externally carried load, and the terrain would not permit a second chance. If an enemy gun was not suppressed there was no alternative for the helos but to continue. They (the transport pilots) were strengthened with the knowledge that following close on their heels were their gunships ready to pick them up if they survived being shot down. Fortunately, these tactics were so successful that during the entire period of the Super Gaggle only two CH-46s were downed enroute to the hill positions. The crews were rescued immediately by escorting Huey gunships.

These missions, however, looked much more orderly on paper than they did in the air and the operation lived up to its name. Only those who have experienced the hazards of monsoon flying can fully appreciate the veritable madhouse that often exists when large numbers of aircraft are confined to the restricted space beneath a low-hanging overcast.

Coupled with this was the fact that the fluffy-looking clouds around Khe Sanh housed mountains that ran up to three thousand feet. No doubt, the aircrews involved in the Gaggle were mindful of the standard warning issued to fledgling aviators: "Keep your eyes out of the cockpit; a mid-air collision could ruin your whole day."

Even though the missions were well coordinated and executed with a high degree of professionalism, it often appeared that confusion reigned because planes were everywhere. A-4s bore in on the flanks of the approach lanes blasting enemy gun positions and spewing protective smoke; CH-46s groped through the haze trying to find the landing zones; the hornet-like UH-1E gunships darted in from the rear in case someone was shot down; and the lone 87TA-4 circled overhead trying to keep his flock from running amuck. During the missions to 881S, the men of India and Mike, 3/26, added to the hullabaloo with a little twist of their own. When the CH-46s settled over the hill, the Marines on the ground tossed out a few dozen smoke grenades for added cover and then every man in the perimeter fired a full magazine at anything on the surrounding slopes that appeared hostile. With some 350 men hosing down the countryside at the same time, the din was terrific.

Neither the deluge of lead from 881S nor the suppressive fire of the jets and gunships kept the NVA completely quiet. The 120mm mortar crews in the Horseshoe were especially active during the resupply runs to 881S and always lobbed some rounds onto the hill in hopes of knocking down a helicopter. These tubes had been previously registered on the LZs and the smoke screens had little effect on their fire; as a result, the Marines frequently shifted landing zones.

The smoke did block the view of the North Vietnamese machine gunners, and they were forced to fire blindly through the haze—if they dared fire at all. The choppers still took hits but nowhere near as many as before the Gaggle was initiated. The CH-46 pilots, poised precariously above the LZs during the few agonizing seconds it took to unload their cargo, often heard the sickening smack that meant that a bullet had torn into the fuselage of their thin-skinned helos.

The members of the two-man Helicopter Support Teams (HST), 3rd Shore Party Battalion, who were attached to the rifle companies were also prime targets. These men had to stand up while they guided the choppers into the LZs and, every few days, they had to attach bundles of cargo nets, which accumulated from previous missions, for the return trip to Dong Ha. This was dangerous for the aircrews as well as the HST men because, during the hook-up, the pilots had to hold their aircraft in a vulnerable position a few feet above the ground with the nose cocked up and the belly exposed to fire from the front. While they attached the bundles, the ground support personnel could hear the machine gun rounds zing a few inches over their heads and slap into the soft underside of the suspended helicopter. Not all the bullets and shell fragments passed overhead; on 881S, the defenders were operating with their fourth HST when the siege ended.

In spite of the seriousness of the situation, the Gaggle was not without its lighter episodes. In one instance, an HST man attached to I/3/26 hooked up an outgoing load and gave the pilot the "thumbs up" when he discovered that he had become entangled in the pile of nets. The CH-46 surged into the air with the startled Marine dangling helplessly from the bottom of the net by one foot. But for the quick reaction of his comrade on the ground who informed the pilot by radio that the chopper had taken on more than the prescribed load, the young cargo handler would have had a rather interesting trip to Dong Ha.

The CH-46 crews also provided a human touch during these missions. When the Sea Knights swept over the hills, it was not uncommon to see a machine gunner on board quit his weapon for a second, nonchalantly pitch a case of soda pop out the hatch, and then quickly return to blaze away at the enemy positions.

At 1st MAW Headquarters, Lieutenant Colonel Carey, who had been an infantryman in Korea before he went to flight school and who sympathized with the men on the outposts, felt that a small gesture acknowledging their continued outstanding performance was in order. Special efforts were made to obtain quantities of dry ice for packing, and one day, without notice, hundreds of Dixie cups of ice cream were delivered to the men on the hills as part of the regular resupply. This effort was dubbed Operation COOL IT. The only hitch developed on 881S where the Marines, unaware of the contents, allowed the cargo to remain in the LZ until after dark when it was safe to venture out of the trenchline. The ice cream was a little sloppy but edible and greatly appreciated.

The introduction of the Super Gaggle was a turning point in the resupply effort. Prior to its conception, the Marines on the outposts dreaded the thought of leaving their positions to retrieve cargo— even when it included mail—because of the heavy shelling. With a dozen Skyhawks pasting the surrounding hills during each mission, this threat was alleviated to a large degree and casualties tapered off. The Company I, 3/26, commander later stated, "If it weren't for the Gaggle, most of us probably wouldn't be here today."

The helicopter pilots, knowing that their jet jockey compatriots were close at hand, were also able to do their job more effectively. In the past, the transport crew chiefs occasionally had to jettison their external load prematurely when the pilot took evasive action to avoid ground fire. When this occurred, the cargo nets usually slammed into the perimeter and splattered containers all over the hilltop. With the Super Gaggle, the pilots had less enemy fire to contend with and did not bomb the hills with the cargo pallets as much; as a result more supplies arrived intact. In addition, the system greatly facilitated the picking up of wounded personnel.

The Marine helicopters continued their flights to and from Khe Sanh throughout the siege. In spite of the obstacles, the chopper pilots crammed enough sorties into those days with flyable weather to haul 465 tons of supplies to the base during February. When the weather later cleared, this amount was increased to approximately forty tons a day. While supporting Operation SCOTLAND, MAG-36 and MAG-16 flew 9,109 sorties, transported 14,562 passengers, and delivered 4,661 tons of cargo.

Colonel Lownds was more than satisfied with the airborne pipeline that kept his cupboard full, and he had quite a cupboard. The daily requirement for the 26th Marines to maintain normal operations had jumped from sixty tons in mid-January to roughly 185 tons when all five battalions were in place. While the defenders didn't live high off the hog on this amount, at no time were they desperately lacking the essentials for combat. There were periods on the hills when the Marines either stretched their rations and water or went without, but they never ran short of ammunition.

Understandably, ammunition had the highest priority—even higher than food and water. A man might not be able to eat a hand grenade, but neither could he defend himself very effectively with a can of fruit cocktail. This did not mean that the men of the 26th Marines went hungry. On average, the troops at the base received two C-Ration meals a day, and this fare was occasionally supplemented with juice, pastry, hot soup, or fresh fruit. The men on the hills subsisted almost entirely on C-Rations and the time between meals varied, depending on the weather.

Within the compound, water was rationed only when the pump was out of commission, and that was a rare occurrence. Lieutenant Colonel Heath's position on Hill 558 was flanked by two streams so 2/26 was well supplied, but the Marines on the other four outposts depended on helilifts for water; it was used sparingly for drinking and cooking. Besides the essentials, the 26th Marines also required tons of other supplies such as fortification material, fuel, tires, barbed wire, and spare parts—to name a few. PX items were on the bottom of the bottom of the priority list because, as Colonel Lownds remarked, "If you have to, you can live without those." On the other hand, mail had a priority second only to ammunition and rations. The men at Khe Sanh received over forty-three tons of mail during the worst month of the siege.

One portion of the airlift that affected morale as much as the arrival of mail was the swift departure of casualties. A man's efficiency was greatly improved by the knowledge that, if he were hit, he could expect immediate medical attention and, when necessary, a speedy evacuation. Those with minor wounds were usually treated at the various battalion aid stations and returned to duty; the more seriously injured were taken to Company C, 3rd Medical Battalion. Charley Med, as this detachment was called, was located just south of and adjacent to the aircraft loading ramp. There US Navy doctors and corpsmen treated the walking wounded, performed surgery, and prepared the litter cases for medevac. From Charley Med, it was a short but often nerve-racking trip to a waiting aircraft and a hospital at Phu Bai. During the siege, the courageous men of Charley Med, often working under heavy enemy fire, treated and evacuated 852 wounded personnel.

Thus the Marine and US Air Force transport pilots, helicopter crews, loadmasters, and ground personnel kept open the giant umbilical cord that meant life for the combat base. Without their efforts, the story of Khe Sanh would undoubtedly have been an abbreviated edition with a not-too-happy ending. On the other hand, accounts of the heroism, ingenuity, and skill demonstrated by these men would fill a book. But there were other things besides manna falling from the heavens at Khe Sanh, and the vital role of the transports was frequently eclipsed by the efforts of air crews who carried a much deadlier cargo.

6

THE REVEILLE ENGAGEMENT

JEFF DACUS

MONDAY, FEBRUARY 25, 1991

At 0530, the desert started to awaken from its blackness. It was still dark, but dawn was slowly pushing the darkness aside. Bravo Company had coiled up about 1,200 meters east of the road that led north to Kuwait City. It had been a long first day of war, but one full of rewards. No one had been hurt, and they had destroyed a great number of Iraqi vehicles and positions. Some, especially Larry Fritts, thought the unit might be getting a little complacent. The war wouldn't always be this easy. Rob Knapp and the other platoon sergeants set up their usual coil. Brian Winter inspected the position and passed the nightly password and countersign. Hawk was situated at twelve to four in the coil, twelve being north; Titan was four to eight; and Viper had eight to twelve. Some tired Marines tried to catch a few winks after a long night driving around in the extreme darkness. Others were keyed up after the excitement of battle and capture of the eight prisoners. Each platoon had two Marines on tanks on thermal watch with two additional Marines on walking duty. Of Forenpohar's crew on *Torture Chamber*, Stan Harris was on a walking post with Brad Briscoe in the turret searching and traversing. Reveille was scheduled for 0545, and the battalion was supposed to resume its advance at 0630. If all went well, they would sleep in Kuwait City the following night.

On board *Torture Chamber*, Briscoe noted blurry shapes to the east in his thermal sight. He called to Harris, and they tried to see without the sight. They also heard something unusual. It sounded like a clanking noise. They found Hart, who, unable to sleep, sat idly talking to Parkison. They asked him about the sounds. At first, Hart was unimpressed. He thought the sounds must be from Marine amtracs, but that didn't soothe Briscoe's anxiety.

Before resuming watch on his tank, Briscoe went to Hart's gunner, Lee Fowble, and asked him to scan the same area. Fowble scanned the area and picked up the images. The distinctive silhouettes of T-55 tanks were streaming across the front, with more appearing each second. "There was no doubt. There was a big column of Soviet-made vehicles out front." Fowble and Briscoe decided they were enemy. Fowble told his commander, "Sir, we gotta shoot these guys! Gotta shoot these guys!" Hart had meanwhile come to the same conclusion. The two captains clearly heard diesel engines.

Hart had been on the farm a long time and easily recognized the sounds of tractors moving. Unlike American tanks, older Soviet-built vehicles had no rubber bushing on their track pins and therefore made the loud, squealing, clanking noise commonly used in Hollywood films to identify tanks. Parkison looked at Hart and calmly said, "Those aren't our amtracs." Hart, the farmer who knew the sounds of different tracked vehicles better than most in Bravo Company, concurred. They scattered for their vehicles.

Hart yelled, "Tanks, Tanks, Tanks, Direct Front!" It had been less than two minutes since Briscoe first saw the enemy.

Marines all around the coil were instantly awake, scrambling for their positions. Turrets were swinging around as jet engines whooshed to life. In the middle of all this activity, Hart jumped aboard his tank and looked into his sight extension. He could see a column of tanks moving from north to south, elevated gun tubes pointing south. "I hopped in my tank and took a look through the thermal sight and identified well over a dozen enemy vehicles out there." The sight shocked him: "I couldn't believe how they came be-bopping across the desert with their guns pointed skyward. They weren't ready to fight us." Hart notified the rest of the company: "Predator this is Hawk 1. Enemy tanks to my direct front! Come on line!"

Fowble urgently prompted Hart: "Sir! We've got to shoot! They're traversing!" There was no time to wait for the entire company to come on line. There was no time for Parkison to give a company fire command. The famous Rommel had once stated, "In an engagement with enemy tanks . . . opening fire early has proved to be the right action and very effective." Bravo Company was presented with the perfect opportunity to put that adage to the test. Hart picked a target and ordered Fowble to fire. "When my gunner fired I saw the round go out and smack a T-72 and blow the turret off." The Marines could clearly make out large numbers of low-silhouette T-72s mixed with a few older, bigger, clumsier-looking T-54/55s.

Even as Hart's round flew down range, Gibbert and his gunner Killian in Titan Two noted the enemy's presence: "There were tanks everywhere, at least thirty." They quickly had their tank in action and fired their gun. Briscoe, on Forenpohar's tank, also fired within a few seconds.

Dacus, in the *Rockin' Reaper*, was asleep on the turret floor, cramped in among metal parts and ammo cans. Edler, his loader, appeared at the hatch and yelled that enemy tanks were approaching. While Edler wiped off condensation on the sights and the driver's periscopes, Brackett took his place in the gunner's seat. Freier, the driver, jumped into his "hole" and started the engine. The *Reaper* quickly joined in as the Hawk and Titan tanks began blasting away in a drumbeat of 120mm music. Hearing Hart on the radio, Dacus frantically motioned Carter, his wingman on the right, to come on line and face east.

Loaders rammed in another shell as quickly as a round was fired. The loud clang of base plates hitting the turret floors was drowned out by the louder crash of main guns. More tanks began firing as their crews were roused from their attempts at sleep. Barker in the XO's tank recalled the abrupt reveille: "We woke up. Then just a few minutes after I got up I noticed I heard the sound of tracks through the fog. Then suddenly someone was racing around screaming. We all jumped in our hogs and fired up the thermals. What we found was 1 or 2 Co. of tanks passing in front of us. We blew the shit out of them. They didn't even know what hit them." It took only a few seconds for the *War Wagon*'s 120mm gun to join in the slugfest.

Perfectly silhouetted against the early rising sun, more Iraqi tanks began to materialize from the dust, early morning mist, and darkness of the oil clouds; more depleted uranium penetrators struck them. Traveling in three columns, the first tank in the righthand column, closest to Bravo Company, exploded into a massive red ball of flame, its turret spinning off. Then the lead tank in the center column and the lead tank in the far column likewise exploded. An Iraqi survivor, the commander of the second tank in the center column, later said, "I saw the tank to my right blow up, then the ones in front and to the left blew up and I knew I was next. I jumped off my tank just as it blew up." His crew was incinerated.

The Marine coil unwound itself as the enemy appeared and the first shots were fired. Hart got off a couple of quick shots that resulted in devastating kills. Hart noted with professional pride, "Every round was hitting." Gibbert's first shot also hit home. Forenpohar's first round went flying off into the sky. He fired again, the flaming trajectory arching into the dark sky. "We screwed up," he said. A quick check proved he had HEAT indexed in the computer but was firing SABOT. That was rectified and his tank, *Torture Chamber*, quickly destroyed a T-72. After that, Forenpohar's crew settled down to the grim business of killing. "Most of the tension was pretty much gone by then. Everybody's pretty frantic, but tired too. We're all yelling 'Tanks out there!' and it brings the pucker factor up some. But you do what you've trained to do. We made sure we had a good laze and good sight picture and just kept rapping out those rounds until we couldn't find anything moving out there."

Seconds later, Viper, facing roughly north and west, pulled itself around on line facing east toward the Iraqi columns and began to pump rounds into the enemy. A T-72 turret flew twenty or thirty feet into the air and crashed back to the ground. An older T-55 in the middle of the Iraqi battalion took a hit and began smoking, probably destroyed. The smoke soon ended, and the tank appeared to be undamaged, so another Marine tank fired and hit it. More smoke but still no catastrophic hit. While T-72s exploded easily, this T-55 took at least five hits. One penetrated the T-55s turret on one side, went completely through, and exited out the other side. The crew was probably killed with the first hit.

The long-rod penetrators of the Abrams SABOT rounds sliced through Iraqi armor with ease. The self-sharpening uranium darts pierced the armor and scattered pieces of white-hot spall (flecks of often fiery metal dislodged by the hit) into the interior of the tanks. Anything flammable burned immediately; ammunition cooked off, fuel and lubricants sizzled. Humans disappeared in a fiery death with nothing left to qualify as remains. Hart noted, "Everything was exploding. Those guys couldn't tell where we were. They had no idea what direction to go; they just knew their vehicles were exploding beneath them."

After less than a minute, amid the loud crashes of tank guns and explosions of Iraqi tanks, the tanks of Bravo Company were all finally on line. It was a frustrating time for many of them. In Second Platoon's *Prodigal Son*, McDonald "began acquiring targets at the far left of the enemy formation, but as soon as I began to engage, suddenly the target would blow up and I had to find something else. That happened over and over . . . I killed four T-72s." He noted the effects of the quick and obvious kills. Visibility had improved, and the crews of the various tanks could see the results of their actions. "Everybody on the tank was ecstatic. We were giving each other high fives. 'You owe me a beer.' 'You owe me another one.'"

Also in Hawk, Brad Hallock on the *Sand Shark* described just coming off watch: "Just as I was laying my sleeping bag out on the back deck of the tank, I heard someone start yelling, 'Tanks, tanks, enemy tanks!' I immediately jumped up and got into the gunner's position." Ray Ransier, the driver, started the tank up, and Hallock hit turret power. "I looked through the sights, I saw I had a laser range finder failure." He informed his loader, Dave Masters, that he "would just engage using 'battle-sight' distance and 'Kentucky windage' to adjust from there." In perfect position, he found the other tanks were just seconds ahead of him. "I also don't recall us needing to pull on line or move at all, because the enemy tanks were right out in front of us. I put my sights on a tank, prepared to fire, and it was hit with a sabot from another tank. I swung and sighted in on another tank; it too was immediately hit by a sabot."

After trying turret power again, Hallock looked for targets. "I kept looking through my sights and watching tank after tank explode. I saw a T55 hit with a HEAT round. I remember watching the tank basically detonate. The turret blew up and off, sparks and flame shot out of every opening, three roadwheels blew off, and for the next hour, the ammo inside the turret continued to cook off."

In Viper, Staff Sergeant Knapp also experienced a system failure. Knapp, the most experienced tanker in the company, calmly shut off all power. When he switched turret power back on, his system was restored. Back in action, his gun nailed two more Iraqi tanks.

Fritts's tank quickly jumped into the action, and "Stuka" Stahnke scored a kill. Unfortunately, the guards to protect personnel from gun recoil were not in place. The heavy, solid breech of the M256 120mm gun struck Fritts's knee a glancing blow as it recoiled. Even the slight blow was painful. His knee was cracked. He continued firing and the tank scored several more kills.

Live targets gradually disappeared after the first ninety seconds or so. Dacus's gunner, Brackett, spotted an enemy tank to the rear of the burning columns. Announcing the target over the radio, Dacus ordered him to fire. The depleted uranium dart sliced through the tank with a blaze of sparks, but an observer called a miss. Nonplussed, Brackett sighted in again and fired. This time there was a gigantic explosion. Brackett quietly whispered, "Game over," and went back to scanning. Later observation of the battlefield would reveal that Brackett had destroyed two tanks even though his tank commander thought he had merely reengaged the same one twice.

The enemy columns had been destroyed in those first ninety sec- onds. Gunners searched and traversed, knocking out any stragglers that were spotted. Hallock continued to fight: "I identified a tank moving out at about 2,000 meters. I fired two sabot; the second round was a hit. To my understanding, that was the last round fired in that engagement."

Despite Hallock's recollection, Gibbert's *When's Chow* fired some of the last shots of the battle. Two dug-in T-55s had been on the field all day but were not engaged because they appeared to be abandoned. Now *When's Chow* took on these two. Gibbert gave the fire commands to "Desert" Dave Killian, his gunner. Killian's shots were excellent, hit- ting the old tanks dead center just a few inches above their protective berm. Unlike the newer T-72s, the T-55s' turrets did not fly off into the air. Both merely burned out.

After a few minutes a new threat to the enemy columns appeared. The Marines saw vehicles approaching from the right, TOW "critters"

(Humvees), moving onto the battlefield. Their arrival signaled the end of the battle. The CAAT (Combined Anti-Armor Team) TOW missile Humvees arrived on the scene and took up the fight. One of the missiles contributed to the most spectacular explosion of the morning. The TOW launcher got the missile off, but just as it approached the target in its slow flight, a faster tank round from Hart's *Crusader* streaked out and struck the Iraqi tank. It was a near-simultaneous explosion. There was a sizzling white eruption, and the Iraqi vehicle completely disappeared. Jackson saw another missile, its heat streak blanking out his thermal sight. Looking through his auxiliary sight, he saw it hit an already damaged enemy tank. The resulting explosion left little of the Iraqi vehicle. He could only think, "This is crazy!"

As the last shots were fired, the Marines for the first time noticed the pitiful figures of Iraqi soldiers on the battlefield. Some appeared to be tank crewmen, others hapless infantrymen, caught up in the vicious tank battle. One Iraqi lay on the desert sand, obviously in bad shape. A comrade knelt beside him. The two appeared to talk, then the uninjured man stood and began to walk to the Marine line. The prone figure raised his hand plaintively and the man returned to his side. A discussion ensued, with the unwounded man several times heading toward the Marines but indecisively turning back again and again. This went on for several minutes. The dark uniforms of the Iraqis stood out plainly on the light tan sand in the gunner's sights. Finally, the soldier on the ground moved no more. Reluctantly, the remaining Iraqi plodded off toward Bravo Company, a pathetic, dejected dark figure silhouetted against the dawn.

The solitary, forlorn character approached Hawk. About twenty yards from the Marines, the Iraqi inquired as to who they were. The reply was "US Marines!" The Iraqi, an officer, then inquired, "If I surrender, will you kill my wounded?" It seemed that the Iraqis had been told that Marines had to kill a member of their own family to enter the elite Corps. Assured that no harm would come to the prisoners, the officer went back to the scene of destruction and began herding others to the Marine position. Hart noted, "It was so easy to kill them that there was no satisfaction in mowing them down with our machine guns so we didn't kill any survivors."

As the dust and smoke receded from the battlefield, Hallock surveyed the scene. "I could see the battlefield better now, and as I scanned, it seemed like there were over 30 destroyed vehicles; T-54/55s, T-62s, and T-72s. Also several BMPs. One of the Iraqis that walked in about 2,000 meters was missing his right arm. He fell down several times while walking in. He used a chunk of wire to fashion a makeshift tourniquet around his shoulder. A group of four Iraqis were sent back into the battlefield to let the others know it was safe to surrender. One group carried in a badly wounded Iraqi who appeared to be missing most of both legs." The shattered groups of Iraqis posed no threat to the Marines, and none carried weapons. Several Marines dismounted to meet the new prisoners. "We treated the wounded. I was inside my tank for most of this, and only got out for a short time to assist watching/guarding wounded while they were being treated."

The Iraqis approaching the tanks with their hands raised, were frisked, and ordered to sit on the ground. The injured received little treatment as the corpsmen were with the log train. The effect of the bloody figures on the Marines was sobering. "Right after the engagement, the enemy soldiers started walking off the battlefield," McDonald related later. "We were pumped up on adrenaline from the tank engagement and now we've got enemy dismounts walking toward us. We trained machine guns on them, but it quickly became obvious that they'd taken a hell of a beating. Some were missing arms, legs—a lot of them were in bad shape. They surrendered, and we had to treat their wounded—no other units were in the area who could do so." Mild-mannered, perceptive Skip Strandberg of Winter's *War Wagon* crew saw it in a more pathetic light: "They would walk in and all of the sudden die." Barker was also impressed with the wretched nature of the Iraqi survivors, observing that "there was a mass surrender. There were at the least 100 troops. It was unreal. There were some that were just all fucked up. Missing arms, legs, hands, fingers, feet, etc. Pretty nasty. But then again they would have done the same thing to me if they had the chance."

Scanning the battlefield, Parkison noticed an Iraqi officer wandering into Bravo Company's line. The bedraggled soldier clutched a green field jacket to his chest. When questioned, the Iraqi explained that it belonged to a young man he had known since childhood who had been killed in Bravo's violent barrage. He intended to return it to the man's family.

Bravo Company coiled up after the Reveille Engagement. Prisoners collected near the Humvee at right center.

AFTERMATH OF MASSACRE

As if by magic, Bravo Company's log train appeared behind the line of tanks. They acted before battalion had been informed. Monitoring the company net, Martin realized the tanks needed support immediately. Led by the bulk of Dittmar's M88, the soft-skin vehicles had dashed across the desert. Briscoe praised them for their quick action: "I think the topper would be when our log train went UA to refuel and resupply us before our final assault on Kuwait City. I couldn't believe it when I saw them busting across the desert to our location. That was the ultimate act of caring that I observed in this ordeal." *Boss Hog* moved up on line and managed to fire one .50-caliber round. The log train

Marines were greeted with the sight of dozens of smoke columns curling up in the distance. Their tanker cousins were milling about, checking over their vehicles and talking in small groups. After the terribly loud sounds of destruction only a few minutes before, it seemed oddly quiet. Many of the Marines gawked toward the east, where fires burned and ammunition cooked off. Some tankers had broken open rations and were eating their breakfast. Several gun tubes were slowly traversing back and forth looking for more victims. Dark shapes were walking in toward the Marine position, and others were collected in a group at the center of the Marine position.

Martin immediately organized the resupply of the tanks and took charge of the prisoners. A service station resupply was set up, and a tank from each platoon backed off the line to visit the ammo truck and refuel. Martin, a former San Diego policeman, and Dittmar, a Seattle policeman, moved among the incoming prisoners. They organized a thorough system of searching the prisoners and arranging for medical care. Martin reflected, "Their casualties were extremely severe. People were missing arms and there were parts of people strewn around in the sand." Corpsmen rushed out to tend to the twelve wounded enemy survivors. Most were infantrymen who had unluckily been on the battlefield. There were only a few survivors from the destroyed Iraqi tanks. Not one of the enemy tanks was serviceable. The tanks, whether T-55 or T-72, were shattered and burned out. Tank combat is vicious, and most of the crews of the destroyed tanks simply vanished, their bodies burned into microscopic oblivion.

Total Marine casualties included a Marine with a hurt knee and a couple of others with fingers crushed by the heavy ammunition doors when moving ammo. Gunny Pineda on *Sand Shark* thought he might have seen a few rounds fired at the Marines. No one else recalled even one round being fired by the Iraqis. Pineda was impressed with the

Hollywood-type quality of the action, thinking about the 1965 film *Battle of the Bulge*. But the sight and smell of burning tanks, the torn and mangled prisoners, and the tired faces of the Marines showed a grim reality that no film could duplicate.

Unloading from their truck, the Recon Liaison Marines boldly but rashly moved out with M-16s bouncing along at high port to secure the battlefield. Martin prudently recalled them. The danger from exploding tank ammunition was too great for them to wander out onto the sand. A total of seventy-six prisoners were counted. One of them erroneously told the Marines that their commander was a member of the vaunted Republican Guards. The story was that the officer was still out on the battlefield hiding in a bunker. The Iraqi prisoners, both those wounded and sound, were loaded aboard trucks and began the long journey to the rear echelon.

Despite later searches, the colonel was never found, but the report of Republican Guards led the Marines to believe they had encountered a Republican Guards outfit. The presence of T-72s, the Iraqi's best tank, reinforced this impression. The Marines were told that they had encountered the 3rd Mechanized Division, and they believed it was the Republican Guards's 3rd Mechanized Division, known as the "Tawalkana" Division. Unknown to the Marines, the Tawalkana was being destroyed by the US Army far to the west in the famous action at "73 Easting." The Marines would learn the identity of their enemy much later. Nevertheless, they had crushed the enemy to their front, purportedly the best Saddam had, and morale subsequently skyrocketed. Despite the lack of sleep over the last couple of days, they were ready to push on to Kuwait City.

The Marines were not impressed with the T-72, a tank thought to be one of the best in the world. Hart said, "The turret flies off. Everything is incinerated to ash. There's nothing identifiable in them and it melts down to nothing. The armor is very thin and it goes up like a candle." Briscoe, an engineer in civilian life, disparaged the Iraqi vehicles: "The only difference between enemy tanks and cardboard targets is the T-72s blow up when they are hit." Forenpohar added, "We blew the turret off every T-72 we hit." He concluded, "The T-72 is a piece of trash." The Marines had also profited because the direction that the Iraqis were traveling left their T-72s vulnerable. "Fuel is stored along the right fender of the T-72 in five or six fuel cells. And they aren't armored, either," noted Winter. Traveling from north to south exposed the right side of the T-72 to Bravo Company. As for their own armored mounts, the M1A1 Abrams? Hart said, "It's the baddest ride on the open desert." Sebens, now riding in a truck after his tank was immobilized due to a mine the day before, surveyed the battlefield. After learning that the Iraqis never knew what hit them, he looked at the M1A1s with their turbine engines and called them "the tool we knew as 'Silent Death.'" Forenpohar said, "You can't touch the bad ride." After the destruction of the Iraqi battalion, the tired but enthusiastic Marines expected a quick push on to Kuwait City.

ADVANCE OR SIT TIGHT?

Knapp wanted a cigar. The urge to slowly chew the end of a good cigar, its distinctive tobacco flavor flowing into his taste buds, however, would be denied. He would have to wait until it was all over, not just this engagement, but the whole war. He was eager to move on and finish it. While leaders in Washington might want to end the war for political reasons or attainment of military objectives, for one Marine, the end of the war just meant a good cigar.

The Marines quickly refueled and rearmed. They were ready to move, to strike, to chew up the Iraqis in front of them. But they didn't move. Instead they milled about, doing operations checks on their vehicles and checking out the prisoners in the center of their tanks. Some wandered to other platoons to swap stories and describe the scenes they had witnessed earlier that morning. Dittmar's TVR personnel went from tank to tank checking to see if any of the machines had a mechanical issue. Comm guys checked out the operation of the company's radios. Fritts limped to officers' call, and the leaders pondered their next move. The company sat for six hours, moving only briefly to where they had been the previous evening near the Candy Canes. There was no blitzkrieg, no fast-moving maneuver warfare.

As the Marines sat and wondered what was going on, Major General William Keys, the division commander, was meeting with his regimental commanders. In a move that would have been approved by British general Montgomery but would have embarrassed German General Rommel, Keys tidied things up. He tried to bring his units on line with First Marine Division on his right and the Arab Coalition on his left. Unfortunately, the Arabs were dragging their feet. To some, the hesitation appeared to be a good move. The procrastination allowed the Iraqis time to pull out of Kuwait, which meant fewer casualties for the Marines. But many of the Marines believed that it would have been better to push on, to take advantage of an opportunity. The Iraqis' counterattack had been crushed and resistance was crumbling. Why give them a chance to reorganize and dig in or counterattack again?

Hart believed the Marines could have been in Kuwait City that evening. Many others shared his view. Not everyone agreed with that appraisal, not least because of a certain attitude toward the Reserve tankers. When first attached to 1/8, Lieutenant Colonel Gombar, the battalion commander, and Parkison had engaged in heated arguments about how the reservists were a "loose cannon" and needed to stick close to the rest of the battalion. Gombar later recalled, "Some of our conversations were not too pleasant. He came to realize that there was safety in numbers, that what I was telling him was not an attempt to stifle his initiative but that it was real guns shooting real bullets and not an exercise at Twentynine Palms, California." After the Reveille Engagement, Parkison knew about real bullets.

Now Parkison was eager to move on. But Gombar was worried about his right flank, as the First Marine Division was lagging a little behind. He complained about Bravo Company, noting that "as a tank outfit, they were working on their own. All their drills were done as a company. Rarely did they come together as a battalion. One problem with 4th Bravo Tanks was getting them to understand they were part of a battalion. I didn't want them racing out 10 or 15 kilometers from the rest of the battalion, getting ahead of fire support and infantry, and becoming extremely vulnerable." Perhaps he hadn't considered using the tanks to lead the battalion and *push* the other companies to closely follow them. As it was, the battalion just sat for hours. At this time the Iraqis had been defeated in every engagement, and they had no organized troops for a viable counterattack. Parkison passed off the lack of initiative by Gombar as the opinion of an infantry officer who had not worked much with tanks. Later Gombar would admit that mechanization, the use of tanks and amtracs together, "was not a normal Marine Corps mission." Even Lieutenant Colonel Cardi of 2nd Tanks, sitting in reserve with his battalion, thought that it was a missed opportunity:

On the second day when it was clear or pretty clear that we had an opportunity to seal the exits from Kuwait of Iraqi forces, that would have been the time to execute a pursuit operation, seize a piece of terrain in and around the al-Jahrah area, and seal off routes of withdrawal. That would have been a very classic pursuit. I think then that

that smacks of some of the principles of maneuverable warfare, and that is, when you find a weakness go for it. Don't get fixed on one single thing. Kind of be fluid, and as the situation develops, take advantage of that particular situation. It perhaps appears as if we got a plan and were sticking to it. I asked that question, because I felt that given those set of circumstances, that would have been a very viable mission for 2d Tanks, for the commanding general to say exploit and seize the crossroads at al-Jahrah and prevent the enemy from withdrawing north along the particular highway.

This "pursuit" would have allowed Cardi, sitting in reserve, a chance to get into the action.

The controversy permeated the leadership of Second Marine Division. Crusty Major General Keys, an Annapolis graduate, was not only worried about his right flank being open due to the First Division being held up but also his left flank, where Arab Coalition forces were lagging far behind as well. "I knew what could happen. I saw a lot of my kids killed and blown apart in Vietnam, so I expected a lot more casualties," Keys said. Colonel Don Richard, one of his aides, also cautioned against an immediate advance: "We wanted to continue the attack but we knew we couldn't just go helter skelter—be foolish about it. There's a fine line between being audacious and being a fool." Why he thought a pursuit was "foolish" is unsaid, but the term could also apply to those who fail to take advantage of an opportunity. Despite the official Marine Corps history disingenuously stating that "the exploitation of tactical situations and rapid execution of orders had become the standing operating procedure for the division," caution ruled the advance. In any event, because of this reluctance to advance, many Iraqis would escape to launch another counterattack against the 2nd Marine Division.

CENTCOM, however, wasn't cautious about advancing. During the previous morning General Schwartzkopf evaluated the situation. He decided the Marines were doing so well that he launched his left hook with the heavy Army units twelve hours early. He pushed his corps and division commanders. He accurately read the battlefield; the Iraqi defenses were a house of cards. He pushed his strong units to seek out and find the Republican Guards and destroy them. Bravo Company sat and waited for the word to move out. It would be long hours before they would move. Fortunately, the Iraqi artillery did not take advantage of the opportunity, another indication of the chaos in the enemy ranks. It was this chaos that the Marines failed to take advantage of.

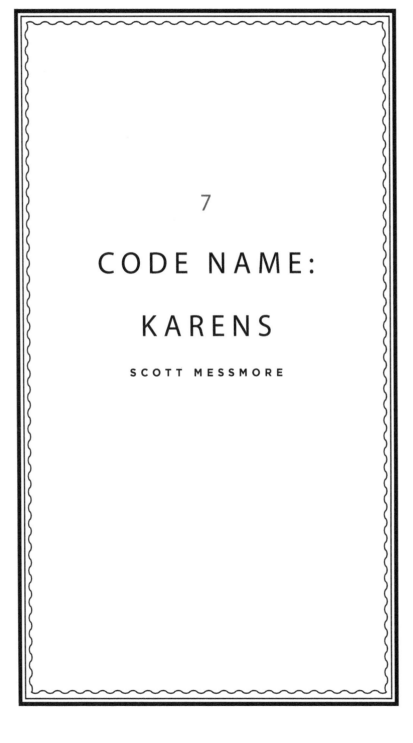

7

CODE NAME:

KARENS

SCOTT MESSMORE

AUGUST 13, 1998

Everything was a go. No one had ever expected to pick up a mission like this. For years every Marine and Navy corpsman in 4th ANGLICO had focused on becoming proficient in fire missions for artillery, naval gunfire, and calling in jet fighters or helicopter gunships to destroy enemy troops and weapons, most of which were designed and built in the former Soviet Union.

Then Hurricane Karen wasted the Big Easy and most of the shoreline towns of the Gulf states. Washington, DC, hadn't had the brains to even consider using a full ANGLICO company after the disaster of Hurricane Andrew cutting through South Florida like a chainsaw in 1992. Taylor had always been disgusted about sitting around listening to news reports of looting, burning, and zero communications after Andrew.

"We could have blanketed the entire area with a radio network and kept Tallahassee and Washington informed with status reports from all the major areas of Dade County," Taylor thought to himself.

Is there rioting in downtown Miami? An FCT team posted on top of the old fifty-story Centrust Building could observe the city for miles using high-powered, German-made Steiner binoculars to spot any unrest or smoking buildings. Handheld lasers could tell the exact range to the danger area. It would've been a snap: you could see rioters or a burning building through your binoculars and shoot a laser to a building next to it. With GPS and maps of the city, all you had to do was take a compass heading to the "target," draw a line from your position on your map showing the distance from the laser shot, and "ta daa": there's your problem area. The city map would show it right at your fingertips: the Dade County Court House on Flagler Avenue. Of course! Criminals are trying to get their thug buddies out of the joint. Or burn their records, or whatever! Get someone over there!

Because we could have placed a heavy FCT team with up to twelve Marines to rotate shifts, our communications ability would've been enormous.

Look to the north and the American Airlines Arena has a large and growing crowd, but there's no rioting. Look to the east; there's no looting at Bayside and no smoke is rising from fires at South Beach in the distance. Look to the south and the skyscraper banks that line Brickell Avenue all seem to be okay. Probably because they hired former military to guard the big banks, but who cares? They're getting it done, aren't they? Looking west, it's a bit too far to see details from the Orange Bowl, but there's no rising smoke in that area. So far, so good. It's hotter than hell, but no hotter than any other South Florida summer.

What this obviously fictitious section is meant to illustrate is the capabilities of Marine ANGLICO and how simple it would be to shift gears to a noncombat scenario. We trained constantly on our communications gear: in the field, at night, in the rain, in the searing heat of South Florida, and freezing our butts off in Norway; Fort Drum near Syracuse, New York; or the Sierra Nevada of Mountain Warfare School in California.

The Hurricane Andrew incident is real and pisses me off to this day after nearly twenty-five years. I was living, writing, and working in Gainesville, Florida, three hundred miles from the Reserve Center in West Palm Beach, and from time to time my car broke down. Of course, when you're in the Reserves, when your car breaks, it's right before drill weekend. I think it's in the Constitution between Freedom of Speech and the Right to Bear Arms, because it happens every time. I called in with enough prior warning to reschedule my drill time. The

Marine Corps has a great policy in recognition of how far its Reserve Marines travel to drill each month and how dedicated they are. If you are excused by the proper person (in my case, my sergeant major), then you were fine and got proper credit and pay as long as you came in to serve within the thirty days before next drill. While I was on the phone, I asked if we were going south to help out in Miami. We weren't. I couldn't believe how dumb this decision, or lack thereof, was.

Here we were, forty miles from, at the time, the worst natural disaster in US history with two hundred US Marines who are constantly trained to send message traffic and keep others informed of the present situation. An ANGLICO company has dozens if not hundreds of radios that cover the UHF, FM, HF, and VHF spectrums of radio frequencies, and the newer models all have an internal SATCOM function. The mission, and Marines, can switch tasks in an instant. Sitting in Iraq with three pickup trucks full of terrorist idiots speeding down the road toward a United Nations checkpoint? Get on your HF radio and call in a fire mission to wipe them out in the blink of an eye. Are you a lone lance corporal sitting on a fifty-story resort hotel rooftop in downtown New Orleans in 2005 and spot a large group of ugly sorts walking south on St. Charles Avenue toward the Garden District? Pick up the handset for the FM radio to alert the local authorities and order the PFC next to you to use the HF radio to alert the SALT team, which will instantly relay the message to the Division Cell at Camp Shelby around one hundred miles away. Obviously, the Division Cell is sitting in a very large room or tent with at least one representative from FEMA, Homeland Security, the FBI, DEA, Customs, each branch of the US military, the Pentagon, White House, and maybe even the governor of Louisiana. Remember the story I told about the OPFOR C-130 full of paratroopers flying directly over my FCT team's position at JRTC in 1995? As soon as I sent that report over the HF net, everyone in my chain of command knew a paratroop attack was going down in real time. If the Division Cell really has their crap together, they wouldn't need a report from the SALT team, as they would be listening to each FCT team's transmission twenty-four hours a day. There is no excuse, then or now, for the way the government handled Hurricane Andrew, and the complete lack of information coming out of New Orleans after Hurricane Katrina, and the media also has a large share of the blame.

In short, this is what I want: ANGLICO FCT teams with up to twelve Marines for three eight-hour shifts stationed on selected rooftops of very tall civilian buildings with clear views of any disaster area, especially the downtown business district, airports, and any officially designated refugee/evacuee centers. Second, battalion-level SALT teams should be placed to monitor all of its assigned FCT teams and relay information to higher headquarters to include the commanding general, governor's office, and also the civilian leadership in Washington, DC, be it the Pentagon, White House, or both. Not only is this entirely feasible, it was possible in the 1970s. Retired first sergeant and wild man Parks Nicolls put me in my place when I told him my best radio shot was with a PRC 104 high frequency radio. On paper a 104 has a three-hundred-mile range, and that's when it's tested under optimum conditions. I performed one solitary radio check from Fort Benning, Georgia, 750 miles back to West Palm Beach, Florida. Nicolls countered with a story from the 1980s when he built a long-range antenna to make a radio check with MacDill Air Force Base in Tampa, Florida, from Sardinia. You know, the little island off the coast of Italy? Radio waves do funny things, bouncing off the ionosphere and thermal gradients, but a six-thousand-mile radio shot is unreal, and SATCOM had not even reached the field yet back then.

Ideally, the federal government would already have a signed agreement with the owners of the tall or critical buildings our FCT teams would occupy. It isn't too hard to determine which sections of the country are disaster prone and what type of calamity you'll be facing when you get there. Lake effect snow doesn't hit Florida; that's Chicago, Cleveland, and Buffalo. Hurricanes don't bother Tornado Alley too often, and raging fires or mudslides mostly go after California, not New England and its nor'easters.

My thinking for a mission to New Orleans would be as follows. I would be leading eleven other scout/forward observers and radio operators into a situation with minimal threat of violence as we would be very elevated, and if I can avoid it, I'd rather not be spotted. Panic-stricken refugees would never cease trying to get our attention, and we couldn't communicate in any way with them, which would only serve to anger them about any rescue efforts. In short, angry, hungry, thirsty refugees are primed to start a riot.

If we're lucky and the Feds found a building with a heliport, the pilot could place my team right on target. The first four Marines charge down the ramp of the helicopter, move off the helipad, drop their backpacks, and perform an armed sweep of the rooftop. Who knows who might be up there? Looters can be ingenious in how they gain access to homes and buildings. If we find any, kick them downstairs, and let the police scoop them up after they've had a fun time walking down fifty flights of stairs.

The second four Marines, including myself, exit the helicopter, run off the pad, and immediately turn on our radio equipment to make contact with higher-ups and send our first status report. The last four Marines will remove the crapload of gear we brought to live in our island in the sun for the next week.

The presently outdated high-frequency radio that I operated for twelve years, the PRC 104, was a true man-packed system, as all of our radios were. That means that they could operate on batteries only and already had an amplifier to boost the radio signal. When you turned a 104 on, it spent sixty seconds tuning to the radio frequency you had punched in. During this one-minute tuning process, it made a steady pinging sound in the handset that could be heard by anyone who was monitoring that frequency. This would be a good sound to the Division Cell one hundred miles away in Camp Shelby. They know what time my team is going to insert, as they created the plan and all of the timelines. If I'm set to land at dawn, which the Louisiana Department of Wildlife and Fisheries lists at 5:37 a.m. on your typical September 1 morning, then within five minutes the Division Cell is expecting to hear all three of my 104 sets start pinging away. To them that means "he's there, he's down, the security team has already run their sweep, he's setting up comm, and the last group is unloading the helicopter." And the Marines I served with, such as Gunny Walsh, would be staring at their watches fully expecting me to start speaking at sixty-one seconds. The pinging stops and I start.

"Lightning one-one, Lightning one-one, this is Lightning one-three, radio check, over," I would call.

"One-three, this is one-one. I read you Lima Charlie. What is your status, over?"

Lima Charlie is Marine radio slang for "loud and clear." Most people think that's just military jargon, but it isn't. It's two separate issues. If you and your buddy are back at base testing radios, usually you'll stand a couple of hundred feet away and send silly little messages back and forth. If a radio is malfunctioning, say, you can only hear every third word, but the signal is very loud because your friend is just across the way, then he's "loud but broken." If he's too far away or his battery is dying (usually the case) but you can understand him, then he's "weak but readable." Radio keywords are essential because they save valuable time on a radio network. A large net could have dozens of people trying to speak at the same time, and in combat, getting shot at just makes things worse. Think of the wasted time if I transmitted that I'm fine, Johnson's fine, Rodriguez is fine, etc., on down the line and then listed all of our equipment. Unless I drop all of our food off the side of the building, it's a given that the MREs are doing just fine snuggled in their cardboard boxes. Meanwhile, other teams are trying to check in at the same time.

Just like a quarterback shouting out play calls at the line of scrimmage, one word can mean a lot. During my time at 4th ANGLICO, for some reason we had a preference for American automakers, while other units preferred colors. If I transmit just one word to describe a situation, I won't be tying up the radio net with too much traffic. It takes a ton of practice, just like the NFL, but it can be just that simple. After the helicopter lifts off, I send my second message:

"Lightning one-one, this is one-three, Buick moving on to Ford, how copy."

"One-three, I copy Buick and Ford. Out."

Buick: We're here with all the gear and all okay. Ford: We're establishing security, setting up all the radio nets, conducting proper radio checks with our SALT and other teams, and then setting up the tarps and ponchos for protection from the sun. Two words and everyone's on the same sheet of music. It's a thing of beauty.

And what a pile of gear we would bring if it was up to me. Each Marine would have full combat equipment with an M-16 rifle with six magazines of live ammunition. I would also bring at least one M-16 with an M203 grenade launcher slung underneath the barrel, not to fire high-explosive rounds but to fire tear gas grenades at any rioters threatening us plus star shell rounds for nighttime illumination. Smoke rounds would be helpful to direct helicopters to rescue landing zones in the immediate area of our building.

For twelve Marines spending seven days on any post requires quite a bit of food and water. At three meals per day, that's 252 meals in twenty-one cases weighing twelve pounds per case. At least seventeen five-gallon jerry cans full of water would be needed for a minimum of one gallon of water per Marine for each day, and most likely would require resupply around day five. Anyone who's ever been through a hurricane can well attest that the days just after the storm have gorgeous blue skies, but it's hotter than Hades outside. With water and MREs alone weighing nearly one thousand pounds and very bulky, I would split them between two wooden pallets; one pallet could easily handle the weight, but they would probably be stacked too high for safety on only one pallet. Twenty-one cardboard boxes of our MREs with our long-range antennas placed on top would work fine after the aircrew attached the nets to the pallet.

After all, the antennas are two of the main reasons we would be frying like eggs on top of a New Orleans hotel. Antennas that don't move too often have a very nasty habit of being seriously blown the hell up after the enemy pinpoints your location. But we're not moving for seven days, and there's no enemy, so it's going to be great to use two separate thirty-foot antennas fifty stories in the air. However, another heavy item we'll need are sandbags, just like in the World War II movies. Out in the field, troops can set up their tents, ponchos, or even antennas with metal stakes just like your family uses when you go camping. On top of a resort, that won't be happening. I don't think your typical billionaire is going to be too happy when he turns on the evening news to monitor the rescue effort he's proud to be a part of only to see a dozen US Marines swinging sledgehammers as they drive metal stakes into the roof of his beloved Crescent City pleasure palace.

With two portable antennas sporting four guy wires each, and some type of anchoring device needed to secure each Marine's poncho to cover their sleep area, I'd call that around fifty sandbags weighing twenty-five pounds apiece. Also, if we had them, I would insist on old-school foldout cots for my Marines to sleep on. I slept in and on some strange surfaces during my time with the Marine Corps, including on the ground inside the Arctic Circle and on the concrete airport runway in Fort Begging, Georgia. But a full week sleeping on concrete won't cut it. Throw in one embarkation box with around one hundred batteries and I think I'm looking at three wooden pallets fully loaded plus each Marine's combat gear and mountain rucksack weighing in at sixty-five pounds. It's a lot, but once we insert, we ain't leaving.

Now it might seem odd that American troops are strictly forbidden from interacting with hurt or suffering citizens in situations like these, but keep in mind why ANGLICO would be there: observation, reporting, and relaying critical information. Living in South Florida for so long, I've been through countless hurricanes. Trust me, people freak the hell out. The worst cases are people who have never been through the process. They don't prepare, they act like a real tough guy, but after the storm they have a look of severe shock, muttering, "I had no idea it would be that bad, I was actually scared." No kidding moron; I tried to warn you. I did warn you. If these folks spot US troops, they're naturally going to run straight for them, even if it's only to welcome them and thank them for help. However, if I'm calming you down, playing with your seriously cute little kids, and getting hugs from the entire neighborhood, then I can't be sending radio traffic on my four-hundred-watt radio truck, now can I? Exactly.

Sergeant John Taylor was a very senior sergeant with nearly ten years of service from California to Norway, the swamps and crawdads of "Loosiana" to the subzero white snow of upstate New York, closer to Canada than Syracuse. Taylor was used to his ANGLICO company breaking itself apart and putting it back together to fit whatever the hell mission the 4th Marine Division headquarters decided to hand off to us. Ironically, 4th MarDiv HQ was in New Orleans, which had just been pounded, punched, and flooded by Hurricane Karen. No one was even positive if the HQ was in operation, so we got our orders and just planned on our own as we have always done.

Every team was going in heavy. More ammo, more radios, more Marines, more slash wire, full-size 292 and 2259 antennas, boxes and boxes of MREs that would most likely be shoved out of helicopters by crew chiefs during resupply, every laser we had in the armory, and, most important, entire pallets groaning under the weight of five-gallon jerry cans full of water. With no need to be on the move, the rooftop OPs would be like World War I artillery spotters with heavy, long-range binoculars mounted on tripods. Made in Germany by Steiner, they could see forever, and Taylor marveled at their quality and the fact that someone in Washington actually let HQMC buy such a pricey piece of gear. Everyone knew we might be stuck on top of a skyscraper with no sun protection for a week.

Oh well, it can't be any hotter than South Florida after our hurricanes, Taylor thought. The assembly hall at 4th ANGLICO was full but very quiet. Each Marine was running scenarios through their fuzzy little heads. Would we take fire? Would I actually have to shoot an American citizen? The rednecks always talk about shooting looters, but it's different when it actually happens. Would the higher-ups forget we're on top of some damn building like the time in Norway when they kept leaving us off flight manifests going back to the States?

Due to the severity of the situation, only the most senior and experienced Marines were assigned to the mission. Officers and staff NCOs had been pushed "upstairs" to the Division level and to lead the SALT teams that would monitor and control the FCT teams stationed atop each building. With so many government agencies involved, we would need Lieutenant Colonel Keith to stand up for us, keep the communications flowing to whoever needed it, and ensure we were looked after.

"ATTENTION ON DECK!" Sergeant Major Mize shouted.

The assembly hall went silent as we all sprang to attention, and Keith walked to the front, standing before a large map of New Orleans. Man, this gig is actually going to happen, went through the mind of each Marine.

"We've all seen the news and we all know the situation," Keith started. "Other than the obviously weird fact that some of you will be spending up to seven days on top of a luxury hotel that usually charges four hundred dollars per night, nothing should come up that you haven't been trained for or performed a thousand times. In fact, all of you have been selected for your experience regardless of rank. Johnson over there is the most junior corporal we have, but he's a wiz-bang radio operator if I've ever seen one. We're putting his ass on the tallest building we can find so Washington can't complain about not getting any good scoop on what's happening in the Crescent City. Sergeant Taylor, he's going with you."

"Aye, aye, sir," Taylor responded.

It was great news and a great relief. Johnson was an awesome radio operator who tinkered with radios and field expedient antennas to get maximum range out of each radio. If you ever had to chastise him, it was that he couldn't keep his hands off of them when they were set up correctly. Keith used a whiteboard to list each team, their assignments, and the avalanche of gear we were taking.

Lieutenant Colonel Keith and Sergeant Major Mize would lead the Division Cell (call sign Lightning 11) at Camp Shelby, a Mississippi National Guard base just up Interstate 59, around one hundred miles from downtown New Orleans. It was a huge training base that had prepped several units for deployments to Iraq and Afghanistan. Shelby was the perfect location to organize the rescue effort and the right place for an ANGLICO commander. SALT Alpha would be led by Major Fernandez (call sign Lightning 12) and control FCT teams 1, 2, and 3, with call signs Lightning 13, 14, and 15, respectively. SALT Bravo would be led by Major Merrill (call sign Lightning 16) and would run FCT teams 4, 5, and 6, with call signs of Lightning 17, 18, and 19.

Each team was much larger than Taylor had ever seen or heard of. Normally a SALT team was attached to a battalion command and led by a senior captain who was a Marine pilot to coordinate air strikes with the Army or foreign troops. On paper around ten radio operators would man the radios to keep him informed of each FCT team's actions and whereabouts. Taylor always found working at the SALT to be just like the old expression that combat is endless boredom interrupted by five minutes of abject terror. You could pull a midnight shift, struggling to stay awake due to eight hours of zero activity. But as soon as the boss sticks his head in the tent or Humvee for a quick update, all hell breaks loose and you get your ass chewed out for not keeping him "in the loop."

On paper an ANGLICO FCT team was led by a Marine captain with a staff sergeant as team chief. Four enlisted Marines were trained as scout/forward observers or field radio operators. Everyone was cross-trained to perform everyone else's job, which is why ANGLICO units never have a second thought regarding placing a junior rank to lead an FCT team. After Hurricane Karen one of those Marines was John Taylor.

As he looked at the whiteboard behind Lieutenant Colonel Keith, Taylor was pleased. This detachment was loaded with more talent than he had ever seen. If a Marine was young, he was smart, energetic, and easy to work with and most likely a cop or firefighter "in the world." The older Marines with more rank had been around the block, and the world, dozens of times, with some going back to ground combat in Vietnam. I love it when a plan comes together, as they said on *The A-Team* television show that Taylor watched as a kid.

Lieutenant Colonel Keith told us the plan.

Somebody at the Pentagon got smart and sent a fighter reconnaissance plane over New Orleans taking real-time photography at low levels but also infrared images to show just exactly where the floodwaters were located. As the SALT teams would be set up on the ground on the edges of the city, we needed to be certain of each dry spot. As the world knows now, New Orleans is a shallow fish bowl. With Hurricane Karen moving north and losing her strength over the American Midwest, the floodwaters should stay where they are and not threaten any SALT team location. Regardless, twenty-four-hour shifts and basic security would be just as critical as in combat.

"All right Marines, here we go. 4th ANGLICO's goal is to create a basic radio network that covers the entire city of New Orleans. As you can see on your maps, Armstrong International is only twelve miles as the crow flies to the convention center, which is gaining stranded residents by the hundreds, if not thousands. You FCT team leaders are there to observe, report what you see, relay messages from other ANGLICO teams to higher headquarters, and respond to any request from myself or your SALT commanders. You are not in the business of riot control, shooting at looters or criminals, or air traffic control.

Some of you FCT teams will be fifty stories or more in the air. That's five hundred feet minimum. It's really nice of you to try and give all of your food to a starving resident, but I can assure you that an MRE dropping to street level from fifty damn stories is going to kill anyone who tries to catch it. You will be frustrated seeing all of the carnage beneath you. But the best thing you can do for these people is to keep higher headquarters informed about what exactly is going on below you. Making accurate and timely reports will allow rescue units to respond to the proper location and not fly around looking for trouble."

It was great to see someone finally got it right. Hell, not even during the Gulf War in 1991 did the Pentagon activate all of 4th ANGLICO. They took one platoon and the rest of us sat around for six months playing "pack your bags, don't pack your bags yet." It drove Taylor nuts and especially hurt his mom. Not now. Two SALT teams would run three FCT teams each while the rest of the company helped run the Division Cell and stand by to insert when needed. The colonel continued.

"We will all fly on four C-130 aircraft from Marine Air Group 42 directly to Camp Shelby, Mississippi. Sergeant Major Mize and myself will establish the Division Cell and link up with the Louisiana and Mississippi National Guard. Now look at your maps, Marines. SALT Alpha will be inserted by two CH-53s at the riverside tip of Algiers Point. Find Jackson Square in the French Quarter, look southeast almost directly across the Mississippi River, and there it is. It's perfect for a SALT. It's a grassy spot about the size of a football field away from rioters or panicky residents, so we won't need to fight off well-meaning people trying to electrocute themselves on our comm gear. A follow-on lift will have the 53s bring in our MRC-138 radio trucks slung load under the bird.

"The Marines of each SALT will be on the first 53 to insert, with the second bird carrying the bulk of the heavy gear and enough provisions for a seven-day mission. Now for our rooftop observation points. Each location has been approved by Washington, and the owners have signed agreements granting rights for observation purposes only, with the US government paying for any damage. I don't need to remind you to leave this place in better shape than when we found it, as that's what we always do anyway. Okay.

"Sergeant Taylor's Lightning one-three will be on top of the sixty-three-story Crescent City Resort Hotel just east of the Superdome. It's less than three hundred meters from the stadium, so you should be able to count people's front teeth with the Steiners we're bringing. Plus, it should provide full view toward the convention center and over the southern part of the city.

"Staff Sergeant Gonzalez's Lightning one-four will be on top of the Louisiana State Supreme Court building right in the French Quarter. The Quarter is an internationally known cultural landmark, and Washington is demanding to know of any foolishness going on ASAP. It's right across from K-Paul's famous restaurant, and down the way from Antoine's, but you won't be eating any shrimp étouffée on this trip, boys.

"Lightning one-five led by Gunny Lorenzo will be on top of the Post Building right next to Harrah's Casino. Gunny, you'll have an easy 'eyes on target' of the entire convention center area just as Lightning 13 will be keeping an eye on the Superdome. For now, everything seems to be calm at the convention center, but there's just a ton of people on site and it could blow up at any moment. You'll probably want to have two Marines with binoculars staring right at it at all times. I would suggest two-hour shifts, but it's your team, so have at it.

"Now, Marines, look to the north shore of the city along Lake Pontchartrain. See the triangular airport? That's the New Orleans Lakefront Airport and it's been in operation since the 1930s. Because the recon flight showed some water buildup in the center of the airport and covering the eastern runways, Major Merrill's SALT Bravo, Lightning 16, will establish their site here, east of the entire airport on the breakwater of the South Shore Harbor Marina. I'm sure the sailboats and yachts of the marina are scattered about like my son's Tonka trucks, but that spit of land is six hundred meters long and more than one hundred meters wide. It's another perfect spot for a SALT team and can monitor the teams on the north side of the city. SALT Bravo will insert using the same methods as SALT Alpha.

"The three FCT teams inserting on the southern shore of Lake Pontchartrain just might end up acting as relay or retransmission sites due to the levee breaks. The Ninth Ward and the University of New Orleans campus are basically lakes filled with muddy water. The levees built along the south shore of Lake Pontchartrain seem to have kept the shoreline, your future observation posts, dry. But the levees are also keeping the floodwaters in the neighborhoods just south of the lake. Infrared from the photo recon run is showing some sections with water as high as nine feet. As more forces penetrate the city, boat teams can use our radio network to transmit or relay message traffic back to Camp Shelby and the command authority. Gunny Duce's Lightning one-seven will insert at Breakwater Park, another marina with a breakwater three football fields long and one hundred meters wide. Anyone visiting any of the marinas is either there to gawk at rich people's wrecked boats or rich people checking on their boats. Either way, they should go about with their sightseeing or planning their insurance claims, so you should be well away from any crowd problems.

"Captain Macantee's FCT team, Lightning one-nine, will insert on the west side of the Pontchartrain Causeway at a two-hundred-by-two-hundred-meter grassy area located just in front of the Pontchartrain Center, where they hold conventions and such. Look along the shoreline all the way west of the city just before where the marsh line starts. See it? There shouldn't be any floodwaters in these areas as fighter recon has shown the bulk of the floodwaters stopped abruptly at the 17th Street Canal, around seven miles east of Armstrong International.

"Lightning one-eight led by Captain Martin have been cleared to operate inside the fence line of Armstrong International. This is where the L in ANGLICO comes from folks: liaison. I need to know the operational level of the airport, any mishaps, crashes, fuel spills, crazy people running around on the runways, the types and numbers of military units as they arrive, and for God's sake keep an eye on the Russians when they land their cargo aircraft. This won't be easy for you Marines with Team one-eight. Jet aircraft and helicopters taking off and landing twenty-four hours a day won't be good for your sleep habits, but hey, we all get the assignments we get. Captain Macantee, I expect you to act as a mini-SALT to assist Martin's team with their message traffic. As the airport comes back on line, the number of radio signals, microwave traffic, and radar waves will probably play havoc with one-eight's radios.

"And let me make this perfectly clear to all of you," Lieutenant Colonel Keith intoned. "Every human being has the right of self-defense, especially you and where you're about to go. But the Rules of Engagement (ROE) are very simple for this operation: You are allowed only to defend yourself or prevent a deadly scenario directly in front of you. You're not there to chase, arrest, or shoot looters. Your job is to tell us so we can send the cops to do it for you. Any questions? Good. Now let's get back to preparing our gear."

This is but one fictional scenario, and I'm sure my old ANGLICO buddies would have a field day tearing it apart and showing me every little fault with my genius plan. But remember back to the weeks after Hurricane Katrina when zero information was getting either in or out of New Orleans. The steps outlined in this chapter would have been far superior to anything that happened in 2005, and yes, my fellow Marines and I could accomplish this very handily. Of course, more FCT teams would be fed into the city as the ground situation improved due to heavier units arriving with more capable communications systems. But two of these six teams would be in a great position to observe two of the worst areas after Katrina: the Superdome and the Convention Center. This isn't to knock the other services at all. The Navy Seabees are great no matter what they do. The Air Force has Combat Control Teams (CCT), some of the most highly trained troops in the military who the American public also knows nothing about. CCT teams are fully qualified to jump in with Army Rangers, Recon, Delta, or a SEAL team and set up a temporary airstrip. Furthermore, they are all fully certified FAA air traffic controllers. I thought of CCT often after Katrina struck the mainland. ANGLICO could have laid a radio net over the city, and CCT could have brought in their mobile radar sets to set up shop at Armstrong International and the Lakefront Airport. If either airport had serious damage to their runways, the Seabees or US Air Force Red Horse Squadrons could repair them in short order. Plus, look at your favorite satellite mapping service online and check out the northwest corner of the Superdome complex. See that giant H painted on the ground? That's an eighty-by-eighty-foot helicopter landing pad that has been run by the City of New Orleans since the late 1990s. Place a CCT trooper right there to control military traffic and more aid could have gotten to those suffering people. Of course, if you plan correctly, they could talk to us in an emergency. Other than the loss of life and property, the other great tragedy of Hurricane Katrina was how much aid the US military could have provided with existing units.

Now for all of you skeptics out there, I can hear you complaining already.

"But Scott, these things are just not that simple. Trust me, I'm a lawyer. I know these things."

Well, actually, counselor, you don't. We've had fifteen years since September 11 to plan, arrange, coordinate, and rehearse this scenario. Yes, the federal government would need to reach out to perhaps a dozen owners of high-rise office buildings, hotels, resorts, and government buildings, and yes, it would probably take a few years to sign a deal. I made up the names of the buildings in the New Orleans scenario, except for the one public building, the courthouse. But go online and look at satellite maps of New Orleans and you can see for yourself the high number of buildings that could be used by troops to keep an eye on the city and relay critical data to Camp Shelby, Baton Rouge, the Pentagon, and even the White House. Very high buildings sit right next to the Superdome and the Convention Center, and if you also research a flood map of the disaster, you'll easily see that both areas were bone dry, just like the French Quarter. In other words a quick report the day after Hurricane Katrina struck would have alerted the authorities to this fact and a helicopter-based rescue effort could have been started. The technology and troops have been in place for decades, and I served with one such unit for a dozen years.

Now being a political science major and huge fan of the US Constitution, the greatest government document ever written, I can assure civil libertarians, the American Civil Liberties Union (ACLU), and various antigovernment types or conspiracy nuts that this plan would in no way threaten American liberties. The Posse Comitatus

Act of 1878, which strictly prohibits federal troops from being used as law enforcement personnel, doesn't apply. While ANGLICO Marines are without question federal troops, who are they going to arrest from the top of a fifty-story skyscraper? They won't be intruding on any Americans because everything they observe will be in full public view, and we've never had any spy tech or eavesdropping capability anyway. Also, information on the locations of potential observation points, helicopter ports, or city parks is all in the public domain anyway. A simple web search would suffice, especially for aviation as pilots need up-to-date data for flight operations. Local police and the Louisiana National Guard, as long as the Guard is under state (the governor's) command and control, will be making any necessary arrests.

For all of you conspiracy lovers out there who are going to scream "Government takeover!" or "Bill Clinton caused Pearl Harbor!," fewer than two hundred Marines are not going to be able to take over a flooded city still occupied by tens of thousands of shell-shocked citizens. One week on station, observe, send radio traffic as needed, and then go home. There is no threat to civil liberties here. Besides, after all the fightin' and fussin' over government use of troops during the Katrina rescue operation, eventually nearly fifty thousand troops were deployed throughout the entire Gulf region from Pascagoula, Mississippi, west to Baton Rouge. (And no, I didn't vote for Clinton, but I know he didn't cause Pearl Harbor either. Let's focus a bit, folks.)

The fictional start to this chapter about using an FCT team in downtown Miami is a bit more true to life than you think. I won't mention the current name of the building as I don't know the folks who own it now, but up until around 1987 the Centrust Building was a shining beacon in Miami. Built with three receding sections, the building would be lit with white light that shone straight up into the night sky. Boat captains sailing in from the Bahamas actually used it as a lighthouse for navigation. During the Christmas holidays it would shine with red and green plus huge ornaments to celebrate the season. Then the boss of the Centrust Bank was charged with nearly seventy counts of fraud and various other criminal acts. Well, it ain't called the Centrust Building anymore, as you can imagine.

But a beautiful building it remains. It's still right in the middle of the city. Best of all it still has a helicopter landing pad right on the roof. See where I'm going? Even if the heliport is no longer in use, a chopper could hover in the open space and Marines could fast rope to the rooftop. A fast rope is a four-inch-thick rope that is just like the old sliding poles in firehouses. With practice you can place twenty-five combat-loaded Marines on the ground, a ship at sail, or a rooftop in less than three minutes. Plus, the pad would be a perfect spot for resupply missions. I can only imagine the incredible view of Biscayne Bay, the Miami skyline, cruise ship row, Star Island, and South Beach across the water. However, my FCT team could report on everything we see and send an instant message to higher headquarters. We held communications exercises for years practicing this exact type of mission. Granted we wouldn't be calling in F-18 Hornets to bomb selected targets in the city (I am a Dolphin fan after all), but we could direct medevac or supply missions to the right areas.

Many political, civic, and business leaders have never served a second in the military and are flat-out ignorant of the US military's capabilities. They failed New Orleans after Hurricane Katrina, and that was nearly fifteen years after Hurricane Andrew, and they botched the response to that storm too. This is the same crowd responsible for the 2008 economic collapse and two Middle Eastern wars with no end in sight.

Lawyers can't do it. MBAs can't do it. The US military can.

8

BLOOD STRIPES

DAVID J. DANELO

INSHALLAH

Corporal Shady Stevens sat inside the Humvee, eyes peeled as he waited for Captain Anderson to finish talking to the hajjis. They were in a village on a ridgeline north of Fallujah. Millions of years ago, that ridgeline had been the edge of the river, which now ran through the southwest corner of the city. Shady was with two lance corporals: radio operator "Kid" Montcalm and his wingman "Sky" Hawthorne. They were watching Captain Anderson as he chatted with a few soldiers from Iraq's latest militia: the Fallujah Brigade.

On May 10, 2004, Major General Jim Mattis took a convoy with several vehicles from the Thundering Third of 3/4 into the governmental headquarters of Fallujah. Their mission was to drive into Fallujah, meet with city leaders—including General Latif (the new Fallujah Brigade commander), the Gay Mayor, and several town sheikhs—and return the city to their control. They had agreed to form the Fallujah Brigade and police the area. Theoretically, the Iraqi government, in partnership with American forces, would control the Fallujah Brigade. It was like accepting a pledge of chastity from a buxom blonde at the Mustang Ranch brothel.

Before the May 10 convoy, Mad Dog Mattis had visited Kilo 3/4 and Corporal Brian Zmudzinski, who were dug in south of the city as part of the siege/cordon. Major General Mattis was easy to recognize because he was the only Marine wearing a desert camouflage cap (a "soft cover," in Marine parlance) instead of a helmet. He walked over to a group of his Marines. Zmudzinski was among them.

"Sir, how much longer do you think we'll be here?" a Marine asked Mattis. The tone was informal but respectful.

"Men, I'll tell you the truth," Mattis said. "I have no idea. It could be days. Could be months. Could be years. I really don't have a clue."

The general clapped the Marine's shoulder and looked him in the eye. "But the best thing we can do is keep our spirits up and take things one day at a time. The folks back home understand that we've got a tough job to do. They'll support us."

Mattis turned to go. "Keep up the good work, my fine young warriors. You have honored your families, the Corps, and the American people. I am very proud of you."

"Oooh-rah, sir!!"

Mattis could have told his Marines to invade Syria, trudge mindlessly through the desert, or swim the Euphrates carrying a pack of lead weights. They would have done anything for him. As it turned out, Mattis was compelled to order his fine young men to do the one thing none of them wanted to do: give Fallujah back to their enemy.

After the Mattis convoy left the city on May 10, all of Fallujah exploded in a victory celebration. Next to the contemptible Sheikh Janabi, General Latif mingled with jubilant crowds who were chanting and shooting AK-47s into the air. The rumor in Fallujah—sort of a Muj version of the Lance Corporal Network—was "the Marines have surrendered!" The Muj said that Mattis had taken the convoy into the city so he could sign the final documents of American capitulation.

On the outskirts of the city—and not knowing the enemy thought his general had just surrendered—Corporal Zmudzinski had other observations. "I just kept seeing assholes riding around in trucks cheering and firing into the air," Zmudzinski said. "I had no idea what was going on, except that I couldn't do anything about it."

A few weeks after the formation of the Fallujah Brigade, Captain Anderson's convoy traveled to a train station on the northern edge of the city. Although the Fallujah Brigade was independently owned and operated by the Muj, funding for the enterprise, per the CPA/Marine/ Iraqi agreement, came directly from the American taxpayer. Vehicles, radios, rifles, and other gear had been issued to the Fallujah Brigade so the Iraqis could "bring law and order" to Fallujah.

The mission of this small convoy that had brought Shady to this village was to pay the soldiers' salaries. The convoy had several stops to make—the train station, a Fallujah Brigade "camp," and a headquarters unit. Each time they went near the Fallujah Brigade, the Marines got the same icy reception.

"Hawthorne, go stand next to the captain and make sure those assholes don't touch him," Shady said. The crowd was mostly teenage punks. They were wearing older Saddam-era uniforms and smoking cigarettes. They sat like schoolgirls, giggling and laughing. One boy had wrapped his arms and legs around his male friend, like a collegiate with his first main squeeze.

Anderson offered his right hand in friendship. They stared back. *La, la.* They waved their hands and shook their heads, smiling, laughing, and pointing to indicate they had no interest in shaking his hand.

As Shady remained perched in the driver's seat of the Humvee, Hawthorne had walked over and stood next to Anderson, who was glaring back while offering a false smile. *"Min Fallujah?"* Anderson asked. His pidgin Arabic was improving. *You from Fallujah?*

Hearing Anderson speaking Arabic made some of the teenagers shift to a more respectful posture. The deferential ones replied, *"Na'am,"* saying "yes" with a formal word. The cockier kids stared back. *"Eee, eee."* Yeah, yeah.

What's it to you, American dog? The hate in their thoughts could be seen in their eyes.

Shady looked over to Kid. Captain Anderson was in a parking lot a few dozen meters away. The Fallujans were all carrying AK-47s. They didn't have magazines inserted, but Shady didn't know that. They were being extremely casual with the muzzles of their weapons.

"If those fuckers flag the captain again, I'm shooting them," Shady said. Flagging meant pointing a weapon at someone, either accidentally or intentionally.

Shady and Kid aimed their M-16s at the Fallujans, who had turned their back to them. Ever since Anderson had been wounded, Shady had felt protective of him. Anderson was the captain, but he had a way of finding trouble. He was used to being surrounded by grunts and had found himself uncomfortable around most of the other staff officers. He cared little for the illicit creature comforts Shady provided for everyone else. Ironically, this made Shady trust him more. They had become something like friends.

Captain Anderson looked over at Shady and waved him off. He turned back to the Fallujans. *"Inti jundi?"* *Are you a private?*

"Na'am, na'am." They had grown deferential. Anderson spoke just enough Arabic to make them think he knew more than he did. It caught them off guard. They were smiling and gesturing more in conversation, a sign of fear as much as happiness.

Anderson and the convoy moved on. It took about two hours to pay each unit. In the late afternoon, one Fallujah Brigade officer motioned to the Marines. "You had better go," he muttered. A few elements within the Brigade had been whispering about an ambush. Annoyed by the entire charade, the Marines left without paying the last battalion—if there was such a thing as a battalion.

Anderson and Shady agreed that there were many things worth dying and sacrificing for. The Fallujah Brigade did not appear to be one of them.

Throughout the Fallujah attack and siege in April, the MEK had sustained a barrage of mortar and rocket fire. Because of this, May 2004 in Fallujah seemed almost serene. As the pressure remained steady on Ramadi and areas south of Baghdad, the May 10 convoy and the "victory" of the Fallujah Brigade brought the American bases around Fallujah a reprieve from mortar and rocket attacks. Like in Husaybah, the lull did not last for long. Instead of bands and parades, sporadic shelling kicked off Memorial Day weekend at Camp Fallujah.

As the sand and summer heat ruined more computer circuits, Shady spent more of his time on base and less on the road. Less action and more boredom raised the demand for libations. His contraband business was now thriving: more of the good stuff was coming in from the Green Zone, and he still had a steady supply of the cheap hajji whiskey.

Holidays in a war zone like Iraq often meant little private celebrations, like the splitting of MRE pound cake instead of fireworks and barbecues. For many grunts, holidays were nothing special—just another day away from home. Memorial Day 2004 was different: the first USO show to be held at Camp Fallujah was coming to town. The performers had specifically asked to play for the Marines.

Weeks before the attack on Pearl Harbor in 1941, President Franklin D. Roosevelt formed the United Services Organization (USO) to handle the needs of soldiers, sailors, and Marines on leave. Throughout World War II, the USO became the hub of activity for community participation in the war effort. Although technically a private organization, every American president has served as honorary chairman since its inception. Volunteers typically outnumber paid staff twenty to one.

Because the MEF Headquarters Group was responsible for Camp Fallujah logistics, both Shady and Anderson were involved in USO show preparations. In April 2004, Shady had gone from being a computer repairman to provisional combat leader. For the USO show, Shady became a provisional concert sound manager. His job was to convert the base chapel into an auditorium. Captain Anderson was one of several Marines escorting the celebrity entourage. The main guests were Ted Nugent and Toby Keith.

Anderson told Shady that he wasn't particularly impressed by the idea of a has-been 1970s rock star and a country musician grooving into a war zone. The captain shrugged off the rumor that Nugent—known simply as the Nuge—and Keith had specifically asked to do a show for Marines as a demonstration of honor and respect. A natural cynic, he thought the whole thing was a gimmick set up to help their careers. He thought of celebrities as prima donnas, craving the spotlight and the glitter of the red carpet without having any substance of character behind their fame.

Flying in helicopters under cover of night, the USO team was supposed to arrive at Camp Fallujah at 10:15 p.m. Sure enough, a pair of helicopters landed at 10:15, but they were the wrong birds. The VIPs had been delayed, and nobody knew when, or if, they were arriving. One earlier show at another base had already been canceled, and the USO party was supposed to arrive at their overnight site in Baghdad no later than 11:00.

Anderson figured they wouldn't show up. After all, these guys were celebrities. Certainly their handlers would force them to get their beauty sleep.

Around 11:30, the twenty Marines at the LZ heard the distinctive whirring of inbound helicopters. A pair of Army Blackhawks landed. After the sand settled down, a man wearing baggy trousers, a T-shirt, and a scruffy beard jumped out of the Blackhawk and wandered out in the general direction. Anderson thought it was a contractor or reporter—a celebrity wouldn't just stroll off a helo in a war zone.

The figure approached Anderson and pumped his hand.

"Hey, man, I'm Toby Keith."

Keith looked over his shoulder and gave a thumbs-up to the rest of the posse. "We're good!" he called back, giving the hand-and-arm signal for the crowd to follow him out. Rather than being handled, Anderson realized Keith was the driving force in the entire operation. Keith was acting more like a squad leader than a country music star. Anderson was surprised.

The entourage of eight people—musicians, military escorts, and USO staff—moved off the bird and over to the escort party. The Blackhawks flew away. Wearing jeans, a camouflage cowboy hat, and a weird triangular goatee, the Nuge was a little farther back in the crowd, but no less animated in his excitement to be with Marines.

Nugent and Keith began walking about, chatting with their admirers, signing autographs, and backslapping. They smiled for pictures taken from the same cheap disposable cameras the Marines had received months before, when a USO volunteer had handed them a brown zippered bag stuffed with items and stamped with the words Operation Care Package as they walked toward the World Airways jet bound for Iraq.

Once things settled down at the LZ, the Marines loaded up for the drive to the chapel. By this point it was past midnight, but two thousand Marines had packed in for the show. Nugent took a seat in a Humvee next to Anderson.

"Whoo boy! It's been *crazy* today!" the guitarist known as the Motor City Madman said. "We woke up this morning in Afghanistan. Went to Camp Anaconda, Balad . . . maybe someplace else. Only reason I know we're in Fallujah is 'cuz we're with Marines." He looked tired, but wired. "Damn good to be with you folks!"

"You had any food?" Anderson asked.

"Not since noon. Uncle Ted don't get too hungry out here on the road," said the Nuge. "We're too busy." The duo was planning to play the night show, fly to Baghdad, sleep for four hours, and then play two more shows the next day.

Knowing they would be at the chapel in moments, Anderson ripped open a couple of MREs and rifled through them. He grabbed the items that could be eaten quickly—peanut butter, crackers, M&Ms, and Tootsie Rolls—and handed them over to Uncle Ted.

The Nuge was impressed. "Yeah man! Improvise, adapt, and overcome, baby!!" He pointed to his belt for emphasis, "If those raghead fuckers try anything tonight, my Glock is loaded, and I'm ready to rock and roll." The Nuge lowered his voice to a conspiratorial whisper. "Just don't tell the USO staff. I ain't supposed to be packin'."

Anderson raised his eyebrows, appraising the situation. Toby: sober squad leader. Ted: goofy lance corporal. He made a mental note to tackle the Nuge if the base took mortar fire—rock star or not, Marines don't react well when weapons are quickly brandished by civilians.

As the Humvees turned onto the main road leading toward the chapel/concert hall, Nugent's door kept slipping ajar. The Nuge fumbled in his pocket, whipped out his Gerber multitool, and jimmied with the hinge until it was fixed to his satisfaction.

The Humvees arrived at the chapel, and Toby and Ted walked onstage, packing six-string acoustic guitars like six-shooters. Shady had rigged a pair of microphones to a speaker system. That was it. High school garage bands have used better equipment.

It didn't matter. Joking that they were "just like Lennon and McCartney, only with guns," Keith and Nugent played a mix of country and classic rock for an hour and a half nonstop. They hadn't showered in three days. There was no manager, no makeup person, and no costume changes. They were tired, hungry, and dirty. But they appeared to be enjoying every minute of it.

Backstage, Shady heard Anderson strike up a conversation with Sarah Farnsworth, the USO chief of staff who accompanied the troupe. "Are they always like this?"

"Yeah," she said, smiling. "Usually we have to tell them when to leave. They always want to stay longer than we can."

At 1:45 a.m., the entourage returned to the LZ. As the Blackhawks landed, Keith and the Nuge offered a final round of handshakes amid the wind, noise, and dust.

"Was it what you expected?" Shady asked his captain.

Anderson smirked. Shady knew of his earlier sarcasm. "Those guys earned my respect," he admitted.

Corporal Craig Atkins pulled his laundry out of the hajji washing machine and walked out to the clothesline. The hajji washing machine was an oversize plastic container with an electric-powered fin attached inside. Marines filled buckets of water, dumped them into the machine, and turned it on. If the Marines wanted a rinse cycle, they had to dump in another bucket of water. Usually the men just took the detergent-filled clothes out to the line and placed them out in the heat to dry, leaving them with soapy stains on their otherwise-clean garments.

Lost in his own reverie, Atkins hung out a pair of desert cammies, a green T-shirt, a brown towel, and a bunch of white socks. The trousers still smelled like the Euphrates. Of course that scent brought everything back. Atkins was more comfortable planning or executing a patrol . . . that was the only time he stopped thinking about it. The guilt never really left.

Sometimes the dreams were good times and memories, he and Schrage laughing about guns or girls. Schrage the City Boy, Atkins the Country Hick. Sometimes he woke up thinking he couldn't breathe. The water was in his mind, but not around him. Sometimes he just woke up scared, flinching involuntarily from imagined or real explosions.

"Need a hand?" Lance Corporal Justin Oliver asked. Oliver, a SAW gunner in the squad, was becoming one of his go-to guys, just like Atkins had been for Schrage.

"Nah, I'm good. Just gettin' a load o' wash clean n' done before we go out tonight." Craig grabbed a pair of clothespins and stuck a white sock next to a green Under-Armour T-shirt.

The Marines had adjusted quickly to Corporal Craig Atkins. He was different from Dustin Schrage—not better or worse, just different. Even out on patrol, Schrage was usually a jokester. Atkins was intense and serious. He rarely lightened up.

"The Cigarette Girl's here," Oliver said. "You gonna buy anything?" Oliver bought town goods from the Cigarette Girl on occasion. All the Marines liked the *hubbous* flatbread, which they sometimes bought or had given to them on patrol by a local in a generous mood.

"Nah. Don't think so." Atkins was truculent.

Cigarette Girl walked up to the pair. She was ten years old, four feet tall, with black hair, black eyes, and tanned skin. She wore a T-shirt and jeans. Her limited knowledge of English had come from lessons courtesy of Fox 2/4.

"*Shaku maku,*" Oliver said.

"Hey. You want the bullshit?" Cigarette Girl asked. She had a bag with cigarettes, lighters, and generic Arabic cans of diet cola. The Cigarette Girl could get anything the Marines wanted—food, drinks, or even hajji whiskey—out in town. The senior enlisted Marines at the Snake Pit had a soft spot for children and thought it would be a nice gesture to let her on base. Meanwhile her parents used her as a proxy to run their own contraband operation.

"La, la. Shukran." Oliver said.

"Please?" Cigarette Girl stopped, giving her best little princess smile. "The bullshit!" She held up her bag of trophies. Cigarette Girl could have sold ice to Eskimos.

"La, la. Go see Mister Richardson." Oliver pointed over toward the gym where another corporal was working out.

"Fuck." Cigarette Girl kicked the dirt and turned her back, walking toward the gym. "Richardson?" she said, smiling and pointing.

The Marines nodded.

"Okay. See you later." Cigarette Girl waved goodbye, innocently chirping with profanity.

Not long after the concert, Shady was up late on a sweltering night, finishing up a cigarette in the smoke pit, the hub of Network life. A mile toward the southern end of Camp Fallujah, an acrid pile of white was rising from the trash pit, where the refuse—like the burn shitters—was disposed of in a homemade bonfire twice each day. Nearby, a cacophony of other headquarters Marines were playing an enthusiastic game of "beach" volleyball. A radio blared.

In the moonlight, refracted from the shadows of the burning trash and volleyball game, Shady saw the silhouettes of four girls sitting on the curb smoking cigarettes. Fatima was there, a *hijab*-covered Iraqi beauty of twenty. Along with the other girls, she worked as a translator for Americans in Iraq.

The oldest of three sisters, Fatima oozed an alluring blend of innocence and insouciance. Her father had been a soldier under Saddam during the Iran-Iraq War, and her mother had been a biologist in Basrah before her marriage. Having learned English from watching movie subtitles, she volunteered for a job as a translator after the American occupation began.

In early 2004, Fatima found work at Camp Fallujah with Titan Corporation, a San Diego–based defense contractor the Pentagon hired to provide linguists. Her Sunni father said she was a foolish girl, but her Shiite mother gave full permission. Fatima hoped to use her job with Titan as a springboard to navigate her way to America. She conspired to forge her father's signature if he would not sign the papers. Grudgingly, he agreed.

As they chatted, Shady became intrigued with her questions and answers. Childlike naïveté mixed easily with resigned acceptance of reality.

"I don't fear the guns, the bombs, the missiles, or the terrorists," Fatima said. "I don't even fear my father. Everyone in my family thinks I'm crazy, but I only fear what would happen if I never took a chance at having my dreams come true."

Shady nodded quietly. In many ways, Fatima was twenty going on fourteen. As they smoked and talked, Shady heard booms off in the distance. He absentmindedly wondered if the rounds were incoming or outgoing; they were well outside the compound, and not loud enough for him to care one way or another. The volleyball game continued. It was a normal night at Camp Fallujah.

"Did they make you join the Marines?" Fatima asked.

"No. I left, then I volunteered to come back in."

This shocked Fatima. "You mean they didn't make you come over here?"

"Well . . . yes and no." Shady told Fatima his story.

Why, she asked, wide-eyed, did you come back in after you had left?

How do I explain this? Shady thought. *How do I explain that I came because I wanted to help . . . I wanted to serve . . . I wanted to defend freedom?* He tried to tell her how he had grown to care very much for other Marines.

"There are good people and bad people in the military, just like everywhere else." Shady explained that, despite his illegal business, he considered himself one of the good guys. He felt like he had a responsibility to do something when his country was at war.

Fatima gave him an odd look that said, "Why did you leave your family to come to Fallujah?" For her, family and tribe were everything. It was only for the hope of a better life that she had left them, and Shady's life in America had obviously been much better than Iraq.

"I'm not much different than you," Shady explained. "The Marines are like family to me. They are my tribe. No matter what I do, wherever I go, I will always be a Marine. And if Marines are in trouble, I will want to be there with them. That's just the way it is."

She asked Shady if he planned to stay in the Marines after his contract was done. He told her he wasn't sure yet. He had just been offered a chance to extend his tour in Iraq. He was thinking about doing it. He made good money with the tax-free salary. Plus . . . he liked it. Being there made him feel like he was actually doing something with his life, contributing to something bigger than himself instead of living the rat race, scrounging for a buck.

Fatima was completely dumbstruck. "Why would you volunteer again for something like this?"

Her interrogation became merciless. "Aren't all these years of wearing the same clothes every day and following the same orders and routine enough for you? You should go back to America! Find a wife! Have a home! Make a family! Why can you not return to your country and help in some other way? Have you not done enough fighting?"

Shady mumbled pithy answers about somebody needing to fight the terrorists, but his mind was elsewhere. *Perhaps hers are the feelings of a girl who has seen too many people die*, Shady thought, trying not to think about the way he had alienated his ex-wife.

Fatima stared back at him, angry that he didn't have enough good sense to return to his beautiful homeland. How could he run away from America and leave such a wonderful place? She was happy that Shady—and the Marine Corps he represented—came and freed her from a dictator's tyranny, but she was unhappy that he was unable to leave it all and go back to his home.

"You know, I danced and sang when I heard the sound of bombs and planes in March 2003," Fatima said, "but I still want you to go back home. Not for my sake, but for yours. Go back to America. You deserve it."

Shady couldn't help but wonder if she would be disappointed if she ever arrived in Washington, DC, or Kennedy International Airport. Would she be able to handle her freedom, or would the same material trappings of most Americans enslave her? Would she groan under the pain of absence from family and familiar cultural surroundings? Would her liberty be mortgaged to a low-paying job or an oppressive husband?

The volleyball game had ended, and with it the late summer recreation. Other than goodnight, little remained to be said. Shady walked away, confused by Fatima's support for his nation and simultaneous disapproval for his own willingness to take personal risk. Despite all of her life's struggle and pain, Shady couldn't help thinking of her as a grown-up little girl.

"I know my rights! This is abuse! I will not go on any more patrols if you keep treating me this way!" H-Money bellowed to Captain Jason Smith, company commander, Bravo 1/5. "You send me on patrol all day while the other Iraqis stay at the MEK and do nothing. This is not acceptable."

"Calm down," Smith said. Lieutenant Stephen Lewis stood behind him, arms folded.

"I want to go back to the MEK," H-Money replied. "No more patrols."

The Iraqi translator, a short, baby-faced Iraqi in his late teens whose Arabic name of Haeder (which means "lion") had been shortened to H-Money by Bravo Company, was in no mood to calm down. As one of Bravo's two Iraqi Arabic translators, H-Money was a scarce and valuable commodity. So valuable that he was averaging two eight-hour patrols a day in the city of Karmah, the town northeast of Fallujah where Corporal Brian Zmudzinski and Kilo 3/4 had destroyed the mosque and killed dozens of fighters/martyrs/angry residents during the battle in April.

After Fallujah was given back to the Mujahideen, Bravo 1/5 withdrew from the city and settled into a more normal routine. They pitched camp at an Iraqi schoolhouse in Karmah and rotated Marines through patrols in the city. They taped up posters, passed out soccer balls, waved to kids, and painted over anti-American graffiti. Occasionally, if they had good intelligence, they raided homes and arrested potential enemies. They found weapons caches and took down IED manufacturers. H-Money was present for it all. H-Money was getting sick of it.

"This wasn't what I signed up for," H-Money said. "I volunteered to serve the new Iraq, not to be treated like a dog."

Smith had had enough of the tantrum. "Listen, I don't care what kind of deal the folks at Titan offered you. You're with us now. Lieutenant Lewis needs you for this patrol. I need you to do it." Smith paused. "I'll give you a day off tomorrow."

Like a slave who had finally vented his spleen, H-Money, whose young body was scarred with torture marks from Saddam Hussein's reign of terror, moved from sullen to ambivalent. He shrugged.

"Okay, captain." It was obvious to Smith that H-Money didn't believe he would actually get a day off.

Lewis and H-Money left and went on patrol. That evening, H-Money came back and talked to Ahmed, the other translator. A Marine knocked on Smith's door. "Sir, H-Money wants to see you."

Smith walked outside. "I apologize for my anger," H-Money said. "I was upset and tired. I do not want to leave Bravo Company."

"No problem," Smith said. It wasn't as if he had never seen a guy get upset. "We really do appreciate what you do for us."

"Then why do we not have the ID cards yet?" H-Money asked. It was a respectful and legitimate question. ID cards carried weight. They meant access through checkpoints and conferred status, both on American bases and out in town. With translators and contracted Iraqis killed at three times the rate of American soldiers and Marines, H-Money and Ahmed knew the risks of aligning with the Americans. It was only fair, H-Money thought, that they should have the privileges they had earned.

Smith nodded. "I'll take care of that," he said. "Go enjoy your day off."

H-Money brightened. Here, for the first time in as long as he could remember, was a man who actually kept his word. Perhaps he could trust the Americans after all.

SOCIAL ENERGY

"C'mon, corporal. Have a smoke," Ahmed said as they walked down the streets of Shahabi, a village east of Fallujah, north of Camp Fallujah and south of Karmah. The mustached Iraqi grinned while offering Howell a pack of British cigarettes.

Howell hesitated. Dirty Steve notwithstanding, cigarettes were typically a no-go on patrol. But Howell knew most Iraqi men smoked, and it would look good to the natives who were watching his reaction. He took a cigarette and lit it, reflecting on the irony of his Iraqi interpreter handing him a British smoke as he stood on a street on Mesopotamia.

Ahmed grinned as they shuffled along, his hand brushing past the forged ID card that sat in his wallet as he pocketed the cigarettes. At Captain Smith's orders, the Marines of Bravo had used digital photography, an English-Arabic computer program, and laminating paper to manufacture a pair of "official" identifications for Ahmed and H-Money. They were as authentic as any other ID cards being made for Iraqis, and the gesture had satisfied the terps.

But in Fallujah, the stalemate was taking a toll on the spirits of the Marines. The Fallujah Brigade openly mocked the authority of American forces by turning the city into a Mujahideen sanctuary. Marines referred to their episodic patrols into Fallujah, which were supposed to act as a "proof of concept" for the Brigade's effectiveness, as a "spoof of concept." The scorching summer heat increased the inverse effect on morale; in addition to the enemy, many grunts battled their own discouragement and psychological malaise.

Because the Fallujah Brigade experiment could not be easily undone—it would take the Second Battle of Fallujah in November 2004 to actually "disband" the unit—the Marines decided to continue the patrolling effort on the outskirts of the city. This included the town of Karmah and the nearby village of Shahabi, where Corporal Jason Howell and Bravo 1/5 continued to maintain their presence at the former UN compound.

While Corporal Shady Stevens was playing sound manager for Ted Nugent and Toby Keith, the grunts of Bravo 1/5 were bouncing back and forth from one job to another. They were on high alert and then off again, which kept them awake at all hours. Tired and disgruntled, Corporal Howell had seen little action since April. His only highlight was that the static routine allowed for more frequent *Maxim*-accompanied visits to the Port-a-John.

Howell finished both the patrol and the cigarette without incident. He had been busy with the new Iraqi Civil Defense Corps—also called the Iraqi National Guard, the New Iraqi Army, and finally the Iraqi Security Forces. Headquarters in Baghdad kept changing the acronyms and, like Depression-era US government programs, the Marines lost track of the alphabet soup of names that uniformed Iraqis were supposed to be called. Despite the myriad of monikers, grunts continued to refer to them as the ICDC, a catchall term that represented individuals whose loyalty to American forces was somewhere between that of the Shahwanis and the Fallujah Brigade.

In addition to training the ICDC, Bravo began working more closely with 1/5's intelligence assets. Human intelligence Exploitation Teams, or HET, were important for American infantry forces in Iraq. A distilled version of HET's job is to recruit local spies, pump them for information, determine if it is useful, and then pass it on to commanders. In Iraq, the HET groups became the grunt-level counterintelligence operators.

After the battle of Fallujah had ended in stalemate, both infantry battalions and HET had turned their attention from Fallujah to the fence sitters in the surrounding villages. In late May, after learning that the residents of Karmah were offended by their presence at the schoolhouse, Bravo Company moved to an abandoned UN Oil-for-Food building in the village of Shahabi. Captain Smith suspected—and the HET Marines confirmed—that many of their sources were also Mujahideen moles. Additionally, the moles were moonlighting as Iraqi Civil Defense Corps employees.

On June 7, Bravo made their move. They raided several houses near the police station in Karmah, arresting several Iraqis-turned-Muj. The afternoon of June 8, while Howell's squad was standing guard in Shahabi, the Muj coordinated an attack on the police station. Although the prisoners had already been sent back to a different American detention facility, the Muj thought they would be able to rescue their captured comrades.

The good news was that the ICDC had, for the time being, sided with the Marines. In contrast to Husaybah, the Marine training in Shahabi appeared to have taken root. Inspired by a mixture of loyalty, nationalism, and fear—not unlike the Marines who had trained them—the Iraqis at the police station were fighting alongside the Americans.

Because 1st Platoon was the quick reaction force for Bravo, they were immediately ordered to the scene when fighting happened at the police station. Along with his platoon sergeant, Staff Sergeant Campbell, Corporal Howell's squad piled into Humvees and drove north, heading from Shahabi to Karmah. As they headed out, they heard a steady stream of AK-47 and RPG fire.

Howell's adrenaline rose. Days before, children had been smiling on the streets in the city, running up to him as if he was their hero. He felt protective of this town and angry at whoever was invading it. Even during the chaos of Fallujah, Howell hadn't had the personal experience of looking through his sights and having a confirmed enemy kill in combat. He still wanted it. Fiercely. Howell would soon get his chance.

What Corporal Howell later learned, based on the identities of the men they fought in Karmah, was that the Muj had come from their sanctuary in Fallujah on June 8 when they were attacking the police station to rescue their comrades. At the time, Howell didn't know where they had come from or why they were attacking. And he didn't care. Those abstract details didn't matter to him.

Additionally, Howell was lost. In the rush to deploy and defend the police station, both Howell and his platoon sergeant, Staff Sergeant Campbell, had left their maps sitting next to their gear. The pair kept driving the Humvees down and back narrow streets, threading and careening closer to gunfire while trying to find a parallel road to switch back to the police station.

"Turn here at Route Bethsheba! This is the intersection we want! Take a left!" Howell and Campbell yelled and gestured over the noise of Humvee engines and gunfire like a pair of fraternity brothers taking a wacky out-of-state road trip.

Making the turn was a good call on Howell's part. One intersection ahead was the police station, where Marines, Iraqis, and Muj were engaging in chaotic building-to-building combat. They had almost driven into the firefight—a bad place to make a wrong turn.

The pair of Humvees pulled into an intersection of alleys two blocks southwest of the police station to plan their next move. Staff Sergeant Campbell's front Humvee found what they thought was a covered position, but Howell's rear Humvee was stuck in the intersection and exposed.

"Pull forward, goddammit!" Howell's vehicle was ramming the Humvee ahead of him like a bumper car. Rounds snapped and whizzed around them; they still couldn't tell from where.

Ever the man of action, Lance Corporal Dirty Steve Nunnery came on the radio. "Corporal, I'm taking my fire team, clearing out this building, and finding some high ground." He dismounted the Humvees, developed a plan, assembled his men, briefed his boss, and moved into action. This took Dirty Steve six seconds.

Dirty Steve ran over to the house, broke a window—cutting his hand in the process—smashed a hole, and dove through it. His fire team followed him into the house and onto the roof, which they hoped would have the standard four-foot wall. In happier days, this made for a pleasant veranda in the cool hours of the morning and evening. Marines and Muj alike used the roof walls for cover and observation.

Unfortunately, this roof had no perimeter wall. With Campbell outside in the Humvee trying to raise Lieutenant Lewis on the radio, Dirty Steve's team ran out of the one house and found another one to clear.

Howell decided the alley was 2nd Squad's key terrain. He wanted to keep control of this narrow road, which intersected several other avenues of approach, and then use them as a foothold to push toward the Muj flank. Howell told one fire team to secure the intersections while Dirty Steve's team started clearing the rest of the houses in the street.

In the second house, Howell found something suspicious. One Iraqi man was standing in a room. He was about thirty years old, with weathered skin, hollow eyes, and a black mustache. Nobody else was in any of the houses. In fact, nobody else appeared to be in the city. Except for this one Iraqi man. It didn't feel right.

They put the man on his knees. Nobody else was there. Campbell was back at his Humvee on the radio. Howell was in the courtyard of the house. The prisoner was Howell's to interrogate.

"You're Mujahideen, aren't you, fucker?" Howell said.

"No, mistah," the man replied.

"Don't lie to me, you sonofabitch!" Howell screamed, putting his face within inches of the man, drill instructor style. "I know who you are, fucking Muj!"

"No, mistah! No, mistah!" The man's eyes widened as his voice trembled.

"*STOP LYING TO ME!*" Howell's veins bulged as he moved his head back and forth. "*YOU THINK I'M STUPID?*"

Thud. The man recoiled back. As his body had moved rhythmically with his screaming, Howell had accidentally banged his Kevlar helmet into the man's face. Surprised, Howell paused.

"Whoa! Hey, corporal, chill out!" Doc Perkins piped up. "Stay cool." He grabbed Howell and pulled him back. Quickly, Perkins examined the Iraqi and slapped a Band-Aid over the cut.

In the small room, the men in Howell's squad looked around at each other. Wordlessly, they all came to several conclusions. First, any further interrogation would be ineffective without their translators. Second, Howell, while going too far with his screaming and head butting, had good combat instincts. This man probably knew things they wanted to know. Third, they needed somebody of higher rank to get the information out of him.

Crack. Howell spun around.

Private First Class Oswalt, whom Howell called "a shitty Marine in general but amazing in combat," had spotted a Muj running through a side street on the other side of the alley. Oswalt had raised his M-16 to his eye and fired one shot, hitting the Muj in the head. The enemy combatant collapsed behind the building he had been running toward for cover, leaving only his foot exposed.

"Got him, Corporal Howell." Oswalt announced.

"Are you sure?" Howell raised his M-16 and looked through his ACOG at the man's foot. It wasn't moving at all. Not even a post-mortem twitch. Just to be certain, Howell fired twice into his foot. Nothing happened.

"Yeah. You got him, Oswalt."

"Hey, Howell," Staff Sergeant Campbell shouted up into the building, "You got a GPS? I'm trying to call in some support."

*Why is this guy on the radio bugging me with this kind of crap while I'm
busy leading Marines?*

Soon Howell got his answer. The 1/5 quick reaction force—the
same cavalry that had showed up for 2nd Platoon on April 13—arrived
within minutes. Accompanying them was Lieutenant Lewis and
Corporal Bob Dawson's 3rd Squad.

Howell was just happy to see Dawson. After the mess they had
gone through in Fallujah, they both felt better whenever their two
squads were working together. Just like the battle of Fallujah, 2nd and
3rd Squads from 1st Platoon happened to be simultaneously in the
fight. 1st Squad was on post.

Lewis walked up to Howell. "Corporal, what's going on?"

As Howell briefed Lewis and Dawson, he made a small mental note
that stuck with him for a long time. The lieutenant came to him first
instead of the platoon sergeant for the explanation. It was a little thing,
but it showed that Lewis trusted his judgment. That meant something
to Howell.

The corporal handed his canteen to Lewis and gestured toward his
empty green CamelBak water pouch. "Sir, could you fill me up?"

Without hesitation, the platoon commander took Howell's canteen and dumped the water into his CamelBak.

1st Platoon was starting to develop social energy.

A man once asked Colonel Clarke Lethin—a wiry, taciturn officer
with black and gray hair who served on Major General Mattis's staff
in three combat zones—what his biggest personal contribution was
to the post–9/11 global war on terror. "I provided the social energy
necessary to keep the cogs moving," Lethin replied.

Social energy? What is that? It is something closely akin to spiritual power, the power that, according to Mattis's favorite saying from General George Marshall, is essential to win wars. To the men of Mattis's staff, social energy was the practical employment of spiritual power. "Spiritual power includes the connection to things larger than ourselves, the feeling and bond warriors have for each other, and the strength to handle any reality," Mattis said. "But social energy is the building of trust and confidence that reduces friction in the heat of battle." Social energy, when established, helps to make the difficult easy.

It's been called different names throughout history. Businessmen have called it "synergy." The Chinese once referred to it as "gung-ho," a phrase that means "all together." The French phrase was "esprit de corps," which literally is "the spirit of the body [the Corps]." Esprit de corps, however, was rarely mentioned in Iraq—French phrases were not en vogue at that time and place in the American military.

"The combination and focused direction of social energy and spiritual power makes a military organization so tight, all the commander has to do is point his unit in the right direction and tell them what they already know," Mattis said. "Social energy is the framework through which spiritual power flows. Social energy is the pipes and hoses. Spiritual power is the fuel."

By this, Mattis does not mean a specific religion, or even an abstraction like "morale." Spiritual power is the unbreakable commitment of a group of warriors, both to each other and to the mission they've been assigned. This phenomenon of spiritual power often happened around Mattis himself, within the small platoon of men he called his Jump CP.

The Jump CP's mission was to provide Mattis with security, communications, and information capabilities while he traveled around Iraq. Commanded by Gunnery Sergeant David Beall, the Jump CP moved quickly—often on extremely short notice—to whatever place Mattis wanted to go. The Jump CP often got into fights with the Muj; of the twenty-nine men who manned the handful of vehicles, seventeen were killed or wounded.

In April, after the first time Mattis's Jump CP was hit, the general called Father Bill Devine and asked him to be present when the men returned to Blue Diamond. "Everywhere Father Devine went, the Marines felt better about both themselves and their mission," Mattis said. "He was a good listener, but not a crutch. He helped the young men find the power inside themselves."

Devine did as ordered, proffering handshakes, hugs, and words of encouragement to the tired and bloodied. As he was talking to the Marines, Father Devine watched Mad Dog Mattis walk back to his office alone. *Who's going to take care of him?* Devine thought. Mattis had charged his chaplain with maintaining the division's spiritual power. Devine wouldn't be doing his job unless he also ensured his boss's spirit was strong.

Later that evening, Devine rapped on Mattis's door and cracked it open. "Busy tonight, general?" Devine asked with his Boston accent.

"Hey, Bill, come on in." Mattis had been reading a book. The general fixed his chaplain with the same quiet stare he offered to his men. "How are the Marines doing?"

"They're doing fine, sir. How are you doing?" Devine pulled up a seat. The pair talked for about half an hour. "I could see strength in his eyes," Devine said, "but also the pain of the loss." He later learned Mattis had personally written award citations that same night for the men who had earned them.

In June, around the time Howell and Bravo 1/5 surged into Shahabi, Mattis's Jump CP was on a road driving west from Fallujah to Ramadi. A convoy of Army MPs was moving in the opposite direction. As the two convoys passed, the Muj detonated a car bomb, killing and wounding men from both convoys. While tending to their own casualties, Mattis's men quickly oriented their focus onto the enemy. The Army MPs followed in trace, and together two units who had never even seen each other hunted down and killed the Mujahideen who had exploded the bombs.

After the second attack, Mattis gathered his Jump CP. He told them that he understood he placed their lives at greater risk because of his frequent trips throughout western Iraq. He implied that perhaps the enemy had learned what his convoy looked like and was targeting him directly for assassination. He offered them the opportunity to be assigned to another unit. "It won't affect my esteem of you at all. There would be no loss of manhood in my eyes."

Not a single Marine accepted his offer.

In a back alley of Karmah, Corporal Howell was dueling for his life.

Twenty feet away from him, a Muj with an AK-47 kept popping back and forth behind a corner and shooting a burst. He was shooting directly at Howell. And every time the Muj exposed himself, Howell was firing at him. It was visceral and personal.

As they exchanged volleys, Howell realized that he had been taking cover behind an empty, rusted trashcan. Five feet away was the armored Humvee that he had rammed earlier like a bumper car. Howell had gotten so absorbed in the hunt for the kill that he hadn't even noticed it. He moved over to the Humvee and opened the door for cover.

Howell felt a jab of pain in his right forearm. He stopped, looked, and found no blood or evidence of a wound. His adrenaline pumping, Howell went back to firing at the Muj, who eventually disengaged and disappeared.

Further down the alley, a white pickup was driving toward Howell. Two men were inside.

"Sir, I've got a white pickup at two hundred meters headed this way," Howell yelled to Lewis.

Where rules of engagement were concerned, white pickups with Iraqi men inside in the middle of a firefight represented a gray area. Technically, they weren't shooting at him. However, in all likelihood, they represented a threat. Again, Howell intuitively sensed that something was off.

Lewis didn't even hesitate. "Light him up!"

Along with two other Marines from his squad, Howell pumped a steady stream of rounds into the truck, killing one man and wounding his partner. Lewis called a ceasefire while another squad of Marines flanked the truck and captured the wounded Muj, speeding him back to the rear for HET to interrogate. The Marines searched the truck and found several RPGs and AK-47s, confirming Howell's instincts.

Lewis looked over at Howell. "There's some traffic on the radio about a lost fire team near this alley."

"You're kidding, right, sir?" Howell had a good idea of where all the Marines were, including those a hundred meters away. He didn't know what unit they were from, but he knew they were Marines. They didn't appear lost.

Lewis thrust the green handset inside his Kevlar to check. "They're stranded somewhere. Go search a couple of blocks with a fire team and come back."

"Aye, aye, sir." Howell had no problem with Commander's Intent. He was happier doing his own thing. Additionally, it was obvious that his squad was having a good day. If he were a basketball player, Howell would have said he was "in the zone."

Howell and three other Marines moved out to a parallel alley in a staggered and dispersed column on opposite sides of the wall. Further down the alley, a man got into another white truck. The vehicle started revving forward *Dukes of Hazzard* style, tires squealing. A mortar system was next to the truck.

This is it.

Howell raised his weapon. He notched the infrared laser chevron that appeared in the center of his ACOG reticle onto the back of the man's head.

Steady.

He took a deep breath. And released it.

"What do we do, corporal?" a Marine with a SAW asked.

Steady.

Howell heard his SAW gunner, Lance Corporal Jeff Elkin, but wasn't paying attention.

Crack.

Howell's first shot hit the mark. Two feet away, Elkin opened up with his SAW, and the other Marines peppered the truck with bullets.

Convinced the man was dead, Howell and the Marines stopped shooting and ran up to the truck. When they ran up to the man, his body was twitching, as if he were receiving an electric shock.

"What the fuck?" Howell shot him eight more times before his body stopped moving.

Concerned about the possibility of a suicide car bomb, the Marines checked for wires running to other parts of the vehicle. Finding no wires, they spotted a white bag with a powdery substance. The man had been strung out on opium, heroin, or cocaine while mortaring the Marines. Howell never found out exactly which drug the men had been using to get high. Throughout Fallujah, the Muj had been found with all of them.

The Marines grabbed the mortar system and ran their hands inside the tube. It was warm, and they could feel the residue of fresh powder. Howell had killed a man who had just been dropping mortars onto other Marines. He was beyond ecstatic.

Howell ran back to Lewis and told him what happened. "Good work." Lewis called a quick meeting with Staff Sergeant Campbell, Corporal Dawson, and Howell. To their frustration, 1st Squad had remained on post. "We're sweeping through Karmah," Lewis said.

Out of breath and still fired up with adrenaline from the kill, Howell didn't hear exactly what Lewis was saying. Something about sweeping through Karmah. Suddenly, Lewis and Campbell took off with Dawson's squad.

Also standing in the house were the HET Marines and their two prisoners—the wounded man from the truck and the thirty-year-old Howell had head butted. "Can you give us a Marine to help with security?" they asked.

Howell looked around at his squad. Other than Dirty Steve, whom Howell needed, there was only one man he completely trusted to act independently. He turned to Doc Perkins. "I need you to stay and do this," Howell said.

"What?"

"Just make it happen," Howell said as he ran off. Confused and somewhat frustrated, Doc Perkins—battlefield medic—grabbed one of the captured Iraqi AK-47s and posted security for HET as they interrogated the prisoners.

As Howell ran to catch up with the platoon, the battery in his radio ran out. Having lost communications, he looked around for other Marines and found none. He vaguely remembered the general plan was to sweep from east to west. Howell and his squad were on their own.

While chaos unfolded around them, social energy and good training formed a powerful combination in Howell's 2nd Squad. They cleared out buildings on instinct, reacting as if they were all different parts of the same mind. When women and children peered out of their windows, the Marines lowered their weapons, took off their Wiley-X sunglasses, and called out. *"Awghf! Stop!"* They gestured and pointed, ushering them to safety.

At one point, the Marines spotted five Iraqi males standing in a building. Although they appeared to be harmless, Howell's squad flex cuffed the men and searched the area. After finding nothing, they cut the men loose, shook hands with them Iraqi style (mild handshake followed by touching of the heart), and let them go. All this happened with no commands. The men just did it.

Running ahead, Howell saw some Marines from another company. A squad from Charlie 1/5, along with their platoon commander, had been training the ICDC for several months. They had gotten caught up in repelling the attack. Howell had never seen them before. One was sitting on a Humvee, bleeding. "Watch out for the fuckers on the roof with grenades," he yelled.

"What are your current ROEs?" Howell yelled back, stopping. Rules of engagement, or ROEs, always seemed to be changing. When attacks were rare, they were restrictive. When the shooting was heavy, some of the Marines tossed the ROEs out the window.

"If it's an Iraqi male, he dies," the Marine from Charlie Company said.

Howell could see the man was exhausted and pissed off. Still, he was proud that his squad had not lost their bearing and humanity. With Spartan discipline, they had killed all the right people and, in their best judgment, not killed any innocents. Howell had taught his men to be discriminating when they pulled the trigger. As much as he had thrilled for his own kill, he knew that the shot was fully justified. Howell had killed an enemy combatant out of devotion to duty, not a random hajji out of vengeance or bloodlust.

Howell and the squad continued running west through Karmah. Just then, Lance Corporal Henderson, a Marine in Corporal Dawson's squad who happened to be driving an Iraqi car, came careening down the street in an Opel sedan he had commandeered. Also in the car were two Iraqi men, a Navy corpsman and a wounded child. The corpsman was treating the child.

Howell and the squad reached the end of the city and found the rest of the platoon scattered near a checkpoint. He posted his squad and ran over to Corporal Bob Dawson, who was relaxing and drinking an ice-cold Iraqi 7-Up that he had just bought from a hajji soda merchant.

"Gimme some, fucker," Howell greeted his best friend in the platoon.

"Anytime," Dawson smiled. Howell gulped the soda.

As the corporals swapped stories, Lewis called a leader's meeting. Everyone was accounted for. The police station had been defended. A large number of Muj had been killed or captured. As the conference ended, several helicopters flew low into the town.

Immediately, scenes from another movie flashed into Howell's head: *Apocalypse Now*. "Walking away from that meeting and seeing the door gunners standing there . . . the propellers thumping . . . hearing the roar of the engines . . . the whole thing was like being in a Vietnam movie," Howell said. "I felt like I controlled the world. I can definitely see how people get addicted to combat. I'll never forget that feeling of power and invincibility."

As soon as air support arrived, the Muj hunkered down. With the town quiet, 1st Platoon patrolled back through the streets they had just sprinted through. Lewis had wanted them to collect all the dead bodies and check them for intelligence. Half of the bodies were already gone. A combination of Islamic tradition—which required burial of the deceased before sunset—and Mujahideen tactics prevented them from collecting most of the dead. "We would walk by and see a fresh bloodstain where a body had been two hours before," Howell said.

Additionally, children were playing in the streets. "It was surreal," Howell said. "An hour before, we were running through, ready to shoot anything. Now kids were waving. Little boys and girls were smiling, giving us the thumbs-up, begging for water or food. They were acting as if nothing had happened."

"We all almost lost it," Howell said. "It was like we had tripped into some alternate reality."

After the psychological jarring from combat to eight-year-old girls giving them the thumbs-up, Howell's squad went back to the house where Doc Perkins, with his AK-47, was waiting for them. They found two dead Mujahideen—including Oswalt's kill on the street—and took their bodies so they could check their fingerprints against other known records. They found numerous weapons stockpiles and took them all.

"We felt like we did something that day," Howell said. "We killed some people and took some weapons off the street and the townspeople thanked us. I couldn't have been any prouder of those men in my squad. They did everything exactly as they had been trained."

Howell went back to the 1/5 headquarters. Several officers interviewed him, asking him to explain why he had shot the men he did. They filled out some paperwork. After that happened, Howell reloaded his magazines. Then he and his squad went back to the warehouse and stood a four-hour shift of guard duty.

One week later, Howell accidentally scraped his right forearm against a wall. He felt something inside it, like a sliver or a scab. He squeezed at the scrape. A sore Howell had not noticed before popped open. Pus, blood, and a small chunk of metal spurted out. The metal was a bullet fragment. Howell had picked it up during his firefight by the empty trashcan. The heat of the shrapnel had cauterized the wound when the fragment entered Howell's arm.

Corporal Jason Howell never said anything to his chain of command about his wound. He didn't want his guys to think he was trying to scam a Purple Heart. Even though he was entitled to the award, he thought his reputation mattered more to his squad's combat effectiveness than his receipt of the medal.

A greedy squad leader on a medal hunt would destroy social energy.

9

FROM BAGHDAD, WITH LOVE

LIEUTENANT COLONEL JAY
KOPELMAN, USMC (RET.)

NOVEMBER 2004: FALLUJAH

I don't remember exactly when I got to the house that served as our command post in the northwest sector of Fallujah, and I don't remember exactly how I got there. It was a couple of days after the Lava Dogs arrived and took over the compound, I do know that much, and I remember that after four days of dodging sniper fire, sleeping on the ground, and patrolling Fallujah with wide-eyed Iraqi soldiers in training who shot at anything that moved, including their own boots, I walked up to the building with a sense of having escaped an abstract rendition of the wrong hereafter.

I remember being exhausted, the tiredness weighing more heavily on me than the sixty-pound rucksack I lugged around, and as I walked through the front door and shrugged what I could off my back, all I could think about was sleep.

That's when I saw Lava for the first time. Only it's not as if I walked in and saw a chubby puppy cuddled up on a blanket undefiled by the world like an overstuffed lamb. There were no squeaky toys, no baby yips, no eyes looking up at me with an artless blue-gray innocence.

Instead a sudden flash of something rolls toward me out of nowhere, shooting so much adrenaline into my wiring that I jump back and slam into a wall. A ball of fur not much bigger than a grenade skids across the floor, screeches to a halt at my boots, and then whirls in circles around me with the torque of a windup toy. It scares me, right? Like I'm tired and wired and anything quick coming at me jerked at my nerves, so I peel back off the wall and reach for my rifle even though I can see it's only a puppy.

Now, before you get all out of whack about me aiming a weapon at cute baby mammals, keep in mind that I just walked in from the streets. Out there, things were spooky, like a plague or a flood or dust from an atomic bomb had just rolled through. Most of the city fled before the US-led attack, and the quiet rang so loud after the bombardment, even windblown newspaper sent your nerves screaming for solid cover.

The day before the offensive started, we dropped leaflets over the city warning the few remaining citizens that we were on our way in, but insurgents inside spit back that they had hundreds of car bombs rigged, booby traps set, and suicide bombers with jittery fingers waiting to go. They'd already dug trenches in the city's cemeteries for the expected martyrs.

In the days prior to our march into the city, our warplanes pounded Fallujah with cannon fire, rockets, and bombs. Because the skies were so crowded, attack jets had only a three-minute window to unload their cargo and clear out before another jet swooped in. Hundreds and hundreds of pounds of 105mm shells, 25mm rounds, and 40mm rounds blasted into Fallujah that night with the impact of meteors from several galaxies away. The aerial bombardment was so spectacular, I—along with ten thousand other Marines waiting to advance on the outskirts of the city—doubted anyone inside would live through it. But plenty managed, and now that we were here, sniper fire came at us from nowhere like the screams from ghosts.

So when this unexpected thing, this puppy, comes barreling toward me in this unexpected place, I reach for my gun. I must have yelled or something, because at the sound of my voice, the puppy looks up at me, raises his tail, and starts growling this baby dog version of *I am about to kick your ass.*

The fur gets all puffy around his neck like he's trying to make himself look big, and then he lets loose these wienie war cries— *roo-roo-roo-rooo*—as he bounces up and down on stiff legs.

I stomp my boot his way to quiet him down, but he doesn't budge and intensifies the *roo-roo-roo-roooos* shooting in staccato from his lungs.

"Hey."

I shove the rifle to my back and bend down. The puppy bounces backward in time to the *roo-roo-roo-roooos* but doesn't take his eyes from my face.

"Hey. Calm down."

He looks like a bloated panda bear, and when he howls the last *rooooo* of the *roo-roo-rooooo*, his snout stretches skyward until his fat front paws lift off the floor.

There's fear in his eyes despite the bravado. He's only a puppy, too young to know how to mask it, so I can see how bravery and terror trap him on all sides while testosterone and adrenaline compete in the meantime for every ounce of his attention. Recognize it right away.

I reach into my pocket, *roo-roo-roo*, pull out a bullet, *roo-roo-roo-roo*, and hold it out toward him in hopes he'll think it's food. The puppy stops barking and cocks his head, which makes me feel manipulative but wise.

"Thatta boy."

He sniffs the air above his head, finds nothing, and then directs his nose toward the bullet. It interests him, and he leans forward for a better whiff of the metal, which surprises me until I notice how filthy my hands are, almost black from a week without washing, and I realize he's smelling accumulated dirt and death on my skin.

I lean forward, but fear gets the better of him and he tears off down the hall.

"Hey, come back."

I stand there and watch him career into a wall. I wince, that's got to hurt, but he gets up, shakes his head, and takes off again.

"Hey, come here."

The puppy stops and looks back at me, ears high, tiny tail rotating wildly, pink tongue hanging out sideways from his mouth like he's crazy. I realize he wants me to chase him, like he figured out he was bamboozled only he's too proud to admit it and now covers up with this *I-was-never-afraid-of-you* routine. I recognize that one too.

He leaps in a circle on paws as big as his face, hits the wall again, and repels into a puddle of daze. I'm, like, mesmerized by the little guy. Wipes my windshield clean just watching him, so I scoop him up off the ground with one hand and pretend I didn't notice his wall slam.

"Tough guy, huh?"

He smells like kerosene.

"What's that aftershave you're wearing?"

He feels lighter than a pint of bottled water as he squirms and laps at my face, blackened from explosive residue, soot from bombed-out buildings, and dust from hitting the ground so many times.

"Where'd you come from?"

I have a pretty good idea where he came from and a pretty good idea where he's going too. I've seen it before, Marines letting their guards down and getting too friendly with the locals—pretty girls, little kids, cute furry mammals, doesn't matter; it's not allowed. So as I'm holding the little tough guy and he's acting like he just jumped out of a box under the Christmas tree, I call my cool to attention.

It's not allowed, Kopelman.

But he keeps licking and squirming and wiggling around, and I remember this part pretty well, because I liked the way he felt in my hands, I liked that he forgave me for scaring him, I liked not caring about getting home or staying alive or feeling warped as a human being—just him wiggling around in my hands, wiping all the grime off my face.

The Lava Dogs told me they'd found the little outlaw here at the compound when they stormed the place, and the reason he was still here was that they didn't know what else to do with him. Because they'd decided to use the compound as the command post, and because this starving five-week-old puppy was already there, the choices were either to put him out on the street, execute him, or ignore him as he slowly died in the corner. The excuses they gave me were as follows:

"Not me, man, no way."

"Not worth the ammo."

"I ain't some kind of sicko, man."

In other words, they had enough pictures already from Fallujah to torture them slowly for the rest of their lives; they didn't need any more. Warriors, yes—puppy killers, no.

The puppy is named Lava, and while I'd like to say my comrades are creative enough to name him for symbolic reasons—like, you know, if they save him, they save themselves—I'm fairly sure they just couldn't come up with anything else.

Lava is the newest grunt, defleaed with kerosene, dewormed with chewing tobacco, and pumped full of MREs.

Just so you understand how tough Lava really is: MREs, officially called "Meals Ready to Eat" but unofficially called "Meals Rejected by Everyone," are trilaminate retort pouches containing exactly twelve hundred calories of food, a plastic spoon, and a flameless heater that mixes magnesium and iron dust with salt to provide enough heat to warm the entrée. On the package, the meals state that "Restriction of food and nutrients leads to rapid weight loss, which leads to: Loss of strength, Decreased endurance, Loss of motivation, Decreased mental alertness," which supposedly coaxes us into at least opening the pouch to see what's inside.

Lava can't get enough of them, though, and learns real quick how to tear open pouches designed with three-year shelf lives that can withstand parachute drops of 1,250 feet or more.

Still, the best part is how these Marines, these elite, well-oiled machines of war who in theory can kill another human being in a hundred unique ways, become mere mortals in the presence of a tiny mammal. I'm shocked to hear a weird, misty tone in my fellow Marines's voices; a weird, misty look in their eyes; and weird, misty words that end in *ee*.

"You had yuckee little buggees all over you when we found you, huh? Now you're a brave little toughee. Are you our brave little toughee? You're a brave, little toughee, yessiree."

And the whole time Lava knows I've got him pegged, and he's stealing glances at me to make sure I see how he's soaking it all up.

The Marines brag about how the puppy attacks their boots and sleeps in their helmets and gnaws nonstop on the wires from journalists' satellite phones up on the roof. They tell me he can almost pick up an ammo belt. They tell me he loves M&Ms.

"Did anyone feed Lava this morning?" someone yells out as "I did" comes back from every guy in the room.

He's like a cartoon character on fast forward, always chasing something, chewing something, spinning head-on into something. He stalks shadows and dust balls and pieces of balled-up paper. He can eat an entire cigar in less than two minutes and drag a flak jacket all the way across the floor. I mean, the little shit never stops. If you aren't dragging him along after you as he hangs on to your bootlaces with his teeth, he's up on the roof tangled in wires or lost and wailing in the bowels of somebody's backpack.

You can't yell at him, either, because even though you are an elite, well-oiled machine of war who in theory can kill another human being in a hundred unique ways, you'd still be considered a freak if you yelled at a puppy. He's completely pampered, kept warm, his sticks never thrown out of his sight range so his ego isn't damaged when he can't find them. I find it all pathetic. At first.

But the newest recruit already knows the two most important rules of boot camp by the time I come around: you don't chew on bullets and you only pee outside.

It's like Lava is everyone's kid. It gives them something to be responsible for above and beyond protecting their country and one another, and getting their brains blown out or worse in the process. He gives them a routine. And somehow, I become part of it.

Every morning we feed Lava his rehydrated Country Captain Chicken with Buttered Noodles and then pile out of the house to various posts across the city. Some Marines patrol the streets, some clear buildings looking for weapons, and some get killed and don't do much of anything after that.

Me, I have to patrol the streets with three wide-eyed Iraqi soldiers who, in their brand-new, US-issued, chocolate chip cammies, wave their rifles around as if clearing the way of spiderwebs. Most still haven't figured out how to keep their rifles safely locked.

They are untrained, out of shape, and terrified. They're members of the Iraqi Armed Forces (IAF)—stouthearted doublespeak for "conquered and unemployed"—who were coaxed by the United States to help root out insurgents in Fallujah before the upcoming national elections.

Several days before we bombed the city, the new Iraqi recruits reported to Camp Fallujah, a few miles southeast of the city, with plenty of promising bravado. When Prime Minister Iyad Allawi made a surprise visit to the camp and urged them to be brave, to go forth and "arrest the killers" in Fallujah, the young Iraqi soldiers cried back with newly developed devil dog gusto, "May they go to hell!"

Things deteriorated quickly though. First we built a tent camp for them just outside the walled safety of the main camp. We called it the East Fallujah Iraqi Camp and hoped the name and the handful of American advisers and liaison officers who also stayed there would boost their courage. The Iraqi soldiers endured both regular mortar shelling of their tents by insurgents and verbal bombardments from the Americans who only had one week to prepare them for their first-ever combat experience. So they were prone to the jitters and often woke up in the middle of the night shooting their un-safed rifles wildly. Thank God they didn't know how to aim.

It didn't help that influential Iraqi clerics publicly threatened the IAF soldiers with banishment to hell, and the insurgent council that controlled Fallujah promised to behead any one of them who entered the city to "fight their own people." In a statement issued by the council just before we attacked, the insurgents stated, "We swear by God that we will stand against you in the streets, we will enter your houses and we will slaughter you just like sheep."

More than two hundred Iraqi troops quickly "resigned," and another two hundred were "on leave." My job now is to babysit some of the few who remain.

One afternoon about a week after I arrived at the compound, a few other Marines and I are patrolling one of the main streets with them. We're in front of a mosque, right? And they're all bug eyed and waving their guns around and I'm a little strung out myself about what's going on around us, only I can't let on because I'm their example of what they're supposed to do and feel and be. But they're so freaked out, they're clearly about to shoot me or one of the other Marines by accident, so I figure the best thing is to make them more afraid of me than they are of the streets—you know, take their minds off it for a little while—so I start yelling.

"Knock that shit off."

And I keep yelling.

"Safe your weapons."

And they keep jerking their eyes one way and their rifles another way.

"I *said* knock that shit off!"

Until I see they've gone into another zone of fear that even I don't have access to, and one of the other Marines, I don't remember who, Tim O'Brien, Dan Doyle, or Mark Lombard, says to me, "Take it easy on them, man, they don't understand English," which kind of ruins my whole show.

"Yeah, well, they *better* learn fast." But I stop yelling and give them a look instead.

Then something rips past us in the air and we freeze. Just like that. It comes from nowhere but explodes a few yards away. Now we're moving fast. Fast.

A second rocket-propelled grenade (RPG) comes screaming our way, and I assess the situation in staccato—taking fire from two directions; small arms, medium machine gun, and rocket-propelled grenades; two men wounded; Iraqi soldiers running for cover; out-numbered in more ways than one.

I maneuver behind the hood of the Humvee to direct the men as Tim O'Brien, up in the turret, opens up with the MK-19 turret gun laying down a base of covering fire so the rest of us can position to fight.

Dan Doyle picks up a squad automatic weapon and fires toward the southwest.

Tim's a primary target in the turret, especially when his MK-19 jams and he has to fight with his M-4—a shortened version of the M-16A4 assault rifle—while he's trying to clear the MK-19 and make it ready to fire again. But it's Dan who gets hit. Blood runs down the inside of his left leg.

"Dan, get into that mosque," I order, but he ignores me and takes off running to get the Humvees positioned so we can evacuate the rest of the wounded, including Mark Lombard, who's bleeding all over the place but is on the radio calling in our situation report anyway.

Bullets and shrapnel ricochet from the hood of the Humvee inches to my right. Blood soaks Dan's pant leg.

"Get your ass into that mosque," I yell again, but he, get this, looks over at me and grins.

"Just a flesh wound."

Two armor-piercing rounds hit the vehicle and tear through its quarter-inch steel plate easier than needles through skin. I fire my M-16A2 and yell for the Iraqi soldiers to direct their fire to the south.

Only I don't see them. Where the hell are they? I have to get the wounded to safety, so when I see them from the corner of my eye crouched numb between two overturned vehicles, I realize we're on our own.

I abandon my M-16A2 for a more powerful squad automatic weapon, then run in front of the Humvee and fire away to the south. This apparently inspires one of the Iraqi soldiers to stick his head out, fire two rounds quickly—using me as his cover—and then duck back in. It's the last I see of the Iraqis for the rest of the thirty-minute fight.

At night we all gather back at the compound, where we cover the windows with blankets and sandbags, clean our weapons, and make sure Lava has something for dinner that he didn't have the night before.

Then the time comes when you have to put back on all your gear, ready your weapon, and sneak out to the portable toilets down the block. We call them porta-shitters. One of my greatest fears during the weeks I stay at the compound is the possibility of being blasted by an RPG in a porta-shitter.

If you survive that, then you bed down and smoke cigars and review the day's events with everyone else who made it.

"We found a weapons cache in that old UN food-for-oil place . . ."

"Yeah, well, we got caught in an alley . . ."

"Yeah, well, we had to transport wounded and they actually fell out of the Humvee onto the street when we got hit with an RPG or something we never saw coming."

They have nothing on me though.

"Yeah, well, my Iraqi guys decided to take their naps during a firefight . . ."

As we talk, Lava climbs up and over our boots, destroys packages of M&Ms, and paws through our blankets for prey.

"They don't have a clue out there . . ."

Then the puppy finds my lap and sits between my crossed legs staring out at the other Marines.

"I mean, how do DC brass ever expect to get these guys to secure their country if we're doing it all for them?"

I untie my boots, and Lava bites at the laces.

"I swear I am going to accidentally shoot the whole group of them if they don't shape up."

As I pull a boot off, the puppy grabs hold of the lace and tugs. I tug back. The puppy growls. I growl back.

"Hey, what's with this puppy anyway?" I ask. "What are you guys planning on doing with him?"

No one answers. Then one of the Marines stretches and yawns and says he's turning in. Others grunt. Lava crawls out of my lap and turns a few circles, flops down, and falls asleep with his nose buried in my empty boot.

Meanwhile, outside on the streets, psychological operations teams blast AC/DC and Jimi Hendrix through loudspeakers, with the additional sound effects of crying babies, screaming women, screeching cats, and howling dogs, in hopes of turning the insurgents' nerves to shreds. They broadcast insults in Arabic, including, "You shoot like goatherders" and "May all the ambulances in Fallujah have enough fuel to pick up the bodies of the mujahideen," which, along with the mortar, grenades, ceaseless rumbling of Humvees, and twenty different kinds of aircraft flying in precise layers over the city including helicopters, attack jets, and small, pneumatically launched spy drones that roam the skies beaming back images to base from automatic video cameras, create a kind of white noise that allows us all to sleep pretty soundly through the night.

I guess they didn't want to answer my question about Lava that night, because like everything else in Fallujah during the invasion, nothing but the immediate was worth thinking about. Really, there wasn't room in your head for anything but what was right in front of you or right behind you or right around the next corner. The future spanned one city block at most. Your dreams consisted of RPGs that missed; lifelong goals were met if you made it back to the compound at night.

So the guys probably weren't avoiding the subject of what would happen to Lava so much as they were ignoring it. There just wasn't any room. But jeez, when a puppy picks your boots to fall asleep in, you do start to wonder how he'll die.

See, I've been a Marine since 1992, when I transferred from the navy, and I know that the little guy is going to die. I knew it right away when I saw him in the hall—*this one won't make it*—just like you could look at some of the other guys and think *This one won't make it because his one eye twitches* or *This one won't make it because he parts his hair on the right instead of the left*—superstitious stuff like that, which you know doesn't make sense but oils your engine anyway. I was thinking *This one won't make it because he's too damned cute.*

I'm also a lieutenant colonel, which means I know military rules as well as anyone, and every time I picked Lava up, they darted across my brain like flares: *Prohibited activities for service members under General Order 1-A include adopting as pets or mascots, caring for or feeding any type of domestic or wild animals.*

NOVEMBER 2004: FALLUJAH

Anne Garrels tells me she sleeps pretty well at the command post. At least there's a roof over her head and a place to set up her satellite equipment, even though keeping Lava from chewing on the wires is just one of this war's pop quizzes for which she hasn't adequately prepared.

I say *this war* because she's attended several. Chechnya, Bosnia, Kosovo, Israel, Saudi Arabia, Afghanistan, the former Soviet Union, Central America, Tiananmen Square, Pakistan . . . you name it, she was there.

Anne's a trip. She can smoke, drink, and swear as well as any of us; knows more about war than any of us; and cares less about consequences than any of us, but here's the weird part: put Lava in front of her, and she kind of falls apart at the seams.

"He's adorable," she says as the puppy gnaws away at thousands of dollars' worth of her radio broadcast equipment, "just adorable," and all the while she's transforming into a soft, feminine, girl-next-door type whom you suddenly wish wasn't married.

But Anne is tougher than she looks. When she first entered the city as an embedded journalist for National Public Radio with Bravo

Company, 1st Battalion, 3rd Marine Regiment, she didn't have a sleeping bag because it was just one more thing to lug around—her broadcast equipment alone weighed fifty pounds. So she slept on the ground for minutes at a time, until bombs or falling bricks or blasts from sniper fire jolted her awake again. I mean, sleeping on the ground in the cold comes in a close second to sitting in full uniform on a porta-shitter worrying about death in terms of lousy ways to spend your time as far as I'm concerned, and she just shrugged it off with something like "Yeah, I'm a little tired."

But then in the compound she finds one of Lava's turds on her socks, and her eyes get misty like she's about to weep, and she says, "Isn't that adorable?" and is suddenly the girl next door again.

Anne isn't like the other reporters—who are usually guys and thus prone to all sorts of issues, not the least of which is preserving their masculinity as they piss in their pants. I mean, I do have to give them credit. They didn't come to Iraq in uniform and yet day after day they hump along after us, dodge the same RPGs as us, eat the same MREs as us, and all the while scribble their notes and whisper into their recorders and try like hell to seem nonchalant.

But not Anne. She flat-out admits that Fallujah scares the hell out of her. If one of the guys said that, we'd probably smirk and spit and examine our tattoos while saying some tough bullshit thing or another, but when Anne says it, it kind of eases some of the tension the rest of us are feeling. Because if all this fazes her, then at least we aren't the closet cowards we all secretly worry we are.

It's like she deserves to say it. She spends her days moving behind Bravo Company block by block, house by house, through a booby-trapped inferno as the Army psychological operations teams broadcast their tapes over the mosque loudspeakers. It gets to her after a while, right? So as she moves through the narrow streets, she focuses

solely on what lies directly ahead, or just above or around the next corner, sweating almost out loud about what comes next. And when she
describes it, your insides scream *What a coincidence!* because you know
exactly what she's talking about, and you almost feel obliged to bow.

So when Lava farts or Lava pees on somebody's boot or Lava shreds
someone's only pair of underwear and Anne bends down and scoops
him up and tells him how brave he is, we all kind of feel okay thinking
so too.

One of the things that I think worries Anne the most is that she's
not telling her radio audience the real story about us. She complains
about it a lot. How can you explain how lethal, how faulty, how funda-
mentally lousy the whole situation is here in general?

" . . . chaotic . . . ," she reports, " . . . moments of sheer terror . . . "

She tries, but she always feels she misses the mark by a few inches.

I understand better than anyone that there are no words to adequately describe how the insurgents seem to communicate with one
another and coordinate their attacks through a series of underground
tunnels that run from mosque to mosque, and how, like some freak-
ish version of a video game, the snipers pop up out of nowhere—on
rooftops, in alleyways, from behind mosque walls—and you only stay
alive to play another round by shooting them immediately wherever
they pop out.

" . . . rarely saw insurgents up close, just outlines through their
night-vision scopes; the scurry of feet on rooftops above . . . "

Or how, without a sleeping bag, the cold night air magnifies the
convulsive jitters that plague you after a while, so when you wake up
one morning to find a Marine's poncho draped over you with no one
claiming responsibility, you think how at this moment, in this place, in
this real-time, hellish virtual video game of hide and go seek, a cash-
mere blanket holds nothing over a dirty Marine poncho.

She doesn't even bother with that one.

We sit up at night in the compound and talk by the glow of the light sticks used to avoid detection by insurgents. We talk a lot, Anne and me, and usually Lava snuffles around us and plays cute, pretending not to listen, but he's taking it all in, I can tell, because every once in a while, when the conversation gets tough and I start, like, talking about something I normally don't and can't find the right way to describe what I've seen or what I've done or what somebody else did and just stop talking, Lava looks up at me and cocks his little head as if waiting—I swear—for the rest of it. So I shrug and finish the story.

Like, the light sticks glow on our faces while everything else around us is dark, so we're on the moon, right?—a million miles away from our gods, our rules, our lives, and I hear my voice plowing through every roadblock and checkpoint without halting, because there's nothing, no gods, no rules, no lives standing guard to stop it.

" . . . parents hate me being in the military, wanted me to be a doctor . . . "

" . . . the marriage didn't work out . . . "

" . . . sure, I want to be a dad someday . . . "

Anne listens and smokes and nods and smokes some more while we talk in the dim glow, and I never worry that she'll turn around and use anything I tell her in one of her radio stories. And I tell her some stuff.

" . . . the first guy I killed . . . "

" . . . found this baby in the rubble . . . "

" . . . his face just exploded . . . "

She seems more focused on the stories of the younger guys anyway, the twenty-year-old grunts just in from basic training who walk around acting tough, like this is no big thing, like they've done this all their lives even though FREAKED OUT blinks on and off across their foreheads in neon. I think she feels sorry for them. She never says that, but that's what a lot of her stories home are about in the end.

Like the story she did about the initial bombing of Fallujah, as they waited on the outskirts of the city for the invasion to begin, when she realized how different this assignment was from any she'd been through before. Unlike the initial offensive against Iraq, for example, when aloof bombings killed anonymous enemies in uniform, this assault turned defensive as soon as it began. The enemy wasn't a soldier hired to shoot back anymore; he was now a civilian who hated you so much he'd down his breakfast, walk out of the house, and then blow himself up in your face.

Most of the Marines in Bravo Company had been in Iraq only two weeks when they convoyed to Fallujah where the new enemy, in a white Suburban van, introduced himself by careening into their seven-ton ammunition-laden truck, taking eight of them with him to wherever young warriors go when they're burned alive.

A few days later Anne interviewed a Marine psychologist sent in to offer counseling, who said the surviving members of Bravo Company didn't feel the expected anger or guilt nearly as much as a sense of disgrace.

"They experienced horrible shame of being helpless," he told her. "Marines hate above everything to be helpless, passive. It's not the way they see themselves, and it makes it hard for them to get back the feeling of confidence."

Anne knew the feeling, but none of it compared with the sense of professional disability she felt in Fallujah. How could you possibly report to people thousands of miles away how perverse it seemed to toss kids a sense of their own mortality with the casualness of a softball?

"Most had yet to experience combat . . . ," she reported. "Soon they would know."

They weren't adults, most were old-ish teenagers, so for Anne, humping along after them was like trying to follow a pack of adolescent pit bulls previously chained up for too many days. Most had just left home—left rented video games, first cars, and part-time jobs—to defend, against all enemies foreign and domestic, the Constitution of the United States, even though many would be hard pressed to tell you what was actually in the thing.

Was that enough? Would people back home get it? She could just come out and say it—*They're too young to be dealing with this, folks. They aren't ready for this, folks. They only just learned to ride bikes, for God's sake, folks*—but she wondered if it would bother anyone for any meaningful period of time.

"They wanted more from life than what they had back home. They believed the Marines when they said, *You can be the best.*"

But she hoped she snared it when she interviewed one young grunt and asked him what his mission was here in Fallujah.

"Kill the enemy, man," he said into her microphone. "Kill the enemy, that's about it."

I don't let Lava sleep with me at first. I always scoot him off toward Anne or somebody else more willing to sleep with a snoring piglet who farts MREs all night.

Then one night Anne says to me, "He's so adorable. What's going to happen to him?"

I give the shrug. "Dunno."

Another night we're talking and she tells me she's scheduled to go back to the States in a few weeks. Lava bounces around on our sleeping bags.

"Good for you." I smile and roll Lava onto his back and scratch his belly until his back paws quiver.

"Then I'm coming back to report on the elections from Baghdad."

I nod and stare down at the puppy, who provides a convenient diversion from eye contact as I tell her that I'm scheduled to rotate out in April sometime. I feel guilty about it. About leaving. But I don't tell her.

"I imagine you're happy about that."

"Sure."

"So what's going to happen to Lava?"

I turn the puppy upright and nudge him away.

"Who knows?"

Lava rushes back, grabs one of my bootlaces, and tugs.

"He is so cute."

"Yep."

I push Lava away again. The puppy turns and faces me as he bends his front legs down and pushes his rear end into the air. He wags his tail and barks. Then he rushes the boots again.

"Cut it out."

So I shove him away, right? I suddenly don't want the little shit chewing on my boots anymore.

"What will you do when you get home?"

Lava regroups and charges.

"Not sure yet."

This time I really push him away, let him know what's what, and he loses his balance and his legs give out while he makes little squeaks of terror and rolls several times across the floor.

"Oh man."

I mean, I can't begin to explain how bad I felt about this. I mean, really bad. You know, I just shoved a little puppy across the floor. So I pull Lava back toward me and scratch the bridge of his nose. He looks up at me all tough and wags his tail like it's no big deal.

"Hey, sorry."

But I feel like shit and let him sleep on my poncho that night, and I think that's how Anne finds her story.

During the fighting, the battalion gained a new member, a tiny puppy they named Lava Dog. . . . Though filthy themselves, they've lovingly washed him down to get rid of the sand fleas.

He sleeps nestled in a Marine poncho.

NOVEMBER 2004: FALLUJAH

General Order 1-A is taken pretty seriously by the military. No pets allowed. That's because they've invested a lot of time and money into trashing your moral clarity, and they don't want anything like compassion messing things up. Your job is to shoot the enemy, period, and if anything close to compassion rears its ugly head, you better shoot that down, too, or you're in some deep, scary shit.

None of us talks about what will happen to Lava, because it means making decisions we don't want to make for reasons we're not being paid to consider in the first place. Frankly, it's easier to just go blow stuff up.

Most nights Lava sleeps outside on the roof of the compound with a group of the BLT 1/3 Marines, but once the weather turns colder, he comes inside at night. That's when he starts bugging me, hanging around looking wide eyed and cute, all paws and snuffles and innocence.

In reality, when he isn't asleep, he's anything but innocent. I personally saw the little monster destroy several maps, two pairs of boots, one cell phone, photographs of someone's kids, five pillows, and some grunt's only pair of socks.

One morning I wake up and find Lava sitting near my sleeping bag staring at me, with his left ear flapped forward and the remains of a toothpaste tube stuffed in his mouth.

"Morning," I say.

He replies with a minty belch and then barfs up standard-issue Colgate all over my sleeping bag.

In addition to forbidding pets, General Order 1-A also prohibits any conduct that is "prejudicial to the maintenance of good order and discipline of all forces," meaning that anything that diminishes morale or discipline is banned. This includes drinking alcohol in countries that don't allow it, entering religious sites without special orders, the theft or destruction of archaeological artifacts, and the taking of souvenirs. Anything that bargains with a Marine's discipline, anything that toys with his ability to shoot and shoot well has to be censored.

I know what's what in that department. During World War II only 15 percent of the troops actually fired at their enemies in battle because most of them didn't want to kill anyone. The problem is that sticky moral compass that discourages human beings from killing other human beings, so over the years the smart guys devised ways to overcome any and all ethical thorns, because not wanting to kill the enemy in combat posed, well, problems. Effective warriors, they decided, had to be trained without regard to moral repercussions.

So after World War II Marines were trained to act immediately and reflexively rather than to stop and think about it first. Through the use of Pavlovian conditioning, we were taught to kill on command. Instead of shooting at the old-time bull's-eye targets, we were taught to shoot at human silhouette–shaped targets that popped up out of nowhere, and the repeated use of pop-up marksmanship ranges combined with fire commands, battle drills, and continued orders to "Shoot!" from authority figures not only controlled our reactions but anesthetized them as well. By the time the Vietnam War rolled around, 90 percent of American troops fired at the adversary. Now killing was as reflexive as answering a phone when it rang, and nothing was supposed to interfere with progress. Nothing.

Another morning I wake to see Lava's entire front end stuffed into one of my boots with his butt and back legs draped out over the side. He's not moving, right? So I think he's dead.

"Oh shit."

Probably from the MREs.

"Oh no. Oh shit."

Lava's body doesn't move at first, but when he hears my voice, his tail starts waving like a wind-kissed flag, and I decide that from now on, he's not eating any more noodles, biscuits, or beans in butter sauce. No more M&Ms. No more toothpaste. Only meat. That's what real dogs eat, meat.

Out on the streets one day during that first week, I discover the Iraqi soldiers with looted candy bars and cigarettes in their pockets, and because we're supposed to train them to be just like us—moral except for the killing stuff—and because looting breaks all the rules, I decide to give them a little additional training.

I pace the ground six inches in front of them with an unopened candy bar clenched in my fist. They wince and lean back.

"Well, excuuuuse me, am I invading your personal space?" I say through the interpreter, letting concern drip like battery acid from every word, because, you know, I have to make an impression here.

The three soldiers try not to move, but their eyes swivel back and forth between me and the interpreter, who is the closest thing they can trace back to the good old days when everyone spoke Arabic and no one yelled at them for eating a little candy.

"Well, I have some information for you pathetic excuses for soldiers." I push my face into exhale range of one of the men and deliver a jab to his chest with each word.

"You have no personal space."

I step back and stare at the unopened candy bar in my hand as if it just fell from a spaceship.

"What is this?"

The three soldiers eye the interpreter.

"And what are these?"

I march toward them, yank packs of cigarettes and more candy bars from their vests, and throw them on the ground with as much passion as I can muster. The soldiers look at the interpreter, down at the loot, and back at the interpreter again.

"Did you *pay* for this stuff?"

The three nod in unison.

"Which *one* of you paid for it?"

The three point to one another simultaneously.

They just don't get it. These guys are supposed to take over their country's security, and here they are acting like the Three Stooges. Disobeying orders threatens survival out here, and while just about everything threatens survival out here including walking, talking, and pissing in the wrong place, lack of discipline is up near the top of the list of sure killers, along with panic, loss of focus, and too much compassion.

"You are less than men for stealing."

I pace up and down in front of the soldiers.

"You humiliate yourselves and the Iraqi forces."

I spit at their feet.

"You are no good as soldiers and I will abandon you here in Fallujah, where you will be beheaded by insurgents."

I rip off my helmet.

"You are nothing but shit."

The interpreter stops and looks at me.

"Go on, translate *shit*. It's not *that* hard."

I throw my helmet on the ground.

"Repeat after me. *I do not steal.*"

The soldiers mumble their response to the interpreter.

"In English. I do not steal."

"In inglezee. I do not sti-il."

"I do not lie."

"I do not lie."

"I am a moron and I worship the ground you walk on sir."

Discipline overrides everything between heaven and earth here, including hunger, exhaustion, fear, homesickness, empathy, guilt, hangovers, snipers, regret, hatred, intestinal blockage, thoughts of suicide, calls to prayer, and letters from home.

"And from this time forth, thy righteous ordinance of discipline will be my guide and I will forgo sex, kill my firstborn, chew with my mouth closed, take no prisoners, do unto others, brush in back, worship my gun, place I before E except after C, leave no Marine behind, oo-rah, praise the Lord, hail Caesar full of grace, Santa Claus lives, Allah is great, yes sir, always and forever and ever and ever, amen."

Poor schmucks. They start praying. They don't even hear me anymore because they're whispering, "Allah, Allah" and trying not to cry, only I see they aren't looking at me anymore but at something behind my back.

I glance across the street and at first only see the usual horizon of a city blown to smithereens. Then I see something moving, and I stiffen and position my gun.

"Allah, Allah."

It takes me a second to focus.

I squint and grip the gun, because my palms start sweating, and my fingers start shaking, and the soldiers keep moaning, and I scream, "Shut the *fuck* up," because I can't hold the rifle steady anymore, because what I see is a pack of dogs . . . "Allah, Allah" . . . feeding on meat, "Oh God," and I think I'm going to puke.

Another morning I wake up thinking someone short-sheeted my sleeping bag because I can't push my feet to the end. It's Lava, who managed to crawl in during the middle of the night and curl up at the bottom in a ball.

"Oh man. This has got to stop."

He snores away, and I don't want to disturb him because it's still too early to get up, so as I lie there enjoying the warmth of his breath on my feet, General Order 1-A starts tangoing around in my head.

Prohibited activities for service members under General Order 1-A include adopting as pets or mascots, caring for or feeding any type of domestic or wild animals. While most of the Marines sleeping around me would admit that it feels good to finally do what they've been trained to do, they don't feel so good about it feeling so good. All the rules and training prove valuable out here, but what the hell do you do with yourself later?

I know what will happen to them later. They won't sleep much, they'll experience panic attacks, they'll avoid their neighbors, they'll drink, they'll snort, they'll shoot, they'll binge on emotional numbness, and that's only if they find some kind of counseling that talks them out of feeling so different from everybody else even though they are different from everybody else.

I tried. I tried breaking the rules once by leaving the fold, when the adrenaline rushes of carrier-arrested landings, airborne operations, and rappelling from helicopters faded and left me itching from the inside out. All the training was fine, all the discipline was great, but what did I do with myself at the end of the day?

When I left active duty, I joined the civilian world working counter-narcotics with the US Attorney's office in San Diego, then wandered into an Internet startup in Newport Beach as an officer of the company, and then into Salomon Smith Barney as a financial consultant.

But it never felt normal. It was like *There has to be more than this.* What's the point? What are the objectives? What in the hell are the *rules?*

Then the attacks on 9/11 kickboxed being normal to a pulp, and I returned to active duty as soon as I could. I deployed with the 11th Marine Expeditionary Unit (Special Operations Capable) to Kuwait and Jordan. Then I deployed to Operation Iraqi Freedom in February 2003 and, by August, found myself assigned as the Special Forces liaison officer for the First Marine Expeditionary Force in Qatar. My third deployment in two years swept me into Camp Fallujah, where I trained the Iraqi Special Forces who are now out here on the streets of this godforsaken ghost town watching stray dogs eat their dead countrymen.

But it feels normal. Despite the bombs and the insurgents and the rubble, it feels like I belong here. And how screwed up is that?

I reach down into the sleeping bag and pull Lava up under my chin. He snorts and snuffles around, and I start scratching his ears.

"What's going to happen to you once we leave, little guy?"

The puppy opens one eye and stares up at me, and I start thinking the stuff we're not supposed to think—about how we're either going to have to shoot him or abandon him on the streets here in Fallujah where for dogs, eating human flesh is normal.

Lava's eyes lower to half-mast as his head drops slowly backward. I blow lightly on his face, because I don't want to be awake alone. His eyes pop open. He looks annoyed.

"What, am I invading your personal space?"

He thumps his tail on my chest.

"Well, you are invading mine."

NOVEMBER 2004: FALLUJAH

After three weeks in Fallujah, I return to the main base with Lava on Thanksgiving Day in a Humvee—which, after serial bombardments, firefights, and crashes, looks more like a secondhand stock car than a High Mobility Multipurpose Wheeled Vehicle that costs slightly less to assemble than the average American mansion.

I have no idea what I'm going to do with Lava, but he loves the loud, rumbling trip, and as I drive and he perches on my lap and drools all over the window and *roos* at the thousands of Fallujah evacuees we pass by, I enter yet another excuse to the catalog of why I'm breaking military rules: I can't help it.

I don't remember exactly when the excuses started, but it was sometime between the afternoon I saw the dogs eating dead bodies and the time I found Lava rolled up in my sleeping bag. After that, the excuses flowed: because the Iraqi soldiers were failing, because I was tired, because so many children hadn't been evacuated by their parents when they'd been warned, because I was out of cigars, because I couldn't sleep at night anymore unless some little fur ball was nestled up against me and breathing on my feet. By the time I'm scheduled to leave Fallujah, I have so many excuses scattered around, I just roll them all up into one big ball of hazy justification and plop Lava in the Humvee.

I call friends and family back in the States and tell them about Lava and ask for help. I call on a cell phone, so I think at first that the silences on the other end are the usual international lag, but I realize, as the silences stretch out, that my friends are trying to place the word *puppy* within the context of words they have concerning me.

See, they're all scared that if I don't get killed, I'll lose my mind in Iraq and end up eating raw meat, collecting weapons, and sending anonymous scary letters to people I don't know. So when I tell them I have a puppy and then there's this long silence, I can sense them connecting the dots between who I was when I left and who they're terrified I'll be when I get back.

Like, when I call one of my best buddies back in San Diego, Eric Luna, and ask him if he knows how to get a dog out of Iraq, I hear nothing for a long time but some static.

"Hey, Easy E, you still there?"

"Yeah, man, I'm here. What did you just say?"

Talking between Iraq and California is expensive and often disrupted, so you have to say everything as quickly as you can. It's an art, and fashioning my explanation into an understandable form that begins with stolen candy and ends with stray dogs eating dead bodies only fuels Eric's worst fears.

"What?" he keeps saying, like he can't hear me.

"RPGs . . . MREs . . . M&Ms . . . "

"What?"

" . . . bloated bodies . . . bootlaces . . . satellite wires . . . psychological operations . . . we're not normal . . . "

"What?"

" . . . and, see, there are these dangerous portable toilets . . . "

"What?"

"Pup-py. I have this pup-py. Can you help me figure a way to help me get him out of the country?"

Eric collects his wits and decides that in order to avoid future repercussions, the best thing to do is to agree.

"Sure, man. Yeah, anything you want."

The trip between the city and camp is only about twelve miles, but it's a pretty tricky stretch, and targeting a military convoy is easier than picking lice off a bald dog.

Contrary to sensible belief, the twenty thousand Humvees they have us driving around Iraq are not all armored vehicles. While their characteristics look cool on paper—weight: 5,200 pounds; engine: V8, 6.2-liter displacement, fuel-injected diesel, liquid-cooled, compression ignition; horsepower: 150 at 3,600 rpm—without armor, they are just big tin cans. We dress them up ourselves with sandbags, metal, and plywood, but that only weighs down the suspension and drivetrain components and creates more shrapnel when we're hit with an RPG or by a roadside bomb.

As a result, convoys make great targets, and in just one easy attack the insurgents can disrupt supply runs, mangle equipment, and butcher troops all at the same time. No suicide required. In fact, they're getting so good at setting off bombs from far away—igniting them with garage door openers, remote controls for toy cars, and beepers requiring only a cell phone call to set them off—using suicide bombers has almost become yesterday's fashion.

The enemy dangles soda cans from trees and packs explosives into roadkill. They hide bombs in girders, vegetated highway dividers, guardrails, trash cans, and manholes. They bury bombs in underground tunnels. They drop bombs from bridges. The convoy drivers keep a specific distance between their vehicles, usually fifty to a hundred meters depending on the dust factor, so the entire herd won't be taken down at once by a land mine.

When the convoy halts for equipment inspection or refueling, every driver stays in his vehicle with the motor running while every other eye scans the horizon 360 degrees and back again. Sometimes one of us will venture out to take a leak, but peeing on the side of the road in the middle of the Sunni Triangle isn't very safe; your chances of being hit are about as high as those for the fat boy in dodgeball.

If you *are* hit while peeing, the following advice is given in our *Lessons Learned* handbook: "RETURN FIRE—Extremely Effective; Continue to move; Do Not Stop!! They want you to do this; Do not be afraid to shoot; . . . anyone not stopping enemy activity is enabling the activity—This makes return fire morally right."

Usually before a convoy moves out, we gather at a staging site where the commander logs us in; the vehicles are inspected; personal items including clothes, food, and water are loaded; and heavy machine guns, grenade launchers, and other weapons are mounted, dusted, lubed, and readied to fire. The commander usually briefs us about new intelligence, the convoy route, radio call signs, and road safety precautions, and follows with immediate action drills if the convoy gets hammered anyway. In our case we left the danger of Fallujah for the danger of the road by just piling things into the Humvees as fast as we could and exchanging good luck salutes with the commander.

So we're driving along to the camp on a tricky road past all these Fallujah evacuees who now live in US-erected tents out in the cold and are pissed off about it. Like, they hate our guts.

The four of us in the Humvee make jokes about the old men in dresses and the fat women behind veils and egg on Lava when he barks.

"*Kill*," we say and fall out laughing, because we think it's so damned funny. "Kill, Lava, *kill*." We're nervous. It helps pass the time.

At first, as the convoy rolls past and the evacuees see this little puppy barking wildly at them through the Humvee's window, I expect them to give us the finger and shout nasty predictions about what will happen to us after we die. I expect any second to see one of the old guys pull a machine gun out of his robe and blast away as he's smiling. I expect burning effigies and hordes of shouting clerics with fists high in the air.

It's all a game really. Monopoly with bombs. Capture the flag with grenades. See, there's this line that's drawn that's just meant to be crossed, and you stand on one side with your goods and they stand on the other with their goods, and the teams lob insults back and forth— "My stuff's better than yours!" "No, my stuff's better than yours!" "Well, I know the referee!" "Oh, yeah? I'm *related* to the referee"— until someone finally steps over the line and play officially begins.

I guess the ref is the only one who really knows who crossed first and under what duress, but at this point everyone's so balled up in the name calling—"Insurgents . . . murderers . . . terrorists . . . fanatics"; "Imperialists . . . infidels . . . invaders"—it doesn't matter anymore who did what or when.

Imagine the old ref up there in the North Pole being all nonpartisan and looking down on this. It's embarrassing. No wonder he doesn't show his face anymore.

And here we are driving by in our convoy past these people, and I can't stop thinking about the dogs. After a couple of days walking around the bodies in Fallujah, you got good at telling which ones the dogs had gotten to—the skin was shredded off the fattiest parts of their bodies, mostly the stomachs, butt cheeks, and soles of the feet— and that, my friend, is some gut-wrenching shit.

But they just stare at us. No rocks. No mutilated American flags. No calls to jihad with weapons raised in the air. Just stares, like they don't have energy to do anything else, mile after mile of them. After a while I start feeling like I've pulled off a brilliant practical joke that went too far and Lava's *rooing* starts getting to me.

"Come on, buddy, cut it out."

But he tears from one window to the other, and one of the other guys tells him to stop, and these faces stare at us through the dirty glass, but it's not funny anymore, and Lava just keeps *roo-roo-rooooing*, mile after mile, face after face, until I think my head is about to explode, *"Knock that shit off,"* and I slam on the brakes.

Lava stares at me. The guys stare at me. The faces, the people outside, stare at me. And they've got that look, all of them, that look that says *Caught your cool off guard, did we?* so I shrug it off, you know, recompose and grin and peel off real fast, leaving the Iraqis in a plume of dust and dirt.

Except as the mood in the Humvee gets back to normal, I can still feel Lava staring at me.

NOVEMBER 2004: CAMP FALLUJAH

As we pull through the gates of Camp Fallujah, the holiday scenery provides what you'd expect from an abandoned Iraqi military installation and former Iranian terrorist training camp taken over by US forces located midway between Baghdad and Fallujah, about eight thousand miles away from Plymouth Rock. Congested landing pads. Humvee graveyards. Rows of portable toilets making some civilian contractor lots and lots of money.

What I don't expect is all the activity at the Mortuary Affairs building with DO NOT ENTER posted at its doors. That's something new. It makes me think of Anne Garrels's stories. I hope she got out of the country okay.

At least the weather is cool, and after stuffing Lava in my backpack and sneaking him into my room in the officers' building, I turn on the heater to keep him warm.

"You okay in here, little guy?"

Lava looks up at me and cocks his head. As I stare down at this cute but fairly drastic breach of military law, I wonder if I've done the right thing. Lava will be vulnerable here at the camp, which under regulations can't harbor any dogs other than the military's working canines. As it is, stray dogs and cats swarm the camp looking for food, and rumor has it that they're being drowned in a nearby pond.

The officers' building is the *worst* place on base to hide a bouncing ball with vocal chords, but the need to decompress from the last three weeks drains me of incentive to do anything but sleep, so I pull Lava up on the cot next to me, where neither of us moves for the next nine hours.

I dream though. Only I dream reality, can't get away from it, even in sleep.

I'm patrolling one of the main streets of Fallujah in front of a mosque and the Iraqi soldiers are waving their guns around and I'm yelling at them to safety their weapons and Tim O'Brien is telling me to take it easy on them, because they don't understand English.

And I turn on Tim and say, "Well, they *better* learn fast," and he starts grinning and saying something, only suddenly his head isn't there anymore, it's on the ground, and grenades explode around us, and I grab up his head and try to jam it back onto the neck of his body, try to make it work again so I can hear what he has to say, only it's not sticking, so I try connecting the tendons from his neck to the tendons in his head only they're all tangled up and sticky and I can't put two and two together, and the grenades keep exploding, and then the eyes in the head in my hands start swiveling back and forth and the mouth starts spewing blood, but it's grinning, it's working, it's spewing and grinning and working and saying, "It's only a flesh wound, man. It's only a flesh wound."

In the morning the bed is soaked, and Lava shivers under the covers drenched in his own pee. It's the first time this has happened since he started sleeping in my bag in Fallujah.

"Humiliated?"

He whimpers.

"Nightmares?"

Lava pushes his nose and then most of his body under the pillow. I hum the Marine anthem to him. His tail starts patting the bed.

"Me too."

I decide I'll risk talking to the dog handlers at the other end of the base where they actually grow green grass for the dogs to walk on. They treat the military working dogs well.

As in Delta Force or the Navy SEALs, the working dogs make up an elite unit that outspecializes any weaponry or high-tech mapping systems the US armed forces possess. Several hundred thousand years of evolution make their noses stronger, their teeth sharper, and their legs faster than any human being alive. That's what the handlers tell me anyway.

Most are Belgian Malinois and German shepherds, and like the rest of us, each possesses his own military service record book and each learns to attack on command without thinking first. Before they ever arrive in Iraq, the trainers tell me that the working dogs attend boot camp at Lackland Air Force Base, where the Department of Defense maintains a high-tech veterinary hospital that includes specialists in pathology, internal medicine, surgery, radiology, and epidemiology who can perform fundus photography, endoscopy, arthroscopy, laser surgery, electrodiagnostics, hip replacements, fluoroscopy, and echo-cardiography in state-of-the-art clinical laboratories, dental suites, surgical areas, radiology areas, intensive care units, and anesthetic recovery rooms.

Boot camp for the working dogs consists of explosives detection and patrol, where they drill, they march, and they pace like any human recruit. The dogs learn the four classics—*sit*, *down*, *heel*, and *stay*—but the command *get him* is added to the syllabus as well. They learn to obey the commands in upwinds, downwinds, and crosswinds in addition to a variety of movements including march, rear march, column left, and column right.

Because of the large number of receptors in their noses and the large olfactory parts of their brains, the working dogs enhance the Marines's ability to detect faint odors and intruders by about a thousand times, with about 95 percent accuracy. A well-trained military dog can detect dynamite, detonator cords, sodium chloride, potassium chloride, time fuses, and smokeless powder.

When the dogs finish initial training, they're issued bulletproof camouflage vests that weigh seven pounds and cost about a thousand dollars each. The vests contain compartments for cold packs to prevent heatstroke and attachments that enable the dogs to be dropped by parachute or hauled up by rope.

Once equipped, the dog is paired with a handler. At Camp Fallujah, the two live and work together—they're rarely apart—and the dog and handler become so dedicated to each other that after two years, the dog is rotated out to keep the pair from becoming too attached. They trust each other to perfection. They know each other's breathing patterns. The bond between them is so strong that if a handler searches a suspect, and the suspect tries to hurt the handler, the dog attacks immediately without any command whatsoever. The dog then bites and holds the suspect down until he hears the command *out*, which means that if the handler is killed or knocked unconscious first, the dog will literally die holding the suspect down as he waits to receive orders to let go.

It therefore comes as no surprise to me when the dog handlers at Camp Fallujah smile and shake their heads when I ask if Lava can hide out in one of the kennels.

"Can't help you, sir . . . "

I'm equally unsurprised when they tell me the closest military veterinarian who can give Lava vaccinations works at a base in Baghdad— some forty treacherous miles away—and because of General Order 1-A, they doubt he'll be able to help.

They wish me luck, though, and give me what I suspect is some very expensive dog food.

Back at the officers' building, I immediately e-mail the military veterinarian in Baghdad. I know it's a risk, but I hope the veterinarian is as understanding as the handlers here at camp.

"I found this puppy in Fallujah . . . "

Then I sit back and think about what the dog handlers told me when I asked what happens to the dogs when their tour of duty is over.

As with the Marines, it turns out, the military working dogs' elite status hurts them in the end. They aren't like other dogs, and because the canine warriors can't simply be debriefed, they have nowhere to go. If a military dog becomes physically unable to perform his tasks in the field—usually when he's about ten years old—a veterinarian deems him as either "nondeployable" or "stateside deployment only" and his military records are sent to Lackland to a full medical review board.

If a nondeployable dog is deemed "adoptable," meaning he probably won't storm local playgrounds and attack small children unprovoked, and if the potential adopter understands the possible risks, meaning he or she understands that small children might provoke the dog who might storm the playground and attack them, then the adopter signs an agreement that absolves the Department of Defense of any liability for damage or injury the dog might cause.

Most of them, though, are deemed nonadoptable. These are the dogs whose entire lives centered on carrying out orders to perfection, who were so devoted to the military that they obeyed to the death. These were the most faithful, dependable, patriotic dogs of the lot, so they're handed "final disposition" papers and euthanized.

I stare at the computer screen in front of me and try hard not to make comparisons. Nonadoptable. Maladjusted. Apt to attack small children on playgrounds. I bleed allegiance to the flag.

I follow my e-mail to the military veterinarian with an SOS to everyone but the gatekeepers of the Emerald City.

"I found this puppy in Fallujah . . . "

Later that day I receive word that I'm supposed to report to the Joint Task Force in Balad to replace a lieutenant colonel, Ignatius "Buck" Liberto, who's going on leave for six weeks. I know the guy, right? So I e-mail him in Balad and ask if he'll take Lava home with him when he leaves.

No problem from Buck's end, but he's flying out on a military plane, and in order to transport a puppy he'll need all of Lava's vaccination papers and approval from brass. I'm thinking that's no big deal until I get the response from the military veterinarian in Baghdad.

He respectfully reiterates General Order 1-A that prevents the Marines from keeping pets, and he further points out that diseases such as leishmania, hydatid disease, and rabies are common among stray dogs in Iraq.

"My apparent lack of concern for this puppy isn't due to not caring. I'm simply following orders, regulations, and my desire to protect the public health of our soldiers," the veterinarian writes.

"What I'm trying to make clear, sir, is that nothing we can do for you is going to assist you in getting the dog home."

Well, shit.

DECEMBER 2004: CAMP FALLUJAH

Dust swirls in the Humvee's headlights as it grumbles in low gear toward the far end of the base. Concrete bunkers, concertina wire, tents, and sandbags appear and disappear before me like quick thoughts, and I notice how much sharper the edges of things seem than when muted by all-out sun. Then again, everything seems weird when you can't sleep in the middle of the night.

It's weird that I'm driving across base. It's weird that it gets so cold in Iraq and that I'm crossing thin-skinned ice puddles under a black winter sky tattooed with stars. It's weird that the prefab metal buildings erected by the Iraqi Republican Guard to train terrorists are now surrounded by US-stuffed sandbags to keep them out. It's weird that the white beam of the headlight seems to stab with violence at whatever I'm passing—the chow hall, a big plastic tub used for Marines who decide to get baptized, a Humvee with a ram's skull roped to its front, the "Morale, Welfare and Recreation" building filled with PlayStation 2 consoles that the psychologists recommend we use to unwind. It's weird that there's war. It's weird that I'm part of it.

Where am I driving? To the Lava Dogs's building.

Why am I driving to the Lava Dogs's building? Because I can't sleep.

Why can't I sleep? Because Lava is in the Lava Dogs's building.

Now that they're back on base, it only seems natural that Lava should visit his uncles who conveniently live as far away from the officers' building as they can.

Only I can't sleep.

I start to nod off, but suddenly, like an alarm's going off, I think, *I've got to leave for Balad in two days*, followed by *Figure it out, Kopelman*, followed by *But how* . . . , followed by *Just figure the thing out*, followed by *Lava's going to get shot*.

See, orders just came down and the Department of Defense hired contractors to kill all nonmilitary dogs found on American bases in Iraq. Seems word got out about the stray dogs eating dead bodies, and while it's perfectly okay for us to make the bodies dead in the first place, it's not quite cool to have dogs walking around eating them. There's some fine line there I guess we're not supposed to notice. Maybe it has to do with cooties.

Anyway, it also turns out that I'm not the only loon who wants to get a dog out of Iraq. There are actually a lot of guys writing home looking for help. I mean, there were all these stories online about it, which I found while Googling "Iraq dogs out" and "Iraq puppy out" and that sort of thing. I was at a complete loss until I found the story about an Army sergeant who said that his unit tried to get their dog back to the United States—but the "dog killers," he said, got her first. They hid her and fed her and then found someone going back to the States who would take her, but then at the last minute, as she was actually in the flight line ready to go and all the guys were saying goodbye, some jerk following orders comes up, yanks her away, and shoots her.

That's the kind of thing that makes you pause and wonder, What the *fuck*?

So I start Googling anything I can think of—puppy passport, help, help puppy, helpless puppy needs passport, help Marine help helpless puppy—I'm feeling kind of frantic about the whole thing and getting nowhere at the speed of light.

As I'm trying to go to sleep that first night without Lava, all this crap is shooting through my head with the velocity of bullets fired in rapid succession. GO-1A. Vaccinations. Bodies. Rules. Regulations. Reasons. Will it hurt? Then as things get weirder and weirder like they do in the middle of the night, the unauthorized thoughts start rolling in to the tune of "When Johnny Comes Marching Home Again," oo-*rah*, oo-*rah*. So I get up, start the Humvee, and drive across base to the Lava Dogs's building seeing all these weird things and thinking all these weird thoughts like how in the *hell* could someone shoot a dog like that? Orders? *Orders?* Since when do Marines follow orders?

When I get there, it's all dark and everyone's zonked out and I can't see Lava anywhere.

"Hey, little guy," I whisper, expecting him to leap into my arms with tail-pounding joy.

Instead I hear this tiny growl, Lava's warning that he's about to kick my ass, and then see this wienie shadow rush toward me with tail erect and fur on end screaming *roo-roo-roo-roooooo.*

Bodies shoot up on every cot.

"Hey, hey, hey, it's me . . . "

"Who the *hell* is me?" someone grumbles as I hear the click of several rifles being readied for some action.

I bend down and pick Lava up. "Shh, shh. It's me. Just me."

The bodies plop back down on their cots. Several pound pillows back into place; several Marines use my name—and God's—in vain.

"Hey, hey, calm down," I tell Lava, who's quivering with delight over what he's done and with what he's found. I sit there for a while in the dark scratching his little ears until he finally calms down and curls up asleep in my lap.

Am I insane?

I am a lieutenant colonel in the United States Marine Corps. I am an officer in a brotherhood that always goes in first, and that pretty much sums it up right there. We're brave to the point of insanity, so being a Marine takes a certain kind of mindset to begin with.

Which means you don't always follow orders.

The common belief is that you go in a boy and come out a man, like they have this magical ability to change who you *are*, but the truth of the matter is, we were insane going in and insane coming out, only now we sing this anthem and know cool martial arts.

Insane isn't the right word exactly. None of us really believes Marines guard the streets of heaven, but how sane is it to *want* to go in first? I can sit aside from this and in a cool, calculated, scientific manner look at it for what it is: not insanity, but a primitive gene that requires some of us to be the fittest and the bravest and the best-est there is, and then the public relations brass throws in the word *proudest* so we don't feel like cavemen on caffeine.

It's not because we didn't belong or didn't like team sports, and it's not because we couldn't afford college or were manipulated by recruiters or dumped by some chick and then had to prove a point. Those guys joined the Army. We didn't have rotten childhoods, we didn't hate math, we didn't bully skinny kids on the playground, and we didn't start fires in the garage.

And it's not like we joined up without thinking about it, or like once we got in they didn't give us time to think about it. Believe me, sleep deprivation, food rationing, and situps make you think a whole hell of a lot about it. We weren't coerced. We weren't brainwashed. Our souls weren't plundered.

We just can't help it.

We aren't cut out for anything else. We were Marines going in and Marines coming out. We don't *want* to take orders.

And you want to know something? I don't care anymore. I used to, when I first joined up. I worried about my parents' objections, my college buddies' sneers, being called a "jarhead" for the rest of my adult life. But hell if I could help it. The minute I signed on the dotted line, I had this sort of out-of-body party that hasn't been matched since.

Oo-rah.

Listening to these guys snore around me, I really like what I am—a Marine. I like being strong. I like being brave. I like going in first. I *want* to go in first, and I'll be damned if I'm going to let anyone shoot my puppy.

10

MARINE SCOUT SNIPERS

LENA SISCO

HAITI: 1993

In April 1993 Mike attended the ten-week 2nd Marine Division Scout Sniper School at Marine Corps Base Camp Lejeune, North Carolina, that trained him to become a Marine Scout Sniper, which awarded him the MOS (Military Occupational Specialty) of "8541." Camp Lejeune is one of the Marine Corps training bases and is called the "home of expeditionary forces in readiness." He learned a wide variety of skills to include shooting stationary and moving targets out to one thousand yards, stalking, mission planning, land navigation, patrolling, sketching, communications, use of supporting arms, and reporting. After Mike's training, tensions on the Caribbean island of Haiti had escalated when the democratically elected Haitian president, Jean-Bertrand Aristide, was overthrown by a faction of Haiti's military regime. Upon hearing that Haiti's military regime had forcibly occupied the government and overthrown Aristide, US forces began operational planning for restoring the government to its people. Armed forces assembled and staged in southern Florida; Puerto Rico; Hunter Army Airfield in Savannah, Georgia; and in Guantanamo Bay, Cuba, preparing to invade Haiti. By October 1993, a rifle company, Mike and his sniper platoon, part of Headquarters and Service Company (part of the 2/8 Battalion), and some headquarters staff of the 2/8 Battalion were issued orders to deploy off the coast of Haiti in support of Operation Provide Democracy. This was different from Operation Uphold Democracy, but it occurred at the same time. The distinction between the two was that the entire battalion did not deploy for Provide Democracy, just the smaller element Mike was in, which was sent to assist with the evacuation of US personnel if it came to that. Mike's mission was to provide security to US forces while they set up defenses on a pier at the Port-au-Prince port facility, which was designated as the access pier for US ships coming to support the operation.

Anyone who has been trained in or involved in real-world operational planning knows that typically the mission is defined first, and then plans to accomplish the mission are designed. These operational plans (OPLANs), also called courses of action (COAs), usually come in threes, and the best of the three COAs is selected for the mission. The crises in Haiti resulted in three COAs/OPLANs. The first dealt with a total force invasion from the land and sea if the United States was not allowed to enter Haiti with permission. The second dealt with a permissive entry still with large numbers of troops who were combat ready. The third fell somewhere in between the first two while still maintaining offensive capabilities. The United States simultaneously strategized for two of the OPLANs in order to set foot in Haiti to help restore the regime. One of the plans, Operation Uphold Democracy, would take effect if the United States was allowed to enter Haiti, and the other plan, Operation Restore Democracy, would take effect if the United States had to enter Haiti forcibly. Talks and negotiations supervened. The military regime, although saying they would relinquish authority back to Aristide, did not, and they continued to rule over Haiti's deteriorating economy. Living conditions were becoming so oppressive in Haiti that thousands of impoverished Haitians were fleeing the country and attempting to illegally enter the United States. The United States had two objectives back then: get Aristide back in power and reduce the flow of illegal immigrants into the United States.

Mike was set to assume the position of platoon sergeant for this mission because the Marine who was the actual platoon sergeant had broken his foot and couldn't deploy. A few days prior to their scheduled departure from CONUS (continental United States), Mike's platoon sergeant (we'll call him Staff Sergeant F) asked him if he would consider leading a sniper team instead of deploying in place of him as a platoon sergeant. At the time Mike was serving as the chief scout, which is the senior school-trained sniper in the platoon. (As the chief scout, he would automatically assume the role of platoon sergeant if the actual platoon sergeant was unavailable anyway.) Mike was prepared to assume that role especially because he had just deployed to Mountain Warfare Training Center in Bridgeport, California, as a platoon sergeant during training and workups (military slang for a period of training and preparations before deployment). He had become tightly knit with the platoon members and was eager to serve in a leadership role. Taking on the responsibilities of this position for a deployment would be a great experience, and even though it would also be a great bullet on his FITREP (fitness report), he didn't care about that; it was all about taking care of the Marines.

Not having made his decision yet while still at Camp Lejeune prior to deployment, Staff Sergeant F had been hearing some rumblings from sniper team members about their apprehension and worry regarding their current team leader. They told Staff Sergeant F that their team leader didn't have the skills or experience to lead them in combat; he had no real-world experience leading a sniper team, and he had only been to sniper training school, with no experience in a four-man scout sniper team. They were about to embark on a real-world operation, and there was no room for mistakes. You can't start over like you can in training. Mike had already been deployed to northern Iraq in 1991 as part of a rifle company for Operation Provide Comfort and to Okinawa and Korea on a Unit Deployment Program (a system for assigning deployments for the Marine Corps) with the same sniper platoon conducting training and bilateral training with the Republic of Korea (ROK) Marines in 1992. As a result, Staff Sergeant F thought it would be a better fit to have Mike deploy as their team leader instead. If any Marine, soldier, sailor, or airman has trust and confidence issues with their leaders, this is a setup for disaster when down range (a term the military uses when deploying OCONUS [outside the continental United States]). Not only does it negatively affect morale, but while deployed in a hostile environment, whether in combat or not, you have enough stress from the high-tempo environment and trying to keep yourself and others safe that the last thing you need to worry about is having an inept leader responsible for your well-being; you need that extra sense of security that comes from trusting your leaders. Mike was faced with a choice: Should he lead an entire platoon on deployment, or should he give that sniper team a leader they could trust on their mission? Mike chose what his heart and mind told him to: he chose to lead the sniper team, and in early October 1993 he deployed off the coast of Haiti as a sniper team leader for Operation Provide Democracy. He flew from Camp Lejeune in North Carolina to Guantanamo Bay, Cuba, with the rifle company, some headquarters Marines, and the snipers. Once they landed in Guantanamo Bay, they boarded a ship that sailed to and was stationed off the coast of Haiti and were told to *stand by*. Mike was on the USS *Nassau* (LHA-4), a Tarawa-class amphibious assault ship, in the Caribbean Sea from October 18 until October 31, 1993. Every day he woke up on the ship wondering if the call would come that day. "I wasn't nervous; I was excited and focused. I had already done two six-month Landing Force 6th Fleet deployments on ships, so I was used to ship life at this point. On my first deployment we did contingency operations off the coast of Lebanon to rescue Colonel William R. Higgins and evacuate other Americans, and on my second deployment we went into northern Iraq for three months as part of a rifle company." Now Mike's sniper team conducted mission planning, rehearsals, and reconnaissance and surveillance (called R&S) both ashore at GITMO and while on board the ship as US planning ensued for invasion.

I remember back in 1997, as part of my workups with the BLT 3/6, I was on the USS GUAM conducting SOCEX (Special Operations Capable Exercise Certifying our MEU [Marine Expeditionary Unit] to be certified Special Operations Capable). We received the warning order (notification of a pending mission) for a training mission ashore in the United States. So we started mission planning to prepare to deploy as the reconnaissance and surveillance element. While doing this, we changed into civilian clothes since we would get off the helos at a civilian airport. A lot of the Marines kept saying, "You think you guys are so high speed because you are wearing civvies." We all just kept doing what we were doing. At one point I went to the hanger deck to inspect my team's gear. We had all of our individual gear and weapons (night-vision goggles, personal rifles, pistols, camouflage paint, MREs [which stands for "Meals Ready to Eat"], etc.), we had the team gear (radios, reporting formats, sketch kits, field expedient antenna kits), and then any mission-specific gear, which was all laid out uniformly on our poncho liners. All the common gear was laid out in the same spot on each member's poncho liner with team- and mission-specific gear in the same spot on each poncho liner as well. I would go through and verify that each item was present and worked. I made sure the radio frequencies were correct and that we could talk to other radios. After the inspection was complete we all would pack our equipment. While this was going on, the other Marines (not in our platoon) seemed to change their tune about us being all "high-speed." I heard one of them say, "Oh shit, that is professional. We don't do anything like that." Like I said earlier, we are professionals and we are professional at what we do.

His mission for Operation Provide Democracy was to take his team of two into Haiti with the rifle company (which was about 140 people), move to high ground, station at posts that overlooked the pier below, and provide security cover while the rest of the company conducted operations at the Port-au-Prince port. Just hours before the United States planned to conduct a full-on invasion of Haiti, President Clinton dispatched a team led by former President Jimmy Carter to try and negotiate with the de facto Haitian leadership. As a result, General Raoul Cedras, head of the Haitian armed forces, signed a United Nations Agreement on July 3, 1993, that called for the legitimate government to be restored. On October 31 Aristide resumed his role as president. Mike and his team were still on the USS *Nassau* waiting off the coast as this took place. "We had a date planned to go in, but instead we got all the ships, three I think, online and did a show of force by coming over the horizon and stopping a few miles off the coast in plain view." Mike's team never went ashore for two reasons: first, negotiations were successful, and second, the United States had just lost eighteen soldiers in Task Force Ranger in Mogadishu, Somalia. They were killed earlier in the month. The national command authority didn't want to have military casualties in two different theaters of operation in the same month. In the end, the United States only had to demonstrate a show of force with the ships coming from over the horizon into full view of the coast of Haiti. It sent the message, "We mean business." Operation Provide and Uphold Democracy had positive outcomes. The United States met both of the objectives: to restore the democratically elected Aristide to power and curtail illegal emigration, and US soldiers didn't have to go into combat—a win-win situation for all. Although Mike didn't see combat on this tour, his decision to lead the sniper team versus the platoon still proved to be the right choice. He had concern for the well-being of the Marines he was leading, and even though they never went ashore, he was there for them and with them if they did. A few days later he got word that he could leave the ship and return back to Camp Lejeune.

"I remember on the morning of the day I was scheduled to leave the ship to go back stateside to assume orders to FAST [Fleet Antiterrorism Security Team] Company, the navy personnel on board were pretty upset about something that happened the night before. It was Halloween, and apparently someone greased up in camo paint for mischief night and put their camo-painted hands all over the ladder rails in officer country. So when the officers touched the rails, they got the paint on their hands unknowingly and then touched their uniforms, getting camo paint all over them. The culprits were never caught." ("Officer country" on a ship refers to where the officer quarters are located; you know this by the blue tile on the floor. If you have never been on a navy ship, you have to use the handrails going up or down the ladders, or you'll end up on your back, or face first, on the deck below.)

While Operation Uphold Democracy planning continued, Mike was flown back to Camp Lejeune, where he would execute orders to FAST Company in Norfolk.

Throughout his training while in the 2/8 Scout Sniper Platoon, FAST, and the Battalion Landing Team 3/6 Scout Sniper Platoon, Mike was learning something else other than honing his shooting skills and good leadership qualities. He was learning that outside of being an expert shooter, critical skills such as observation, reporting, and the use of supporting arms (which would be calling in mortars, artillery, and close air support [CAS]) were just as important to the success of the overall unit mission as taking a single successful shot. As he was taught, what they do as a four-man team can have huge impacts and implications for the battalion and beyond. "With one wrong shot, killing an innocent individual can have implications far beyond the battlefield. There are political and social implications, as well as personal, and you have to live with it." Yes, he was a highly trained weapons handler and could engage targets with his M-40 out to one thousand yards, but as he states, "You have to remember, if I, or another team member, fired a direct fire weapon, that would clue the enemy that someone was in the area, and they would start searching for us. Maintaining concealment from the enemy to observe, report, and study their tactics, techniques, and procedures (what we call TTPs) is critical." He isn't concealed just to take out the enemy with his bullets; he's there to report on enemy locations and movements, to assess safe routes for friendly forces to use, and to stay undetected by the enemy, and you will see how this played a big part when he was deployed to Mogadishu, Somalia.

MOGADISHU: 1994

Mike was initially designated to go to FAST Company back stateside to help teach sniping skills, but when he got there, the company commander had other plans for him. The commander thought Mike would benefit both personally and professionally from gaining a better understanding of the FAST mission support role by assigning him to the next platoon deploying to Somalia. While deployed to Somalia, Mike would learn the unique capabilities of a FAST Platoon, which included things like close quarter battle (CQB), armed convoy escort operations, high-risk personnel security, and personal specialized armament. The role of the FAST is to detect, deter, and defend against threats, with a focus on antiterrorism. FAST Company platoons provide a limited-duration, expeditionary security force to protect vital naval and national assets. A common FAST Company mission is serving as security reinforcements at US embassies around the world. FAST maintains forward-deployed platoons at various naval commands around the globe and is also based in the United States, acting as alert forces capable of rapidly responding to unforeseen contingencies worldwide. Each FAST Company is equipped and trains with some of the most state-of-the-art weaponry. Unlike in an infantry platoon, in a fifty-man FAST Platoon every Marine is not only trained and qualified on a rifle and pistol, but they are also trained on the medium and heavy machine guns, MP-5, and shotguns. Only snipers and DMs (Designated Marksmen) are trained and equipped with designated marksman rifles (DMRs) and sniper rifles. The 0351s (MOS for Infantry Assaultman) are the only ones trained on SMAWs (shoulder-launched multipurpose assault weapons), and 0341s (MOS for Infantry Mortarman) are the only ones trained on M224 60mm mortars.

Although the FAST Platoon had all of this armament to bring with them to Somalia to help protect the US embassy and all its personnel, the ambassador said they couldn't bring SMAW rockets or 60mm mortars into the country because they were too offensive in nature. The ambassador wanted to maintain the appearance of a more defensive posture than offensive. Even though his FAST Platoon only wanted to bring in the mortars to fire illumination rounds to light up the area in front of embassy, they still weren't able to. Mike said this was a very typical scenario: "We would tell the ambassador, 'This is what we need to bring into the country to protect you,' and the response would be,

'You can't bring all that in here, and you can't set up there; it's my rose garden.' That's how it went."

In Somalia, FAST had been rotating platoons on four-month rotations to guard the US embassy compound in Mogadishu and the ambassador while he traveled outside the compound. Mike was excited to deploy to Somalia versus staying stateside training, and it turned out to be a great career move for him. Mike deployed as a rifle squad leader with the FAST Platoon. Aside from his sniping duties, he had also been trained in CQB (room clearing), combat fighting (engaging the enemy at close proximity, about thirty meters, with personal weapons), Enhanced Military Operations in urban terrain (combat conducted in urban areas such as towns and cities), and convoy operations (which involves planning, organizing, and conducting convoy movements). In addition, Mike attended basic Forward Observer (FO) courses in his last unit, where he learned how to call for fire with mortars and artillery as well as close air support. "Basically, you are the observer on the ground and call via radio to the mortar or artillery Fire Direction Center with coordinates to where you want them to have the mortar and artillery to land. Or in the case of CAS we acted as the terminal controller. Think 'JTAC' now, but this was before they termed it that. We would contact the pilot and give them coordinates to the enemy location and our location as well as any other friendly forces." JTAC stands for joint terminal attack controller and is the term used in the United States Armed Forces for a qualified military service member who, from a forward position, directs the action of combat aircraft engaged in close air support and other offensive air operations.

As part of the FAST Platoon's workup, US Air Force personnel trained Mike, Sergeant T, and Captain B how to call for AC-130 gunship fire missions. "A lot of the Marines I keep in touch with today are from that time. I get messages to this day about how much of an effect

I had on them back then; you'll see in a story I share at the end. It is very humbling!"

Prior to deploying to Somalia, during their CRE (which stands for Commanders Readiness Evaluation; it was an exercise where FAST would evaluate and certify the platoons who were ready for the deployment), Mike remembered a funny event that eased any concerns he had about who he would be deploying with. "It was the second night of the CRE, and we had been up for most of the last forty-eight hours. To try to get into our heads they would play music on a loop over and over again over a loudspeaker. The music they chose was Barney. I woke up about 0200 to Barney singing about peanut butter and jelly. I hear 'peanut, peanut butter and jelly' and as my eyes focus I see my Marines dancing around and waving an MRE peanut butter packet in one hand and a jelly packet in the other in sync to the music. I just started laughing. I knew this was a great bunch of guys and I would have no worries about us over in Somalia!"

The day came in mid-June 1994, when Captain B, Mike's platoon commander; Sergeant T, one of the other squad leaders in Mike's platoon; and Mike flew to Somalia as an advanced party (which means they arrived prior to the rest of the platoon) to the United States Liaison Office (USLO) in Mogadishu, Somalia.

I know that to this day I still smell things and flash back to Mogadishu and the "shit shacks" outside the walls along the Dead Cow Road and south of Market Street. Shortly after the whole platoon arrived in Mogadishu we had an in-brief by the CI [counterintelligence] Marines there assigned to the USLO on the Task Force Ranger raid [which was the Battle of Mogadishu on October 3–4, 1993, commonly referred to as "Black Hawk Down," when two US Black Hawks were shot down by rocket-propelled grenade launchers] and watched the footage from that day. We watched a forty-five-minute clip of the raid; the Black Hawk going down and how quickly they were swarmed by Somalis. It drove home to me how quickly the Somalis can come out of nowhere and close in on you.

A few days after his arrival in the country, Mike found himself on the roof of the "White House." The White House compound sheltered the FAST Company Platoon, which provided security for the embassy, and their command operations center. The State Department personnel stayed there, and all of the armored Suburbans and the armored HMMWVs (high-mobility multipurpose wheeled vehicles) they used for their armed convoy escorts were kept there. It was the old living quarters of the US ambassador. The ambassador and his staff had moved into trailers in the same compound. They had large, ten-foot-high walls built in front of the trailers for their protection.

It was midafternoon in June, and Mike and Sergeant M, the senior sniper from the platoon he was relieving, were on the rooftop of the White House compound going over the range card. "It was the rooftop post manned by a FAST Marine but wasn't the dedicated sniper post until later in my deployment." (A range card is a hand-drawn document that graphically represents the range distance to specific locations that is easily recognized by the shooter and observer and terrain in front of you. It lays out the assigned target reference points with the corresponding distance and azimuth to that location as well as the data you need to dial on the scope to hit a target at that location.) While baking in the Somali sun and inhaling the scent of burning trash, Mike glanced around the area that stretched out in front of him and noticed two tribal clans fighting on the dusty streets below outside the compound. "They usually started midmorning and continued through most of the day." He diverted his attention off the range card and down to the streets below. He could see there were about twenty to thirty clansmen, and they were armed with AK-47s, PRK machine guns, 12.7 and 14.5 machine guns, and rocket-propelled grenades (RPGs). Within minutes, the tribal clansmen started shooting at each other. They were approximately three hundred to four hundred yards away from where Mike was standing. It was a full-on firefight. Minutes later, Mike heard the crack of a bullet piercing the hot air as it passed overhead. "I looked at Sergeant M, he looked at me, and I asked him, 'Are they shooting at us?' Sergeant M just looked at me and shrugged his shoulders. We didn't know if they were shooting at us or if it was just spillover fire from the firefight below. So . . . we continued to go over the range card. We didn't call it in, because with just the one shot it could have been just a stray bullet or a ricochet. But then another round cracked closer this time. We looked at each other and shook our heads, saying, 'Yep, they're getting closer.' After another round passed even closer, we thought, 'Oh shit! They are getting a bead on us!'"

Sergeant M looked through the scope of his M-40, and Mike glassed the area with binoculars. They were as low as they could possibly get while still trying to observe the surrounding area and the clansmen, and then another bullet came whizzing by, but this one passed right between them. "I dove right and he dove left! Once I checked on Sergeant M, the other sniper, to make sure he was ok, I turned the crank of the TA-312 [field phone] and radioed to the COC (Combat Operations Center) saying that we were taking fire. Their reply was, 'It's just spillover fire.' My reply was they were full of shit! Sergeant M agreed with me. We never could identify the shooter. I had loud ringing and was deaf in my left ear the rest of the day; Sergeant M was deaf in his right ear. I have issues still today with my ear from that shot.

We observed the area but couldn't ID the shooter. We didn't take any more fire that day."

The FAST Platoon Mike was in was broken down into two sections; Sergeant T led one and Mike led the other. The platoon had two school-trained snipers, Corporal R and Mike; three Designated Marksmen (DMs); two lance corporals, L and P, and Corporal M (he was a DM and also a graduate of Amphibious Reconnaissance School [ARS]); and Corporal B, another ARS graduate. They all assumed and carried out the duties of their "normal" jobs: squad leader, fire team leader, and so on.

In Mogadishu we only did snipering when a situation arose. Conducting reconnaissance and surveillance is not as exciting and sexy as conducting the assault or being in the assault element. We didn't do this type of work at FAST; I did it when I was at 3/6 [Battalion Landing Team 3/6 Scout Sniper Platoon]. Usually we would insert two or three days before the assault to conduct preassault reconnaissance and close-in surveillance. We would observe the target building to confirm or deny information (for example, was the target individual or the device really there?). We would try to recognize any patterns, such as the location of guards and where they patrolled, we would try to identify areas that were commonly used and those that weren't, and we tried to identify any entrances and access points to the buildings, etc. But a lot of it was lying motionless hour after hour with nothing going on and having to be as still and as quiet as humanly possible. You start to hear your breathing, and it seems to get louder the quieter you are, and you think to yourself, can they hear it? We wait there until we link up with the assault force so we can guide them to the target, and cover them by precision rifle fire if needed. In essence, the assault force has what some would call the cool job of raiding the building, but they need our info and precision rifle fire to cover them.

Just a few days later another incident happened.

A few weeks after my platoon arrived we had a few days to turn over with 1st Platoon FAST; then they departed, and we, 2nd Platoon FAST, took over. I was on the roof again doing some sketches of the area to document the terrain in front of our position to ensure nothing changed over the time we were there. Dead Cow Road, named from the previous platoon, and you can guess why, paralleled the compound wall in front of me. Market Street was slightly off to my right and went perpendicular away from the compound and into the Medina Hospital area. Further off to my left about five hundred to six hundred yards ran Afgoye Road, which paralleled Market Street. Dead Cow Road dead-ended into Afgoye Road. I assigned different teams to sketch the area in front of the compound and the abandoned building at the intersection of Dead Cow Road and Market Street. I wanted to make sure no one added to the debris or knocked out any shooting ports close to one of our posts. A shooting port is the window we shoot through. While I was sketching the area, I observed a few technical vehicles pull up on Afgoye Road and stop. A technical vehicle, or "technical," was usually a pickup truck with a mounted crew-served weapon on the back. We had compiled a list of technicals we had observed over time. We would report them in detail when we saw them, but after the third time we put them on the list. We found that some of the clans would change weapons on the same vehicle to make it appear they had more technicals than they really had. The area between Afgoye Road and Market Street was pretty much open terrain except for some piles of trash, rocks, and rubble here and there. The right side of Market Street had a stone wall that stood about four or five feet tall. A large number of clansmen got off the back of a technical and some cling-on trucks on Afgoye Road. (We called large dump trucks or box-type trucks that would transport large numbers of people who would literally cling on or hold on to the vehicle "cling-on" trucks.) They started to spread out and in groups of two to four behind large rock piles that were spread haphazardly across the open area in front of me. They began bounding (bounding is when one group would move from one covered position to the next while the others cover their movement by either observation or fire) one group at a time as they worked their way down to Market Street. I looked over at the Marine on Post 2 (also on the roof of the White House) to make sure he was observing what I was . . . and he was. I continued to sketch while keeping an eye on their progression. Once they reached the stone wall on Market Street, they began to spread out fairly evenly as if manning a defensive position. Then I noticed one clansman move from position to position, talking and pointing to each individual as if assigning sectors of fire. They weren't aiming at the compound or me; they had moved left to right in front of me and were to my right now. After this guy went to each individual he called them all into a huddle. They talked for a few minutes then broke up, got on the technical and the cling-on truck, and drove off. I was left with a very disconcerting feeling in my gut. I asked the post stander if he was going to call that in to the COC. He said, "What do you mean? They didn't shoot anything." I was like, "They just did a rehearsal! They got online, bounded by teams all the way to the wall where the leader assigned sectors of fire. And then they conducted a debrief!" His reply was, "Oh." I couldn't believe it. We just watched this event go down together at the same exact time, and he couldn't put two and two together. We [snipers] aren't trained just to shoot or to shoot when we are being shot at; we are trained to assess, to analyze, and to observe. Throughout my training and the years of service I had in up to that point I was able to put it all together. After I finished the sketch I was working on I told the COC, as well as Sergeant K, our intel [intelligence] Marine assigned to the platoon from the Marine Corps Security Force Battalion, about what I observed.

It wasn't long before another, similar incident happened.

On another afternoon, a few weeks later in July, the COG was out taking pictures of different technicals driving by and happened to capture a picture of a dump truck carrying a quad-mounted gun from a ZSU-23–4. (We referred to three smaller rotating groups of post standers and their supervisor as the Corporals of the Guard. The "COG" specifically refers to the leader/supervisor, which was normally a corporal.) One of the regular (infantry) Marines (we called them "post standers") on Post 2 didn't see it. The COG turned over the camera roll to Sergeant K. He turned it over to a co-located agency to develop. The pictures confirmed what the COG reported. At that point I felt like we needed to have the snipers and DMs consolidate and stand Post 2, not just infantry Marines. This was the second time an infantry Marine on Post 2 missed a significant event. No fault to the Marine; he wasn't trained in observation skills at our level of analysis, plus it was too large an area to observe for one Marine. I brought it to Captain B's attention, and he agreed that Post 2 needed to have the trained observers such as snipers, DMs, and amphibious reconnaissance school graduates to stand that post. Post 2 was the critical post because from Post 2 you had a 360-degree observation of the whole compound. We could see and cover all the other posts on the compound.

In August, Mike took over the R&S section. "We broke up into three, two-man teams: Corporal M and I, Corporals R and B, and Lance Corporals L and P (who just happened to be partners at DM School). From that time until we got the word we would be pulling the USLO out of Mogadishu, we stood six-hour watches—six on, twelve off— for over a month. Once we started standing post on the roof, we worked with Sergeant K to help figure out the atmospherics and track the clans throughout the city. He used our reports to help fill out a twenty-four-hour pattern analysis sheet. Anytime there was a gunshot in the city, we would log the time, direction, estimated distance (from Post 2), and the number of rounds fired in a notebook. This helped him, along with other assets, to track Aidid's clan throughout Mogadishu." See, they aren't just shooters.

Some background information on General Mohamed Farrah Hassan Aidid: he was a former intelligence officer under Somalia president Mohamed Siad Barre's regime. Barre suspected Aidid of planning a coup d'état and imprisoned him for six years. Aidid's clan managed to overthrow Barre. With no successor to Barre's regime, civil war broke out, and "warlords," a term born in Somalia during this time, were claiming to be the de facto rulers of the country. Aidid was one of these "warlords." On October 3, 1993, President Clinton sent in elite US forces to capture Aidid and his militia in Mogadishu. Many of you remember what ensued, which was captured in the movie *Black Hawk Down*. (Mike was off the coast of Haiti in October 1993 when this event happened, but he watched it as his in brief when he arrived in Somalia.) The United States withdrew its forces soon afterward, and the United Nations left Somalia in 1995, after which Aidid declared himself president of Somalia in June 1995. On July 24, 1996, Aidid and his militia were in battle with the forces of warlords and former Aidid allies. Aidid was wounded by gunfire during the fight and ultimately suffered a fatal heart attack on August 1, 1996.

(As a side note, after Mike left Somalia, while in 3/6 Scout Sniper Platoon with then Staff Sergeant K, the S-2 Chief [S-2 stands for the intelligence section of the Marine Corps], he used this same pattern analysis technique again in Egypt to help track firing and other incidents in the area of operations. While he was on patrol with his sniper team, when they heard gunfire, they would halt, take a knee, and the assistant team leader would get out the GPS and get a grid while Mike shot an azimuth and estimated the range. He would call all that information back to the battalion. Once he did, they picked up and started moving again. They repeated these steps every time they heard gunfire. The other team leader started to pick up on the calls and quickly started doing the same. Now the battalion was able to triangulate where the fire was coming from.)

Around early September we got the word the USLO was going to be pulling out of Mogadishu, so our platoon restructured for this move. All the embassy gear had to be moved to the airport in preparation for a flight to Kenya. One section was guarding the gear at the airport, another section was escorting the convoy, and myself and a group of about eight to ten Marines were holding down the embassy compound. As the platoon was getting ready to depart on a convoy, one of the posts reported that a checkpoint was being manned by local clansmen on Afgoye Road just inside our area of observation, about six hundred to seven hundred yards away from Post 2 in the compound. As the SOG (sergeant of the guard), I went to the roof of the White House to Post 2 to survey the situation myself. I called the platoon commander to inform him there was indeed a checkpoint set up by the locals, and it was being manned by a few clansmen and a technical that had a 106 recoilless rifle on it. The clansmen were stopping vehicles and people to extort money to pass— yes, you can do that in Somalia. The platoon commander told me to take it out (the makeshift checkpoint) if they aimed their 106 recoilless rifle toward the compound, because it was capable of punching holes in our perimeter walls and the walls to the White House, which was where our embassy was located. I said, "Roger that." As the convoy departed, my sniper partner Corporal M and I manned the roof; me with my M-40 and Corporal M with his DMR and the M-49 spotting scope in between us. We set up and with the appropriate range dialed on the scopes. After about an hour or so I decided to check the rest of the post, since I was the SOG and we only had a handful of Marines left to guard it. It was quiet, and the technical wasn't aiming at the compound. About twenty minutes went by, and I get contacted by Corporal M on the radio saying the checkpoint had left. "Good," I thought to myself. I told him to put my rifle in its case but to leave it up there, and we both returned to the COC, which was on the first floor of the White House. Thirty minutes later I got a call that the checkpoint was back up, and now the 106 was manned and pointing at the compound! M and I jumped into action. We both put our gear on, our helmets and our ranger vests, and raced back up to the roof. Our ranger vests were green camo vests that had a small arms protective insert (SAPI), which was a thick ballistic plate sewn in the front to stop bullets. In 1994 that was not the normal gear that Marines had or used, because that technology hadn't made it to the regular infantry units and was generally only for special operations forces, but we were issued them over there. As soon as I got to the post, I looked through the M-49 spotting scope we had left set up. Sure enough, the 106 was manned and pointing directly at us. I bent down to get my rifle out of the case and set it up on the sandbag. I quickly double-checked the range card and the data on the gun, racked the bolt, and sighted in. In those short few seconds that it took me to do all of that, the Somali local who was manning the 106 spun the rifle away from the compound and jumped down off the technical.

Mike didn't know what to do: Should he take the shot, because when he first got to the roof his rules of engagement (ROE) were met? There was a weapon and potential violence of action. In his mind, the fact that the 106 was just aiming at the compound was violence of action. One shot from that would have breached the wall enough for the enemy to make entry. On the other hand, he was thinking about what he saw when he was actually behind the rifle, which didn't meet the ROE. In the back of his mind he thought if things got bad and it turned into a shit storm, there were only seven other Marines on the compound to defend it; but he had no doubt that they could defend it competently with the prepositioned posts they had set up. His concern was the bigger picture: What happens if the returning convoy gets stuck out in town because there was an attack on the embassy, or the USLO can't pull out because of an uprising in Mogadishu—what if it turns into another Black Hawk Down incident? Again the thought of the long-range implications, not just about taking a shot, but all of the follow-on consequences. "I made the decision in a split second; I didn't take the shot. As part of the years of training I have gone through, I learned how to take the shot, when to take the shot, and sometimes more importantly, when not to take the shot. You have to look at the bigger picture and think about the unit's mission, not just my team's mission. I feel I made the correct call that day. I don't think the Somalis realized they were aiming at the compound but quickly realized it as we were running up the outside steps to post two on the roof; hence why they scrambled to move the rifle and jump off the vehicle."

The United States pulled the US flag down on September 15, 1994, when the last of the diplomatic personnel and the Marines from FAST Company 2nd Platoon departed the American compound in Mogadishu. The diplomatic personnel went to Nairobi, Kenya, and the Marines went to Mombasa, Kenya, then back to the United States. Mike's Somalia deployment gave him real-world experience and the confidence that would help him throughout the rest of his career. "I enjoyed this mission so much that I remember as my platoon time was winding down getting ready to head back home, Sergeant K and I were going to ask to stay and transfer to the platoon replacing ours just so we could stay, because of the tremendous responsibility we had as sergeants. I'll never forget the steak and lobster grilled up on Sundays! That was some of the best lobster I have ever had!"

KABUL: 2004

It was fall of 2004 when the Marine Corps had redesignated the 4th Marine Expeditionary Brigade (MEB) to be an Antiterrorism Brigade. The infantry battalion that fell under 4th MEB(AT) was being sent overseas to guard high-risk posts providing external embassy security. "The Marine Security Guard (MSG) was the internal security; think dress-blue-clad Marines as interior guards at the embassies. We were tasked with external security. I was assigned to 'F' Company 2/6; the battalion that fell under the 4th MEB(AT). My battalion was assigned to send Marines to the embassies in Iraq and Afghanistan to provide security. One company was assigned to be the quick reaction force (QRF) in Afghanistan for Afghanistan's President, Hamid Karzai, during the elections. One company was assigned embassy security in Kabul and one company in Baghdad, Iraq. My company (F Co) was sent to Kabul."

While serving as a rifle company gunnery sergeant in Kabul, Afghanistan, as part of the 4th MEB(AT), Mike was stationed at the US embassy compound in Kabul with his rifle company (minus approximately ninety Marines). Shortly after his company relieved the previous company there, while on post, one of the DMs spotted two men outside the compound with a cell phone and binoculars. They reported the suspicious behavior to the advanced targeting intelligence cell (ATIC) section—the collective group of Marines comprising intelligence Marines from our battalion and counterintelligence Marines. The Marines from the ATIC cell quickly got their gear on and set out to find these individuals. The DMs didn't have any reference points close to the location of these two individuals, and because of this, they had a difficult time trying to guide the ATIC Marines to the exact location. The area was large and open and had few identifying terrain features or manmade structures to help narrow down the location. Mike was up on the roof with the DMs while they were trying to guide the ATIC Marines to the targets.

I was kind of kicking myself in the ass for not seeing this problem sooner. I went down to the ATIC section and got one of the intel Marines to print me off overhead imagery of the embassy and the surrounding area. I got a ruler, made some tick marks, gridded out the whole thing, and put letters across the top and numbers down the left side. We taught and used GRGs [gridded reference graphics] in my last unit, Special Operations Training Group, and at 3/6 Scout Sniper Platoon, very successfully, so why not use it now! Unfortunately, it was too late to help that night, and we lost the two targets. I made copies of the GRG I created and passed them to all the posts to use in the future to help identify exact target locations in situations when you have nothing else to go by. I flew back to the States a week later and was told by the Company 1st Sergeant that the ambassador liked it so much, they did it on a larger scale and covered the whole city in this method.

There may not be anything sexy about gridding out an area, lying motionless in a position for hours observing, or standing by on a ship running mission rehearsals, but that is part of being a sniper, an efficacious sniper, and you have to love all parts of the job if you want to be a US Marine Chief Scout Sniper.

AFTER THE COMBAT

In October 2009 I was transferred from the Gunner at 2/2 to the Infantry Training Battalion, School of Infantry at Camp Geiger in North Carolina. 2/2 had just deployed to Afghanistan. Once 2/2 started taking casualties, I started going to visit them at the hospital in Bethesda (Maryland) so they could see a familiar face. On one such trip to Bethesda in late November or early December, I was walking through the halls on my way to one of the Marines's rooms when I heard a voice. As soon as I heard it, I said in my mind, that's "the freak show." I backed up and saw the name on board outside the room: "SSgt R." I could hear him talking, so I knocked on the door and went in. He was lying in the bed with his foot in traction. He had survived an IED [improvised explosive device] strike to his Oshkosh MRAP, and his foot took some serious damage. In the room with him were his wife and father. A minute or so after I entered the doorway to the room, he kicked his wife out. I felt very uncomfortable and wasn't sure what was going on. Once she was gone, he turned to his father and said, "Gunner Carr was my first squad leader. When I reenlist, and every day, I try to be half the Marine and man he trained me to be. And that I do what I do because of how he trained me and the leadership he showed me while we were at FAST." That blew me away. I only ever did what I was trained to do, and that was to take care of my Marines and train them to the best of my ability. I tried to teach my squad at FAST something every morning, simple classes like the elements of call for fire, how to cross danger areas, reporting, how to make field expedient antennas, etc. I didn't realize I had such an impact on their lives. I was truly humbled.

Being sent to FAST and then deploying to Somalia and Iraq then to Afghanistan ultimately landed Mike in a successful place today. And now he is a retired CWO4 Marine Gunner.

I met the best group of Marines I have had the pleasure of serving with. I have just about done everything I want to. My only regret is the toll it took on my marriage and ultimately my family. Before I would go on my combat deployments, I would start compartmentalizing feelings and prepare myself for what I had to do and what I might see. In doing so, I inadvertently was distancing myself from my wife, who needed me to be there for her emotionally because she was battling her own struggles worrying about my safety, having the full responsibility of taking care of our children, and everyday life situations. I cut off my emotions to prepare for the emotional stress I knew I was going to have to endure, and she took it as cutting off my emotions to her. If I could go back in time, would I have done things differently? Yes, one thing. I see the toll it has taken on my kids, sharing time between their mother and me. If I could go back in time, I would have tried to express my emotions better so she could understand what I was going through. I wished I could have communicated better. We are divorced now, and my kids have grown up with my deployments and the divorce. They have taken the greatest toll. It breaks my heart to see the pain I have caused them. My son Michael and my daughter Laura are two special and amazing people. And when I see how they have really come into their own, I feel so proud. They give me my most pride and joy. I'm retired now, and I have given what I can to this country; now it is time to focus on them.

FIRST DEPLOYMENT, FALLUJAH: 2005

Dave deployed to Fallujah in 2005, some nine months after Phantom Fury; he relieved 1st Battalion/6th Marines (1/6). There was a period of calm between Phantom Fury and when 1/6 departed, but the fighting picked up again around the fall of 2005. "IEDs (improvised explosive devices) were big then."

Dave landed in Kuwait like everyone else who is on their way to the "sandbox." From there, he hopped on C130 to TQ (Dave can't remember the name; everyone just called it "TQ"). That was the first time he had been on a C130. He doesn't know how many of them were in the plane, but he says they were all packed in there like sardines. The pilots had to do evasive maneuvers as they landed because of the threat of commonly occurring RPG (rocket-propelled grenade launcher) attacks. Dave remembers one of the guys in his platoon, who had been on this flight before, looked over at Dave, who was holding a .50-caliber SASR (special-application scoped rifle, pronounced *sass-ser*), which weighed about thirty pounds, and over the roar of the engines he yelled to Dave, "Let go of the SASR!" Dave didn't think he heard him clearly. Confused, he kept a grip on it. As Dave watched, this guy removed his hands from his gun and signaled to Dave to do the same. Still confused, Dave complied and let go of his SASR. They were in their approach, spiraling down through the air like mating eagles, and all of a sudden the SASR became weightless and hovered a few inches above the deck. He thought that was pretty cool; it took his mind off of possibly being shot at by the enemy, at least. Dave was nineteen at this point, the youngest guy in the platoon.

He didn't have a clue as to what was going on, yet he seemed to be quite at home amid the chaos, excitement, and fear. As the SASR hovered, and not knowing if he should be more excited or scared, he began to reflect on how he got into that seat on that plane that day. He was living his dream, or soon would be. The plane landed safely, and everyone went immediately to a tent for the indoc brief (the safety brief for this country). The tent wasn't a typical Army green military tent you'd picture in your head; it was a Bedouin tent with tassels hanging everywhere. The indoc brief covered what to do if they came under enemy attack, what bunkers to take shelter in, and so on. Then they were told to grab some rounds (ammunition) and chow, then get settled in and prepare to move in the morning. Dave went to his assigned living quarters (another tent) and was lying on his cot with a bunch of other guys.

All of a sudden the air raid sirens blasted off; this was about twenty minutes after the indoc brief. He had no clue what was going on; he assumed they were going to take incoming fire. He jumped off his cot, grabbed his flak, and looked around to notice none of the other guys were moving. One of the sergeants was just lying there calmly on his cot, listening to his headphones. He rolled over and said to Dave, "Don't worry about it. Number one, we're in a tent. If you get up and run, one of those rounds will find you. And two, if a round comes in here, that flak is not going to do you any good. So just lay down, get some rest, and relax." Dave thought to himself, "Well, okay then. I guess I can do that."

They never heard any impact, so they weren't sure why the air raid sirens went off. Apparently it was commonplace that the sirens went off half the time for no reason. I asked Dave if that sound put the fear in him, as I would imagine it would me, and he said, "It wasn't overly scary; it became as common of a sound as the local fire department whistles back home."

His first night in Iraq had come and gone with no incidents. Now was his first official day "in country." Dave mounted a truck that would take him to his camp, Camp Baharia, right outside of Fallujah. "It seemed to take forever to get there. It's a pretty well-known camp; it was like a resort where all the nefarious activities went on with Saddam's sons. We were taken to our hooches (their living quarters) and then got another indoc brief." They were told they were in an active combat zone and to make sure they had their weapons with them at all times and ammo close by, because they might take direct fire. They were supposed to get two hot meals a day at the chow hall there, but for some reason Dave doesn't ever recall having two hot meals a day while he was in Iraq. The food wasn't cooked there; it was brought in from elsewhere. It was like a giant tub of slop, but it was hot. He lived mostly on MREs ("Meal Ready to Eat" packages) or whatever they could find in town, which he preferred over the MREs or the slop.

Dave's team's first mission was to Saqlawiyah (they called it Saq), a town west of Fallujah. It was a pretty, green, and lush area with lots of palm trees. Dave and his team went over the plan of where they were getting inserted and what they had to look for. No kill targets or anything cool like that. They were just assessing the lay of the land and getting their feet wet; this was his very first mission in combat. (His team leader had already been in combat before.) There were four of them setting out for a three-day mission. (Reminds me of *Gilligan's Island* when the crew set out for a three-hour tour and disaster followed.) Approximately twenty minutes after they got inserted into the town, weighted down with all their gear, they started taking several rounds of small arms fire. The rounds were hitting close by, so they were sure they were targets, but nothing impacted them, and then suddenly the fire ceased. They weren't sure if their positions had been compromised. Dave's team held off on returning fire. Was the enemy shooting at them or not? They didn't really know, because everyone out there still carried an AK-47, so someone may have been shooting at a wild dog or something. With no more fire, they proceeded to walk around for a few miles, without getting shot at, and got picked up by the HMMWVs again. They did a data dump of information they had collected for the Marines in the HMMWV so they could report it up the chain of command, and then the trucks dumped them off again in another area. And that's how it was for three days straight. Getting picked up, dropped off, no casualties, no shooting, just stealthily collecting information and reporting it.

Sniper teams are inserted and extracted in such a way as to conceal their activities and whereabouts. How they are able to do this is by syncing up with conventional forces in the area. For example, when Dave's team needed to be extracted from a particular area, they would radio the regular forces patrolling in the area so they could pull over at an exact location, get out to do a security haut, and then Dave's team would sync up with them covertly on the streets. Then they would all get back inside the HMMWV and drive off target. This is the same technique they used to get inserted in a particular location. As the HMMWV drove off target, Dave's team would unload the information until the next stop, where they would all get back out of the vehicle, but only the regular forces would return, while Dave's team would sneak off on foot under the cover of the natural and man-made terrain features around them. In theory, no one knew they were being dropped off. Then they would be on their own anywhere from forty-eight hours to ninety-six hours. To survive on their own for that amount of time, they carried everything they needed, which equaled a lot of weight. Dave carried an M-16A4, thirteen magazines of roughly 360 rounds of ammunition, 200 rounds of ammunition for the SAW (the light machine gun), two or three hand grenades, two or three smoke grenades, a thermite grenade, a small amount of demolitions, usually some detonating cord and C4, two or three radio batteries, extra rounds for the sniper rifle, an M-9 pistol and sixty rounds for the pistol, water, food, and a booby trap kit. Everyone had their own load, but they were all usually carrying well over one hundred pounds of gear per person. Depending on the mission and the area, they would hunker down in various places for various amounts of time. Dave will never forget what happened during one particular time when he and the three other members of his sniper team were on the inside edge of Fallujah, concealed in bushes; it was a good position where they could hang out for a couple hours and get a shot off. It was one of the team members' time to rest, so he lay down on something and said, "I don't know what this is, but it's comfortable." It was pitch dark out, so none of them could see what it was. When the sun started to come up the next morning, they saw what the guy had been sleeping on . . . he had been sleeping on a dead dog all night. Because everything smelled over there, they didn't notice the stench of its carcass. They left that spot soon after sunrise.

Sometimes they were able to find water pump houses or well houses to stay in overnight, and sometimes they just needed to commandeer someone's house. This was not uncommon. When they had to do this, his four-man team would come up to a courtyard wall (most houses in Iraq were surrounded by a courtyard and mud brick walls), and because Dave was the smallest guy on the team and was a gymnast when he was younger, he was always the first over the wall. His team members would toss him over the wall with his 9mm as fast as they could so he could open the courtyard gate and let the rest of the team into the courtyard before they let themselves into the house. He got good and comfortable being the first over the wall, so he always did it.

The first thing that goes through your head is, "Did anybody see me?" Then, "How the hell do I open the gate?" Once I got the guys in, we'd move all of our gear inside and close the gate as quietly as we could. We would try to open the door to the houses; we didn't kick the doors down. I got good at jimmying the locks and getting in. The occupants were usually sleeping in the house or on the roof in the summer, because they all had flat roofs and it was cooler up there. But in the winter we'd go in and try to figure out where the head of the house (male) was inside the house. We would wake him up at gunpoint. We would tell him, in our horrible Arabic, "Wake up your family, and we are going to move them all into one room. We are not here to hurt you, but your house is ours now, and if you try anything, we'll kill all of you." I know it sounds barbaric, but this is at a time when you couldn't trust anyone, and no matter what you were, if you were in a US military uniform, you were being shot at. Oh, and being a sniper meant you usually had a bounty on your head anyway. We would stay there as long as we needed, usually until nightfall, with at least one of us having constant watch over the family. Once we needed to leave, we would call for an extract. Because the family would spread the news that we were there as soon as we left, that entire area would become unsafe for us. We would throw a smoke grenade if we had to meet up with the vehicle. After three or four days out on our own, we were pretty beat down, supplies were low, and we were hungry.

Dave tried to eat what the locals ate. "They were skinny dudes who could run, jump in sandals, so they were doing something right; they were eating stuff that gave them the energy." Dave kept a journal of recipes he picked up from eating the local food, which he enjoyed. He ate a lot of rice with short-grain pasta in it, mixed with raisins or chopped-up dates, a lot of chicken, yogurt, round flat bread, a lot of potatoes and tomato-based products, ground beef in fried dough, goat, and cucumbers. The Euphrates ran close by, so there was a lot of vegetation, and crops grew well. There was a good amount of farmland and a decent amount of food to eat.

The coolest mission I went on, I don't remember if was a week and a half or two weeks, we were out, but we linked up with a company and we pretty much became forward scouts for them. We would go into an area looking for IEDs and whatever other sort of trouble was around. We were given free rein. The company didn't have a mission per se for us; all they wanted us to do was to push forward to find safe locations for the company to sleep at night and just sort of sneak around scouting the area. So we were essentially freelance scouts. I have pictures of the four of us in the middle of nowhere; we look like nomads, just wandering about (of course, stealthily). We gathered a lot of intelligence in those weeks; the Company detained a lot of people and answered a lot of priority intelligence requirements, and we never took any shots.

WHAT'S DIFFERENT?

"What's different about sniper platoons is that each one is set up slightly different and is unique to the people in the team. It's not like the rest of the Marine Corps, where if you are in a rifle company you know what happens in a rifle company in another battalion; you have the same mission and composition. This is not the case in sniper platoons." Sniper platoons run four- and five-man teams; some even break down further into two-man teams. There are even different weapons used and assigned among the teams. What makes a sniper platoon unique and special is that the individuals on the teams are hand-selected. Snipers don't get assigned to a sniper team the way infantry Marines get assigned to a rifle company. Snipers know who they are going to be assigned with and why. After you indoc into the sniper platoon, which is basically like a draft, the team leaders hand-select who they want on their platoons and teams. They handcraft the teams by knowing what each individual brings to the team, both personally and professionally. Dave states that because the teams are hand-selected, there were never any real personality clashes. If problems came up among them, they were able to sit down and hash them out fairly quickly with no long-term consequences. This relationship is further enforced within the teams because the team members usually do not wear rank, and they were all on a first-name basis. "No one was 'above' anyone else." Of course, if they were back in the rear and had to do a dog and pony show, they assumed and wore their rank and titles, but after that, they went back to being Joe, Bob, Tom, etc. When they were on a field operation, every team member had a say. Even though the senior guy would ultimately enforce the command, the junior guys could voice their concerns about it. They all contributed their opinions, and they were all asked for them, because their ultimate goal was to not get killed. "If any one of us on a team gets killed, the probability of another team member getting killed is high. We have no backup; we back each other up." Dave says sometimes they got on each other's nerves, just like your friends and family do, and they would fight. Once he got in a fistfight with a team member and lost horribly. And a week before this interview with him, years after this fight, the guy he lost to spent the weekend with Dave at his home, hanging out, drinking beer, and having a good time. "Nobody from outside the teams or platoons dared confront us. We were a band of brothers, just like the entire Marine Corps, and if an outsider challenged or provoked one of us, they would get the wrath of the entire team, or platoon."

THERE'S FALLUJAH, THEN THERE'S CAMP FALLUJAH

As a sniper, Dave worked for the conventional forces battalion, so technically he did not fall under Special Operations Command (SOCOM). Even though sniper schools are "special operations" schools and everything snipers do makes them "special operations" capable, they technically are not Special Operations, nor do they fall under the command and control of SOCOM. "So by the rules it puts us in a gray area. Even though we can be directly attached to Special Operations Forces (SOF), we were not SOF. Does that make sense? I was attached to a SEAL team once for a month. And even though we had gone through similar training and conducted ourselves operationally the same, we were not SOF, and they had cooler gear and equipment than us. When I first was attached to the SEAL team, I thought, I can't wait to see these guys in action!" But at the end of the day he realized they were doing the same TTPs (tactics, techniques, and procedures) as he did, and he thought, "We're not that different. Although they would beat my ass in the water any day." Luckily, he was in the desert. "So what does that make me? I went to a Special Operations School, I support Special Operations as an asset, but I'm not Special Operations. I don't know where I fall." A common question of Marine Scout Snipers.

Dave says there's a huge rivalry between infantry and noninfantry Marines. "All snipers come from the infantry. Snipers and infantry all go through the same training; initially, it's those of us who want to push ourselves to get selected into a more specialized school who go on to become snipers. Yes, snipers carry cooler gear and have more freedom to operate independently, sometimes with no oversight, but there wasn't a rift between snipers and infantry. I would say the bigger rift was between staff NCOs (noncommissioned officers) and us (snipers). We were considered to be more of subject-matter experts (SMEs) than they were, and it pissed some of them off." When Dave's team had to stay with the infantry, they were their guests. Dave's team knew most of them personally, and they liked having snipers alongside them because they were an asset to the infantry; in turn, the snipers liked having the infantry close by because when they got into a "shit sandwich," there was somebody around with a lot more firepower. So there was really no rift between the sniper teams and infantry; the rift was between infantry and noninfantry.

This may sound trivial, but it's something that drives us (snipers and infantry) insane. Fallujah and Al Anbar were bad, dangerous areas. There were just always a lot of people getting killed; we were basically on the front lines of it all. You see people being blown up and shot, enemy and friendly, it's just the way it was. The city proper was very small, about three to four miles wide. It's a very dense city, but not a large city; it was definitely not as big as Washington, DC. Camp Baharia was just outside of Fallujah, where the battalion in charge of the city was located. That was a relatively safe camp. But then you had Camp Fallujah, the largest base in the area. From what I understand, it actually encompassed more area than the city of Fallujah did. It was insanely big. So they operated like a normal base with morale boosters like USO shows, organized runs, and all sorts of dumb contests. They had an awesome chow hall, and everyone had to wear rank and blouse their pants with boot bands, you know, normal Marine Corps base activity, but in a war zone. When we came back from our missions, we didn't think we were hot shit by any means; heck, we didn't even run into that much combat. But when we would talk to people after we returned home from deployment and I would tell them I was in Fallujah, they would say, "Oh, me too." It was nice, because you could talk to them about something you had in common, something that others might not understand, so it was nice to have others to talk about the shit you saw and had to live through. I would say, "Oh, you must remember the blue mosque . . . "; everyone who is anyone operating in Fallujah knows about the blue mosque. Whenever you passed by it, you got shot at, no matter what time of year, day, etc. And then they would say, "No, I was at Camp Fallujah, I was never outside the wire in the city." Dudes would go there for a year and never leave the camp. I would think, wow, how could they have been for a year and never leave the camp, never see the "real" Fallujah? The surgical center was at Camp Fallujah, so all wounded went there. One particular day I remember we were out and some guys got wounded, and it was faster to get the wounded to Camp Fallujah Surgical than be medevaced out by a helo. We were all piled in a truck, and the guys driving the truck drove straight through the main gate to Camp Fallujah. They weren't hauling ass, but they were driving with a purpose; we had to get to the surgical center. It was standard operating procedures at the time that all vehicles entering Camp Fallujah had to stop and all persons inside had to clear their weapons before being let through. Well, we didn't do that. We radioed the gate to tell them we had wounded and we breezed through, obviously thinking it was okay because lives were at stake. As we are passing through, this female Marine lieutenant, who is running in PT gear no less, is trying to flag our vehicle down to make us slow down on base. She had no concept that there was a war going on outside the gates of that base. While people are out there getting shot up, she's running in PT gear, yelling at us to slow down! That aggravated me. It seemed some people stationed there were more focused on PT and parties than the war that was going on around them. And these are the same people who come back and thump their chests while saying that they were in Fallujah during the war. While they were being entertained by USO shows, we would be running extra missions because they didn't want the base getting attacked during the show. And we did so gladly, that's what we signed up to do, but then they turn around and yell at us for driving too fast on base to get to the surgical center to save a guy's leg. Pathetic.

YOU'RE NOT ALLOWED TO EAT IN MY CHOW HALL

"I remember one mission that we were sent on, with a twenty-minute notice, which was an absolute cluster fuck, and what happened after was a kick in the teeth. We were sent out in the middle of nowhere, somewhere outside Fallujah, I really don't remember the exact location, which took us forever to get to, to babysit this bridge because intelligence reporting said something was going to happen. We were out there for a week, and all we saw the entire time was one dude taking a shit, I kid you not. I was on the gun, dialing in on this one dude as he's getting close to the bridge, and then he drops his pants and does his business." Dave's team was out there for approximately five to seven days, which he said felt like forever. It was just the four of them living in a hole. They stunk like shit. They had gone out totally sanitized, meaning they didn't wear nametapes or rank insignia, nor did they carry Geneva Conventions cards.

We were told go out with nothing, so we did; but that wasn't the real reason. We weren't doing covert operations; the real reason why we were sanitized was because if something happened to one of us while we were out there, our families wouldn't see it on the news first, they would be notified appropriately before they'd see their son's dead body being desecrated by insurgents on the 6 p.m. news. If we carried ID cards, the enemy would know who we were and take advantage of it by disgracing us and parading our bodies on TV for propaganda before our families could be notified that we had been killed in action. We didn't want to be cowboys; we wanted to protect our kin. Nevertheless, we had to explain this to the regular forces every time we were seen on Camp Fallujah without our ID cards. We're snipers; we already had bounties on our heads.

At the time of this bridge-watching mission, Dave's sniper team's parent command hadn't deconflicted their mission and presence with the other operating forces in the area. So there they were, in a concealed position and unrecognizable because they were covered in mud, just the four of them, with no way of distinguishing that they were even US citizens, aside from their nice white teeth. As they were watching the bridge, waiting for any type of action, they saw a Cobra come over them, a US-owned attack helicopter. There were initially excited because there wasn't supposed to be anything out there, so at least they could "roll tach" (change the radio frequency so they could talk to air). He kept circling them. And then he started tilting. Dave thought, "Oh shit, we are being targeted by our own forces! I thought, we should have probably put out some air panels right now. He was tilting, so we didn't know if he was going to start a gun run or what. We later found out they didn't know we were there, and they spotted us and were targeting us! So we threw out air panels, which were big orange sheets of plastic cloth to signal to them that we were not the enemy." (You can put air panels on anything that needs to be identified from the air to signal aircraft.) Can you imagine getting shot by one of your own because of a lack of deconfliction? Unfortunately, it happens, and it wasn't the first time it happened to Dave's sniper team. Fortunately, they didn't get shot, and the Cobra saw the air panels.

Aside from the guy taking a shit and the Cobra targeting us, at the end of those five to seven days we saw nothing, we accomplished nothing. So when we got picked up, we were taken to Camp Fallujah to get something hot to eat. Mind you, five to seven days living on MREs and water rations, that means no showering, no shaving. We stunk, we looked like hell, we had tons of facial growth, our hair was long, we were dirty, but above all, we were hungry. We were so excited that we were going to Camp Fallujah to eat. It had been almost three months since we had a real meal. We got to the gate, and this time we cleared and cleaned our weapons. Our weapons are an extension of us; we are nothing without them, so we take excellent care of them. We go to the chow hall, and we are denied access because we didn't have our ID cards. Remember, we went out sanitized, meaning there was nothing on us that could give away our identities; we were ghosts out there. Our hearts sank. We just wanted this one small pleasure. So a USMC captain sees us and vouches for us and gets us into the chow hall. We all got our food, sat down, and start eating. As we ate, we began to realize that food was something we had taken for granted, because we were so thankful for it. All of a sudden we start to notice everyone who is sitting around us is getting up and leaving. We just looked at them wondering what's going on? What don't we know? We didn't care, we continued to enjoy the food. About ten minutes go by, and a different USMC officer comes up to us and says that we are too dirty to be eating in his chow hall. He made us leave the chow hall. At least he allowed us to take our food and finish eating outside. We felt humiliated; we had been treated like dogs. Unfortunately, that became a common experience for us. Like I said earlier, they had no idea what a war really was, the dirty stench of war. I wanted to tell him, "This is what guys who fight the war look like, and you won't let us eat in your chow hall!?" He even had the audacity to ask us why we didn't shave. Let's see, because one gallon of water weighs eight pounds. I drink a gallon a day and I'm out for four days. That means technically I'd have to carry thirty-two pounds of water, and I can't do that. All I can carry is about three gallons, so I can carry everything else to stay alive. So maybe he could understand why I'm not wasting any of my water to shave when I'm out in the field. We continually had to explain this to people. Water was a big issue, and we were told we just had to plus up on water to survive out there, but we simply couldn't. It weighed too much.

CONDITIONED TO WAR

Dave remembers coming off a mission with his team inside the city of Fallujah, and an infantry squad came by to pick them up. The infantry squad was out doing "presence patrols," a show of force to let the locals in the area know they were in the area and, of course, observing them and all activities going on. The squad just happened to walk by the house Dave and his teammates were staying in, albeit as uninvited guests, and they walked out the front door as the squad passed by and fell in right behind them. He said he was sure everybody knew what they were doing and that they had just come from that house, but at least they had protection. The squad was going to escort them back to the center of the city where the government center was, the large compound he thinks was called the "CMUC" (pronounced *see-muck*), but he can't remember what it stands for, where US forces were staying. Before entering friendly lines into the CMUC you always had to request permission via radio. "As we walked up to the gate, we were on foot, not in a vehicle. Someone in the squad saw something that looked suspicious. It was a dead dog with what appeared to be wires coming out of it. So instead of asking permission to enter, he radioed the CMUC to tell them that there was a possible IED in the area. No sooner did he say, 'Be advised there's a dog that appears to have wires . . . ,' over the radio, when Ka-Boom! The dog blew up! And without missing a beat he picks up where he left off: 'Never mind, request permission to enter friendly lines.' The dog blew up, before he could even finish calling in the suspected IED. Using dead dogs as IED was popular back then. But that's how it was, you get conditioned to war and it conditions you. You just got used to things that would be horrific here, but there, it was just another day." And for those animal lovers, like myself, who are cringing while reading this, Dave tells me that these were not dogs that you have as household pets; they were wild, vicious, and mostly rabid dogs that would attack. It doesn't make it a whole lot easier to swallow, but a little bit easier.

"SS" BOLT

Dave returned from deployment after seven months. He got back and was sent to a lot of schools: Combat Marksmanship Instructor, SERE

(Survival, Evasion, Resistance, and Escape) School (where he turned twenty years old, still not old enough to legally drink), Mountain Scout Sniper School, and Desert Warfare training. He postponed predeployment leave so he could go to Urban Scout Sniper School with Special Operations Training Group. Then he went back over to the sandbox for his second deployment to Fallujah in 2007. This time Dave led a five-man sniper team. Their weapons were different; they had some experimental weapons. Dave carried the XM3 short bolt-action 308; Mark 11 (MK11), which were all suppressed; 308s; M107s; and M40a3s. The gear had really changed in one year. But what hadn't changed was that one year later he found himself in the same hooch that still had the "SS" symbol that his previous sniper team spraypainted on it a year earlier.

So back at the same hooch a year later, Dave said the vibe was different this time. They knew it was going to be a lot more relaxed this deployment; not necessarily less dangerous, but fewer combat engagements. The forces there had done a great job keeping ordnance out of the city, so the IEDs were less dangerous because they were made more from homemade explosives now rather than ordnance. The most prominent IED makers had already been targeted and killed. Attacks were on a smaller scale, and overall things seemed to be getting safer. They still dealt with serious casualties, guys losing limbs and bleeding out. During one attack Dave had become the guy in charge of the observation post, and somehow he became in charge of a squad. He didn't know the guys. They were from another company, but because he had more stripes on his arm than anybody else there and the guys that were his senior were lying on the ground bleeding, he had to jump up and assume the position of squad leader, as well as team leader. "I got indoctrinated pretty quickly."

PINNED DOWN

You know on his previous deployment Dave had become the first guy over the wall because of his stature and his physical aptitude. So this time around he kept it up and was still the first guy over the wall. "I wanted to be. I didn't want these guys to get killed, and I really didn't want to have to explain to their parents why they weren't coming back. So I'd rather take the risk of being the first over. I was twenty years old at that time. I was in charge of the team, but I wasn't the oldest."

He'll never forget one combat mission during this deployment:

It was the craziest thing that happened to me, even though it's just a typical day in the life of a sniper. I wanted my team to get some rest, so I left them in the rear and went out with a platoon that was going into an area I wanted to survey to find out how my team could sneak in at night and do our thing in the near future. So I asked the platoon if I could tag along. We were in the city proper and my team was at Baharia, and all of a sudden we started hearing a lot of chatter over the radios, then gunfire and explosions. I could hear the stress in people's voices on the radios. We find out a MTT (Military Transition Team), who were training the Iraqi Army, were getting attacked about four hundred yards away. It was afternoon, and we made our way to their location. We weren't prepared to see what we saw when we arrived on target. You know it's a bad scene when you see an M-4 that's been blown in half, flak jackets littering the street covered in blood, and pockmarks everywhere from hand grenades. I saw one dude huddled and crying in front of a vehicle, the one vehicle that got hit and got separated from rest of the convoy. This guy turned out to be a major, who got a Bronze Star out of it, go figure, but there is no fire at this point. Everything has stopped for the moment. There is a lieutenant in the back of the Humvee that the major is huddled in front of who is dead. I found out he got shot by an enemy sniper. Later we found out the entire ambush was initiated by that sniper. Some of the guys were trying to get the major to tell them what had happened, but he was shell shocked. All he could tell us was that they were ambushed and took fire from all directions. No sooner does he relay this, we start getting lit up. There are four medium machine guns that had us in a crossfire ambushing the shit out of us from elevated positions. They were on top of a building, and they had us pinned down at this point. There were a lot of them. I was firing my M-4 on semiautomatic, and I was running out of ammunition; I had 360 rounds with me. Because of the way the ambush was set up and the position of the vehicles, this particular vehicle can't turn around and get off the target. We have dead and wounded, and I ran out of 5.56mm ammunition in seven minutes. The five of us were pinned down in this street just watching the enemy pop up through my iron sights, and we're shooting back. Not good.

Dave kept tracer rounds at the bottom of his last three or four magazines to alert himself that he would run out of ammunition soon. He was shooting his 556 at targets popping up from a wall about twelve feet away, and the rounds were just skipping off the top of the wall because it was so thick, and the tracers were burning out. At this point he thought to himself, "I have to try to keep the heads down of the enemy so we can get the wounded out. I've got no more ammo, and I just can't sit here waiting to get shot." So he gave his rifle to his friend Chuck and told the guys to lay down cover fire for him while he advanced forward without any cover. For some reason he was the only one who had some hand grenades, so the only thing he knew he could do and had to do was try to take out the enemy machine gun positions with his hand grenades. "The first thing you learn about hand grenades is to never throw a hand grenade up. But in this situation, I either throw the hand grenade up or die. The choice was easy." So he ran up to the twelve-foot wall and tossed a grenade up over the wall onto the roof. It ended up knocking out one of the machine guns. Fire ceased just long enough for them to throw some smoke grenades, get into the vehicles, and get everyone off the ambush site. He got a Navy and Marine Corps Achievement Medal (NAM) with a *V* (the *V* device is a miniature bronze or gold letter *V* that stands for combat valor) for that day.

Dave was modest as he explained how the remaining survivors and deceased all got out of there because everyone did what they were trained to do. All he did was throw the hand grenade that ceased fire long enough for them to buy the time they needed to do what they all were trained to do, and that's how they all got off the target. But he ran out in the middle of an ambush scene, with minimal cover fire (remember they were all running out of ammo), and used his hand grenades in a most unconventional way. But that's war. They do what they are trained to do and think on their feet and react accordingly. The crazy part about it was he just happened to ask to go with this platoon to do a recon mission for his team. They just happened to be in the area where this ambush had taken place, and he just happened to be able to support during the ambush.

We get trained on how to not wander into an ambush. We know what to do and what not to do, but there were Marines out there who needed saving, so you go into the situation no matter what, you want them to do the same for you if those actions lead to an ambush. By all the signs it was the quintessential ambush pattern. The hit vehicle was in an alleyway, basically a cross street that wasn't wide enough to where you could turn a Humvee around; you couldn't fit two Humvees side by side. If you think about how the dimensions of the Humvee came about, they are built as wide as they can be to be able to get through the narrowest alleyway in Europe. In retrospect we should have known the enemy was waiting for the first responders to get to the hit vehicle, and it was an ambush just waiting to happen, but when you are in it, you only think, those are our friends, they are Marines, and they are wounded. You don't give a shit what could happen; you go in there and help them.

Without the mental and emotional capacity to make a split-second decision while his life and the lives of others are on the line, and without the courage to trust his ability, perhaps Dave wouldn't have followed his gut instinct to run the gauntlet of fire and do what he thought was the only hope of getting those people out safely that day. Perhaps I would have never gotten the chance to interview him and share his story with you. Thankfully, he did follow his gut instinct and trusted his years of training and a year of combat experience, gained all before the ripe ol' age of twenty-one, and is alive today to talk about it.

SOURCES

"Belleau Wood" from *Miracle at Belleau Wood: The Birth of the Modern U.S. Marine Corps*. Alan Axelrod. Essex, CT: Lyons Press, 2018.

"Infamous Day: Marines at Pearl Harbor: From *Infamous Day: Marines at Pearl Harbor*. Robert J. Cressman and J. Michael Wegner. Marines in World War II Commemorative Series. Washington, DC: US Marine Corps Historical Center, 1992.

"Taking Mount Suribachi" from *Closing In: Marines in the Seizure of Iwo Jima*. Joseph H. Alexander. Marines in World War II Commemorative Series. Washington, DC: US Marine Corps Historical Center, 1994.

"Assaulting Inchon: Korea 1950" from *U.S. Maine Operations in Korea 1950–1953, Volume II, The Inchon-Seoul Operation*. Lynn Montross and Captain Nicholas A. Canzona, USMC. Washington, DC: Headquarters Historical Branch, USMC, 1955.

"Supplying the Embattled Marines at Khe Sanh" from *The Battle for Khe Sanh*. Captain Moyers S. Shore II. Washington, DC: History and Museums Division Headquarters, US Marine Corps, 1969.

"The Reveille Engagement" from *Desert Storm Marines: A Marine Tank Company at War in the Gulf*. Jeff Dacus. Essex, CT: Lyons Press, 2023.

"Code Name: Karen" from *Call Sign: Lightning, Inside the Rowdy World and Risky Missions of the Marines' Elite Anglicos*. Scott Messmore. Blue Ridge Summit, PA: Stackpole Books, 2017.

"Blood Stripes" from *Blood Stripes: The Grunt's View of the War in Iraq*. David J. Danelo. Blue Ridge Summit, PA: Stackpole Books, 2006.

"From Baghdad, With Love" from *From Baghdad, With Love: A Marine, the War, and a Dog Named Lava*. Jay Kopelman and Melinda Roth. Essex, CT: Lyons Press, 2006.

"Marine Scout Snipers" from *Marine Scout Snipers: True Stories from Marine Scout Snipers*. Lena Sisco. Essex, CT: Lyons Press, 2016.

www.ingramcontent.com/pod-product-compliance
Lightning Source LLC
Chambersburg PA
CBHW031240240425
25624CB00006B/12